## RIO VISTA JOINT UNION HIGH SCHOOL

1. Students will be responsible for the loss or damage to books.
2. Grades will be withheld until all books are returned or accounted for.
3. Students will return books to teachers on leaving school.

| NAME | RECEIVED | RETURNED | TEACHER |
|------|----------|----------|---------|
| Spivey, Tom | 4/21/66 | | |
| Paula Byrd | 4/24/67 | 6-1-67 | |
| | | | |
| | | | |
| | | | |
| | | | |
| | | | |

# The World

# of Communism

*General Editor:* HOWARD R. ANDERSON

# The World of

ANSWERS TO THE
100 QUESTIONS MOST
OFTEN ASKED BY AMERICAN
HIGH SCHOOL STUDENTS

**Houghton Mifflin Company** . Bo

# Communism

# Rodger Swearingen

DIRECTOR, SOVIET-ASIAN STUDIES CENTER

UNIVERSITY OF SOUTHERN CALIFORNIA

EDITOR: HOWARD R. ANDERSON

## ABOUT THE AUTHOR AND EDITOR

**Rodger Swearingen** is Associate Professor of International Relations and Director of the Soviet-Asian Studies Center and of the Research Institute on Communist Strategy and Propaganda at the University of Southern California. He is co-author (with Paul Langer) of *Red Flag in Japan: International Communism in Action, 1919–1951*, and has written other books and articles in professional Journals.

**Howard R. Anderson** taught high school classes in history in Michigan, Iowa, and New York. He has also been on the faculty of the State University of Iowa, Cornell University, and the University of Rochester. His field is the teaching of history.

# Contents

# CONTENTS

## CONTENTS

# Acknowledgments

First of all let me acknowledge those many colleagues everywhere without whose dedicated efforts in the field of Soviet affairs, Chinese affairs, and World Communism this book could not possibly have been written.

I am indebted in a special way to Leo Gruliow, editor of the *Current Digest of the Soviet Press,* for taking time from a busy schedule to go over the preliminary draft of a large portion of the manuscript. His comments, additions, and suggestions have been invaluable. Charles Malamuth (Research Institute on Communist Strategy and Propaganda, University of Southern California) reviewed the final manuscript and made many important suggestions.

Charles Thompson, Paul Langer, and Leon Gouré (all of The RAND Corporation) read the final draft of the entire manuscript, as did Col. Clyde McBride, until recently U.S. Military Attaché in Moscow (currently, Research Institute on Communist Strategy and Propaganda, University of Southern California). Their suggestions have been of greatest value. Franz Schurmann (University of California, Berkeley) reviewed the portion of the manuscript on Communist China. His specialized knowledge of this important field contributed materially to the final version

A special word of appreciation is also in order for the staff of the Institute for the Study of the USSR in Munich. Their generous assistance in providing recent information on a number of questions helped assure that the final version would be as up-to-date as possible.

The perceptive comments on Communist China by such men as Edmund Clubb (New York), Doak Barnett (Columbia University), and Theodore H. E. Chen (University of Southern California) were most helpful. Howard Boorman (Columbia University) provided the answer to the question of the Chinese Communist elite. Alice Hsieh (The RAND Corporation) furnished information and ideas on Chinese military and nuclear affairs. Joseph Kershaw (The RAND Corporation) was most helpful with suggestions relating to the Soviet economic scene

Richard Pipes (Harvard University) added useful suggestions on the question of nationalities in the Soviet Union. Donald Treadgold (University of Washington), Marin Pundeff (San Fernando Valley State College), Mark Neuweld (Systems Development Corporation, Santa Monica), and Reverend Michael Hamilton (University of Southern California) supplied suggestions on ideology and history. Gene Sosin (Radio Liberty) made useful comments on education and recreation in the Soviet Union. Thomas Hammond (University of Virginia) and Frederick Barghoorn (Yale University) furnished important formulations in the field of foreign policy. David Cattell (University of California at Los Angeles) made suggestions on the treatment of Soviet government that were also helpful. Richard Brynildsen (University of Southern California) briefed material on the American Communist Party.

Several persons who are knowledgeable in the area of the school curriculum were most encouraging and helpful. To Mr. Allan Fink, of the office of Superintendent of the Pasadena Schools, I owe a special debt for urging me to undertake this task and for continuing helpful suggestions and advice. Mrs. Howardine Hoffman and Mrs. Elizabeth Pellitt of the Los Angeles County Superintendents' office also have been most generous of their time and suggestions. Dr. Louise Seyler, Deputy Superintendent of the Los Angeles City Schools, and her colleagues have also been encouraging and helpful. Finally, I should like to thank Dr. William M. Melchoir of the Long Beach Unified School District for his assistance and suggestions.

It remains to thank my student assistants and loyal secretary. Jim McCloud and Miles Campbell worked weekends, evenings, and odd hours tracking down bits of information. Susan Schreiner was also helpful on this score. Betty Bowman, my secretary, spent evenings and weekends typing the manuscript.

Rabbi Edgar F. Magnin was kind enough to write especially for the book a brief statement entitled "Judaism Versus Communism."

It goes without saying that, except where attributed, the organization, presentation, style, viewpoint, and conclusions, as well as any mistakes in fact or judgment, are my own.

                                                    Rodger Swearingen

Such events as the Korean War, the bloody suppression of the Hungarian revolt, Red China's take-over in Tibet, the wall in Berlin — this increasingly militant behavior of the Soviet Union and Communist China has aroused the American people. To contain World Communism the United States is making use of trade and aid, armaments and alliances, information programs and education. Today our federal and state governments, churches and patriotic organizations, laymen and teachers are agreed that young Americans must be taught the facts about World Communism. That is the reason many schools are introducing courses about Communism and also the reason why this book has been written.

*The World of Communism* has been prepared to answer the questions Americans are asking about Communism. The material in this book is based on long years of research by government and private agencies, university centers, and individual scholars. Professor Swearingen's own research in this field is well known. In addition to interesting narrative, *The World of Communism* includes specially prepared maps of the Communist World; charts explaining the Soviet political system, comparing the growth of Soviet and United States economies, and depicting the race in nuclear armaments; pictures of Communist leaders, communes and collective farms, Communist propaganda efforts and technological achievements.

Teachers can use *The World of Communism* in their course in American and World history, American Government, and Problems of Democracy. The book will also prove useful to those who are developing new courses or units on Communism.

Howard R. Anderson

x

# Introduction

Should American students study about Communism in school? With the increasing recognition by Americans in all walks of life that Communism has become an urgent and serious threat to our democratic society, parents, teachers, school administrators, and other patriotic Americans are concerned about better preparing themselves — and YOU — to meet this challenge. Many schools have already instituted units or courses designed to teach the facts about Communism. Others plan to do so shortly.

How do the students feel about it? After all, it's your country, your life, and your future. To help us find a meaningful answer to this question, obviously we must turn to the students themselves. First, let us look at the results of a "student opinion poll" taken in early November, 1961 at the John H. Francis Polytechnic High School in Sun Valley, California. Polytechnic could be any high school in America. Eight hundred students in the government, history, and contemporary American problems classes answered a brief questionnaire on the subject. Here are the results:

Q. How much of a semester should the teaching of Communism take up: A, one fourth; B, one half; C, an entire semester?
A. A, 33 per cent; B, 29 per cent; C, 38 per cent
Q. Should Communism be taught as part of a history class?
A. Yes, 58 per cent; No, 42 per cent
Q. At what grade level should it be taught: A, 10th grade; B, 11th grade; C, 12th grade?
A. A, 13 per cent; B, 21 per cent; C, 66 per cent

1

Q. Should it be an elective course?

A. Yes, 41 per cent; No, 59 per cent

Q. Should Communism and Democracy be compared in this course?

A. Yes, 84 per cent; No, 16 per cent

Q. Do you feel a student can understand Communism without a basic background of World history?

A. Yes, 26 per cent; No, 74 per cent

Q. Are teen-agers mature enough to understand the concepts of Communism?

A. Yes, 87 per cent; No, 13 per cent

Q. Do you feel the teaching of Communism in high schools will confuse the students?

A. Yes, 11 per cent; No, 89 per cent

Q. Should teachers of courses on Communism have special training before being allowed to teach this subject?

A. Yes, 95 per cent; No, 5 per cent

As interesting and important as these statistical responses are, they do not answer satisfactorily and directly the original question: "Should students study about Communism?" It turns out that young America is not unanimous on the question, that there are two very different attitudes toward the problem. These divergent views are eloquently reflected by two Sun Valley seniors. Should the schools teach about Communism? Peggy Otchis says NO! Frances Wolf says YES! Each of these short essays is typical of the feelings of many young Americans — for there are students such as Peggy and Frances in high schools across America.

## NO — by Peggy Otchis

Any attempt to teach Communism in high schools would be completely ridiculous. Most teen-agers do not care about Communism, don't know what it is, and wouldn't want to spend class time learning about it. To confuse a high school student with the concepts of Communism would be . . . [unwise]. To train a teacher to be objective in the presentation of this subject would be impossible.

In a booklet published by the Los Angeles City Schools entitled "Point of View," the policy to be practiced . . . [in] . . . studying . . . current issues is made quite clear.

It states [that] the classroom atmosphere must be free from . . . [emotion] or partisanship. This means teachers are not to take a specific point of view; instead they must present both sides. How many of our teachers would be willing to present two sides on Communism?

The booklet also strongly recommends [that] the discussion of controversial issues be deferred until sufficient facts [are available to insure] . . . discussion [based] upon REASON. . . . Obviously, Communism is a controversial issue and could not be discussed in accordance with the recommendation.

When the word Communism is mentioned, how does the student react? He perks up and is ready to fight and defend himself. From what? He really doesn't know and he couldn't care less. . . . He is thoroughly confused by all the terms he has heard, and doesn't want to be bothered with them. Capitalism? Communism? So what? He still has food to eat and a date this weekend.

Suddenly, people have decided that high school students should be told about Communism. Students have only two junior high school semesters of World history in the ninth grade,[1] and they remember little of it. This is too weak a basic background [for the] study [of] Communism. At this time, students are just beginning to see the need for money and are realizing the value of a job . . . and now they are to be confronted with Communism. . . .

At the present time, few . . . teachers have had college courses on Soviet affairs. They should not be permitted to present Communism to students without such a background. . . . Who will train the teachers and what materials will be used in the classrooms? It would be almost impossible to develop valid charts, films, and recordings [for use] . . . in classrooms. It would also be quite costly. Who would evaluate these materials? Even after a full course in Communism, teachers would not be able to present the subject without undue emotion entering [in].

As you can see, there are many unanswered questions. In this

---

[1] The courses referred to in these essays are those taught in the Sun Valley high school. Courses vary from state to state. World history, for example, is more often taught in the tenth grade.

case, something is not better than nothing at all. We are not
ready to teach Communism in high schools. To attempt it now
would only result in confusion . . . and would be an utter waste
of time.

## YES — by Frances Wolf

A pack of crimson comrades is standing atop . . . the Kremlin
today, shouting a [challenge] . . . to the democratic forces of the
West. The [challenge is] . . . to fight the strangest of all wars,
the cold war of ideas. And the United States is right in the middle
of the battlefield.

The question which we must raise is: How do we fight the
enemy? Certainly we must use the best weapons available, and
many people will think of the H-Bomb, the multimegaton bomb,
the atomic warhead, or the missile. Yet, in our frantic search,
many of us overlook the most powerful weapon of all, the weapon
of knowledge. And the [place to] . . . arm ourselves is in our
high schools.

We must start teaching the dynamics of Communism . . . not
as a haphazard one-semester [experimental course] on the "menace" of its economic theory, but as an integrated program for
junior and senior high school students.

In the junior high school, the program must start in the seventh
grade, with not only the prescribed geography course, but with
a careful study of the geography of the USSR. In the eighth
grade, when the student is introduced to American Government
and both World Wars, he should study the 1917 revolutions [in
Russia] and the growth of Communism, just as he studies the
American Revolution and the growth of Democracy. And finally,
in the ninth grade, as he studies [World] history, he must study
the . . . tsarist regime [in] Russia and what led to its downfall.

On the senior high level, the most barren area is the tenth grade,
with little or no [instruction in] social studies. Here we must
concentrate . . . on the original Marxian doctrines and how they
were . . . [modified by] Lenin. We must note the clashes . . .
within the Communist Party which followed the death of Lenin.

In the eleventh grade, we must integrate the prescribed United

States history course with European history and . . . [describe] the growth of Communism. . . . And finally, in the senior year [the student] . . . must be offered one semester in comparative economics to [make clear] . . . Communistic and Capitalistic economic theories. His Senior A semester should be spent in a study of the very latest events . . . in the Soviet Union.

Certainly . . . some adjustments . . . [will] have to be made. Our teachers will have to [take part in] a crash program. . . .

[Whenever a] war strikes, is not the average young man hastily trained . . . [for service] in a matter of months? In the very same way, we cannot wait for years . . . [to] be absolutely sure our teachers are "ready". . . .

We must teach our young people the facts about Communism. We must put this most powerful weapon in their hands. The bullets are IDEAS. The trigger is UNDERSTANDING. The time is NOW.[2]

* * *

How would you evaluate these essays? Which of Peggy's arguments do you find most convincing? Try to add some points of your own to Frances's arguments in favor of studying about Communism in high school. Some of the facts and suggestions in Chapter 1 of this book, "Exploring the World of Communism," will help you clarify your own views on the subject.

[2] Both essays from Campus Section, *The Los Angeles Examiner*, November 4, 1961.

# 1 Exploring the World of Communism

## What is the world of Communism?

The world of Communism is a strange world only vaguely familiar to the majority of Americans. By the world of Communism we do not mean merely those lands and captive peoples behind the Iron and Bamboo Curtains. We also mean the realm of the mind — Marxist-Leninist ways of thinking, writing, and speaking. Included, as well, is the region of the domestic Communist, particularly Communist activity here in the United States. These areas are all tied together by Communist theory, Moscow-Peking foreign policies, and an interlocking network of World Communist organizations. This is the world of Communism. How much do you know about it?

## Why bother studying it?

Why study the world of Communism? It's not our world. True, but it is increasingly our problem and the problem of all free peoples. J. Edgar Hoover, the Director of the Federal Bureau of Investigation, in his thoughtful book, *Masters of Deceit,*[1] puts it

[1] Holt, Rinehart and Winston, Inc., New York, 1958, p. v.

6

this way: "Every citizen has a duty to learn more about the menace that threatens his future, his home, his children, the peace of the world. . . ."

One of the cardinal rules of military strategy taught at West Point and at military academies throughout the world is "Know your enemy." The Bolsheviks declared war on the capitalist world in 1917. Today Communists everywhere make no secret of the fact that they regard the United States as their principal enemy. Khrushchev said recently that he intends to "bury us." Our grandchildren, he assured us, "will live under Communism."

The record, thus, is clear on one point: The Communists have declared war on us. To be sure, it is not a hot war fought with guns, tanks, aircraft, or nuclear weapons, but it is a war all right — a war waged with ideas, propaganda, economic aid, trade, culture, and espionage.

A more polite term for this gigantic world conflict is competitive coexistence. But perhaps the time has come to call a spade a spade. We are presently engaged in a life-or-death struggle for which we are ill prepared — historically, psychologically, or politically. Our study of the world of Communism at the high school level has to date been largely confined to the quaint dress and "strange" customs of the people of Russia and China. An occasional controversial film has also been shown here and there from time to time.

But when the stakes are the survival of our way of life, we would do well to find out something about the rules of the game. It would be helpful also to know as much as possible about the number, strengths, and weaknesses of the players on the opposing team. And finally, we had better learn all we can about the system, formations, and specific plays employed by the coach on the other side — lest we be taken by surprise, overwhelmed, and defeated.

## How much do we know about the subject?

Winston Churchill described Russia as a "riddle wrapped in a mystery inside an enigma." But that was years ago. Intensive research and experience during the past decade have taught us much about the subject. The stranger will still become hopelessly lost in the world of Communism without some kind of guide or road map. The essential point, however, is that we now know quite enough to define and sketch accurately the theories or ideology, the political and economic system, and the daily life of the world of Communism. The problem is no longer diagnosis. It is communication.

Once we come to understand the Communists — what they believe, how they think, the basis of their system, the record of their rule, and the realities of life behind the Iron and Bamboo Curtains — the mystery disappears. And when the clouds have lifted and the mist has cleared away, what do we find? We see two massive power centers and a World Communist movement operating with goals and rules quite different from ours. But they are goals and rules which can be identified and studied. Once understood, these goals and rules help explain much of the mystery of the theory and practice of the system. A look at life in Russia and China today further serves to demonstrate the difference between reality and propaganda. It also supplies a vivid contrast between the open societies and the captive peoples, between freedom and slavery.

## Where do we get the facts?

World War II plus fifteen years of research have combined to bring the Soviet Union, Communist China, and World Communism into clear focus. We now have all the facts needed to put together a fairly accurate picture of the world of Communism. Where do these facts come from? Here are some of the most substantial and revealing sources:

(1) **The Communist press.** Hundreds of magazines and newspapers are printed in the USSR and Communist China. Topics range from speeches by Khrushchev or Mao and texts of Five and Seven Year Plans, to letters to the editor. Western specialists trained to distinguish between facts and propaganda and to read between the lines find these an indispensable source of information.

(2) **The secret files of the German and Japanese governments**

**captured by the Allies at the end of World War II.** Besides intelligence reports on every aspect of Soviet and Chinese Communist affairs, these files include thousands of documents, stolen or captured by the Germans and Japanese. Together this case-study material provides both historical perspective and patterns of behavior. It helps us distinguish facts from propaganda.

**(3) Soviet defectors, escapees.** Millions of Russians, East Europeans and Chinese have fled the tyranny of the life behind the Iron and Bamboo Curtains. Their numbers include high-ranking military personnel, doctors, managers of collective farms, government and Party officials, code clerks, intelligence agents — in short — former "Communists" from every walk of life. Intensive interviews with thousands of these living sources of up-to-date information provide perspective and detail and add immeasurably to our accurate and intimate knowledge of the world of Communism.

**(4) Former Free World Communists.** Some of the most important Communists in the Free World have defected. Many high-ranking American Communists have left the party in disgust. Their numbers include several one-time Party Chiefs with broad international contacts. Now anti-Communist, they furnish a wealth of information on the operations of World Communism.

**(5) Reports of United States governmental agencies.** Government departments or agencies regularly issue reports on aspects of the problem. State Department and FBI or Justice Department reports on Communism at home and abroad are typical of this valuable source of information.

**(6) Foreign government reports.** A number of foreign governments regularly publish reports on Communism within countries of the Free World. The Japanese Government, for example, periodically issues a *white paper* on Communism in Japan. So do some other governments. Such detailed material deals with all phases of Communist movement for the years covered by the given report. From these reports we obtain specific data: names, places, events, tactics used, Party organization, and strength.

**(7) Eye-witness accounts by foreign diplomats and visitors to the Communist countries.** These commentaries add to our recent knowledge of conditions within the countries behind the Iron and Bamboo Curtains. The British Ambassador in Moscow, the Indian Ambassador in Peking, an American student in Leningrad University, an American university professor, or the French military attaché to the Soviet Union, can tell us much about the realities of life behind the curtain.

**(8) On-the-spot coverage by newspaper, radio, and TV correspondents.** The life of a foreign correspondent in a Communist country is very different from his life in a country of the Free World. His activities as a correspondent are often strictly controlled by the government. He is not allowed to seek stories freely or always to report the news as he sees it. If he is too well informed, too eager, or too imaginative, he may be asked to leave the country. Nevertheless, a great deal of useful information on life and events is reported by hard-working members of the press, radio, and TV stationed in Moscow, Warsaw, or Peking. While the United States does not recognize the Chinese Communist Government, some of our allies do. Hence we are not entirely cut off from on-the-spot coverage of Communist China.

Several hundred American, European, and Asian research scholars with a knowledge of one or more of the essential foreign languages are busy — even as you are reading this page — analyzing, sifting, testing, comparing, and putting together the facts on Russia, China, and Communism. It is their findings to date that make possible this volume.

## A word of caution

A word of caution may be in order. This is a subject on which, as suggested, many hundreds of mature scholars have spent their lives. On many aspects of the subject there is no general agreement. Do not be discouraged if some of the ideas are so strange as to be literally *unthinkable* at first. Do not expect more than a new horizon of understanding from this brief introduction to the vast world of Communism.

Students with a spirit of adventure, an inquiring mind, will want to read more deeply on some of the topics. To this end, a list of suggested readings has been included for each chapter.

## Organization and approach

How does one go about presenting such a complex subject in one slim volume? Let us talk about how this book grew.

High school students have one great talent: They ask fundamental questions. They may not always get adequate answers, but they keep asking. Communism has clearly become one of our major problems. It has been called, I think quite correctly, the burning issue of our time. But, to date, few authoritative answers and little reliable reading material has been available to the inquiring student. The result: frustration and confusion. Why not attempt to answer some of these questions?

This book, then, is written in response to the specific questions asked by high school students and teachers throughout America. The answers, as we shall see, briefly survey the theory, organization, systems, strategy, tactics, and life of Communism in the USSR, Eastern Europe, China, and America. Three appendices: "A Glossary of Communist Jargon and Double Talk", "A Compact Bookshelf on the World of Communism," and "Key Sources of Current, Up-to-Date Information," include further food for thought.

## One final suggestion

One final suggestion! Don't be satisfied with a brief or incomplete answer. Don't take the Communists' word for it. In fact, don't take any one individual's or organization's word for it. Dig out the facts. Ask more questions. Read more about Marxist-Leninist theory and practice. Read what some of the brilliant critics of Communism have written. Challenge Communist arguments. Above all, learn more about your own country. Remember, there are two tests that Communism cannot pass: The first is the test of truth; the second is the test of comparison.

In this way you will be able to confront Communist lies and distortion with organized truth. In this way you will be able to demonstrate to others — and to yourself — the superiority of our American system and our democratic way of life.

# 2 What Is Communism?—Marxist-Leninist Theory and Beliefs

## Communist Theory

### 1. What is Communism?

An authoritative dictionary defines Communism as:

1. Any system of social organization in which goods are held in common; as, Brook Farm was an experiment in *communism*.
2. A doctrine and program based upon revolutionary Marxian socialism as developed by N. Lenin and the Bolshevik party, which interprets history as a relentless class war eventually to result everywhere in the victory of the proletariat and establishment of the dictatorship of the proletariat, and which calls for regulation of all social, economic, and cultural activities through the agency of a single authoritarian party as the leader of the proletariat in all countries so as to achieve its ultimate objectives, a classless society and establishment of a world union of socialist soviet republics.[1]

But the complex, controversial term "Communism" cannot easily be reduced to a dictionary definition or a simple explanation.

[1] *Webster's New Collegiate Dictionary* (G. & C. Merriam Company, Springfield, Massachusetts, 1960).

Certainly, today, when we use the term, we do not ordinarily refer to any of those early Christian or utopian experiments in sharing, such as the Brook Farm. Modern Communism is many things.

**Communism is a philosophy of history, a view of society and the world.** A century ago, Karl Marx, whom the Communists regard as their spiritual father, taught materialism, atheism, and the evils of private ownership of industry, agriculture, and business generally. He believed that "class-struggle" ("haves" against "have nots") explained all of human history. As the "oppressed" workers (proletariat) became more and more numerous and miserable, they would eventually rise up as a class against the capitalists who exploited them. This proletarian revolution, Marx was convinced, was bound to take place in one after another of the advanced, industrialized, capitalist countries of Europe and in the United States as the middle class became poorer, and the desperate swollen working class finally sought to liberate itself. But Marx was wrong. The middle class has not disappeared; it has grown in size, wealth, influence, and importance. The worker "as a class" has not become more miserable; his lot has improved markedly, especially in the democratic countries. Foreigners who have visited the United States observe that the "workers" in America live better than the "middle class" in Europe. Communism came to relatively non-industrialized Russia and agrarian China, not to industrialized Western Europe or America. Revolution did not occur automatically. It was imposed by force.

**Communism is a political strategy and a social system.** Lenin overhauled Marxism at the turn of the century and forged it into a political weapon for reshaping society. Lenin was the master of organization and of the strategy and tactics of revolution. (For the story of his life see page 46.) He saw the need for a corps of revolution-makers, a "vanguard" called the Communist Party. A revolution, like war, Lenin said, has to be planned, organized, and skillfully executed. It doesn't just happen. And when the revolution is over and the Communists are victorious, this vanguard will eliminate the opposition and organize every facet of the political, social, and economic life of the nation. This "dictatorship of the proletariat" would prepare the road to pure Communism and hasten the day when the state will "wither away," to use Marx's term. But state or government power in all the nations under Communism has not shown the slightest tendency to "wither away." Quite the opposite. The Communist socio-political system has become, in practice, a ruthless, one-party, totalitarian machine run by a few men at the top.

**Communism is an economic system.** Communism is an economic system of total planning, collectivization of agriculture, and regimentation of workers and peasants. The State owns virtually everything. It operates all sectors of the nation's economy. There are no private businesses, no effective labor unions, and, of course, no strikes. The Government runs all enterprises from the railroads to shoe stores and lunch stands. The Government determines both salaries and prices. In order to assure maximum resources for development — to build new factories, bridges, or apartment buildings — the Soviet Government simply pays extremely low salaries while keeping most consumer prices high. Virtually every phase and aspect of life is thus planned and controlled — from the cradle to the grave. The individual becomes a quiet, small cog in a big machine.

**Communism is a world-wide conspiracy.** Nor does Communism confine its goals to domestic issues or its activities to the home front. Its stated aims are the destruction of capitalism, the subversion of the free societies, and world domination. Its revolutionary activities, which radiate from Moscow and Peking, are extensive and world-wide. Communist Parties in the nations of the Free World are part of this world-wide system. Lenin suggested in 1923 that the road to Paris is by way of Peking. Khrushchev said in 1959, referring to the United States, "We will bury you!" Communists believe that their system will eventually triumph throughout the world, and they are working twenty-four hours a day to that end.

**The Communist ideal and Communist practice.** What Communism is supposed to be was put this way by Stalin (and it has not been fundamentally revised by Khrushchev):

The anatomy of the Communist society may be described as follows: It is a society in which
(a) there will be no private ownership of the means of production, but social collective ownership;

(b) there will be no classes or state, but workers in industry and agriculture managing their economic affairs as a free association of toilers;

(c) a national economy organized according to plan will be based on the highest technology in both industry and agriculture;

(d) there is no antagonism between city and country, between industry and farming;

(e) . . . "from each according to his ability, to each according to his needs";

(f) science and art will enjoy conditions conducive to their highest development;

(g) the individual freed from bread and butter cares and of the necessity of cringing to the "powers that be" will become really free. . . .

*In practice*, Communism in this sense does not exist anywhere in the world today, and it seems unlikely that it ever will. The Soviet Union today is a far cry from the model described by Stalin (see Chapters 4 and 5). The commune system in China, designed as part of the "great leap forward into Communism," has proved neither successful nor popular (see pages 144–145).

The other Communist countries behind the Iron and Bamboo Curtains — the "People's Democracies" of Eastern Europe, North Viet Nam, and North Korea — have economic systems and social conditions that are patterned after the Soviet model. These bear little or no resemblance to either the Marxist-Leninist ideal or to current Communist propaganda claims.

But Communists continue to push the same propaganda line. Khrushchev said recently:

> The paid agents of capitalism . . . attempt to scare people who know little about politics with the bogey of Communism. What is socialism, and what is Communism? It is a social system under which there is no exploitation of one man by another. All means of production belong to society and are used in the interests and for the good of that society. To put it more simply, socialism and Communism mean a better life for working people than they have under capitalist conditions.

As we shall see, the facts do not support Khrushchev's words. The reality is quite different from the claim.

## 2. *Can Marxism be explained in a few words?*

Terms such as "historical materialism" and "surplus value," along with the idea of "class struggle," contain the essence of Marxism, the Communist view of history and of human society. Such concepts cannot be easily explained short of a detailed description and analysis of Marxist theory. But because they are so important to the world of Communism, we dare not pass them by unnoticed.

**Historical materialism and the dialectic.** Marx's materialist conception of history, called historical materialism, is generally accepted as valid, or true, by Communists. This basic theory is also called *dialectical materialism.* It says that the nature of so- cial and political institutions in a country is determined solely by the economic forces which form the nation's foundation. All human development, in this view, is shaped by material forces. There is no soul. There is no God.

Marx borrowed the concept of the dialectic from the German philosopher, Hegel. This dialectic process of reasoning says that every line of thought proceeds like a snowball until it goes too far, becomes exaggerated, and is no longer true. Then this *thesis* or assumption generates an *antithesis* or counter-assumption. Out of this clash of ideas comes a *synthesis:* an idea which contains the essence of the truth of both, but which is really superior to the combination of its parts, on a new higher plane. Now the progression of thought starts all over again and repeats itself in a continuing line to eternity.

This dialectic is what gives Marxism its so-called "scientific" quality. Marxists claim this is the key to *prediction.* Once the thesis and antithesis have been identified, the synthesis can be *predicted!*

In this way, Marx traced human history from slavery through feudalism to capitalism, dividing society at each stage into the exploiters and the exploited, the ruling and the oppressed classes To Marx, government was always merely a reflection of the economic arrangements, the instrument of the dominant economic "class."

In this view a country with a capitalist economy *must* necessarily have a government directed by bankers, stockbrokers, and loan sharks. This is why Communist propaganda today claims that the United States is controlled by "Wall Street" business interests. The notion of a balanced "capitalist" economy, run by the elected representatives of the people and including elements of business, labor, farmers, and other interest groups, was not part of Marx's limited understanding of reality. Nor do the Communists today admit such a possibility.

The antithesis of capitalism is socialism, which Marxist-Leninists believe will lead to the new synthesis, Communism. But, as we shall see, the *socialism* of the Marxist-Leninists (Communists) differs from socialism as presently practiced in a number of countries of the Free World. (See page 19.) Socialists in Free World countries may call themselves Marxists. This does not mean that they are Marxist-Leninists and under the discipline of Moscow.

**The labor theory of value and surplus value.** If the class struggle and the dialectical materialist interpretation of history constitute two keystones of Marxism, the *labor theory of value,* which gives rise to the term *surplus value,* is the third.

What is the value of something here in America or, for that matter, throughout the "capitalist" Free World? Except for keepsakes and sentimental items, things are generally worth as much money as they will bring when sold. Prices are fixed by supply and demand: How many of the items are there, and how many people want them badly enough to pay a high price for them?

Marx substituted for this "capitalist" notion the "labor theory of value." Things are worth, he said, only the amount of labor necessary to create them — that is, what it costs to produce them. If a "capitalist" hires a worker to produce a pair of shoes that the capitalist then sells for twice the amount he paid the shoemaker, the difference is surplus value. This *profit* the capitalist pockets. It is this "surplus value," siphoned off by the capitalist, which Marx identified as the root of the problem, the basis of exploitation. Thus, according to Marx, the capitalist, himself idle, "lives off the sweat of the worker." By reinvesting his profits, Marx concludes, he becomes a bigger and bigger capitalist, forcing small capitalists out of business.

Political economists have pointed out many things wrong with this theory, among them (1) no provision is made for justified rewards to skilled and responsible management (Marx assumed that all capitalists are bad); (2) on the other hand, Marx taught that all workers are good — identical, interchangeable, equally talented and productive; (3) it does not take into account the costs of sales and promotion, or the risk that money might be lost as well as made under the free enterprise system; and (4) it ignores the fact that the more that is produced, the more there is for people generally.

## 3. *What is Leninism?*

It has been said that Lenin turned Marx on his head. By this is meant that Lenin's idea of the urgent need for a "vanguard" of revolution-makers suggested that Marx must have been wrong on one fundamental point: The revolution could not be expected to take place as Marx suggested it would, more or less automatically, for economic reasons. The "masses" — the majority — didn't seem likely to make a revolution. It would have to be the work of a minority. It clearly needed direction, a push! Accordingly one of Lenin's main contributions was his theory of the *elite* (or small corps of leaders) and his accompanying strategy and tactics of revolution. He demonstrated how a minority party, the Bolsheviks or Communists, could by skillful organization, clever propaganda, political and military training, and well-developed strategy defeat a confused, undisciplined enemy — even when the enemy forces were vastly superior in numbers. This is an important point which applies to the situation in the world today.

Lenin's second major contribution was his theory and definition of *imperialism*. Lenin defined imperialism as the final stage of capitalism, that stage when in order to keep their economies from collapsing, the capitalists reach out for new territory and new markets in Africa, Latin America, the Middle East, and Asia. He predicted that the capitalist powers would eventually start fighting among themselves. By this definition, only a capitalist country could be imperialist. This also explained something else: why the economic crisis and workers' revolution prophesied by Marx for these advanced, industrial societies had not taken place. The capitalists had been keeping their economies going artificially by exploiting the resources and cheap labor of the underdeveloped nations of the world.

Stalin summarized and defined Leninism as "Marxism of the era of imperialism and of proletarian revolution." Leninism has thus become an important half of the theory of Marxism-Leninism on which Communism throughout the Sino-Soviet world is based. Communists today accept Marx's teachings on history and human nature, but Lenin is their guide to political warfare and international relations.

# 4. Is there a difference between socialism and Communism?

In the nineteenth century the words "socialism" and "Communism" usually meant the same thing. However, the roots of socialism can be traced to non-Communist thinkers. The Frenchman Rousseau and the English industrial reformer Robert Owen both advocated forms of public control and ownership of industry before Marx did. Some socialists like the English Fabians, though greatly influenced by Marx, did not accept his views on the necessity for armed revolution. In the twentieth century, after the Bolshevik (Communist) seizure of power in Russia, the socialists split away from their co-operation and alliances with Communists, putting forward less ambitious goals and preferring parliamentary techniques to Communist violence. The socialists in the Free World today advocate the transfer to the state (nationalization) of only the major sectors of industry and hold that middle-sized and small industrial enterprises as well as farming should preserve their economic independence.

In many democratic states, such as Sweden, Norway, Denmark, and West Germany, the socialist parties have even removed from their programs the demand for nationalizing heavy industry. Socialists in the Free World largely maintain that they can bring about improvements in the position of the working class through legislation.

We may say, then, that socialism differs from Communism in at least three fundamental ways. (1) Socialists are committed to *political democracy*, working within the framework of the individual country's constitution and using parliamentary means; (2) socialism is not committed to the policies put forward by Moscow or Peking; and (3) socialism is more moderate, less given to extreme solutions (such as total nationalization).

The fact that the official name for the Soviet Union is Union of Soviet *Socialist* Republics should not confuse us concerning the distinction between Communism and socialism. The Soviets have appropriated the term socialism as they have the word democracy, but they assign their own special meanings to these terms (see Appendix A).

What has been said to clarify the differences between socialism and Communism should not be interpreted as advocacy of the former.

## 5. *How does Trotskyism fit into the picture?*

Trotskyism takes its name from Leon Trotsky (1879–1940), one of the two men who made a revolution in Russia. The other, of course, was Lenin. Russian revolutionaries expected that their revolution would sweep right across Europe. For a time, indeed, their hopes were borne out by post-World War I uprisings in Germany, Hungary, and elsewhere. But these uprisings quickly died down.

Stalin then formulated a Russian nationalist policy — concentrating first on building up Russia as a Communist country, which would be a center for world revolution while World Communism bided its time. Trotsky advocated pushing ahead with the program of world revolution without delay.

In Trotsky's own words: "The completion of the socialist revolution within national limits is unthinkable. . . . the socialist revolution attains completion only in the final victory of the new society on our entire planet."

After a prolonged, bitter feud with Trotsky, Stalin succeeded in having his former comrade-in-arms removed from his high position (1925), expelled from the Communist Party and exiled to Central Asia (1927), expelled from the USSR (1929), and finally murdered in Mexico by a Soviet agent (1940).

In present-day Soviet propaganda Trotskyism is branded as fascist, counter-revolutionary, and "undemocratic."

## 6. *Have Stalin and Khrushchev contributed to Communist theory?*

Stalin was more a practical politician than a student of theory. He did make one major contribution to the development of Communist ideology: the concept of "socialism in one country." He argued (successfully against Trotsky as we have seen), that a "final victory of socialism" in the USSR was essential as a guarantee against "imperialist intervention" and "the restoration of capitalism" in the USSR. Build the USSR as a citadel of socialism! Workers of the world unite in defense of the USSR! These were the slogans. Stalin insisted that his "Russia first" theory was in accordance with the best Leninist tradition. In reality it brought a new emphasis to Communist theory and practice. Soviet power and a territorial base now became factors quite as important as abstract Communist ideology and permanent revolution.

Khrushchev has so far made one major change in emphasis in Marxism-Leninism-Stalinism. It is too early to state whether or not this "new line" should be considered a fundamental alteration of Communist theory. Certainly it is highly significant and goes beyond the usual Communist zig-zags in strategy and tactics.

From 1918 until the Twentieth Party Congress, held in 1956, the Communists had always maintained that "one more imperialist war is inevitable." After 1945 this line took the form of "the inevitability of a third world war." Then, at the 1956 Congress, Khrushchev stated that another world war is "*not* fatally inevitable." This reversal of position is caused by (1) the destructiveness of hydrogen war (nothing would be left of the Soviet Union either!), and (2) the feeling of the Communists that they can accomplish their mission by means short of world war — negotiation, propaganda, economic penetration, blackmail, subversion, and limited war.

### 7. Can Titoism be analyzed briefly?

Titoism is sometimes also called National Communism (to distinguish it from "international" Communism). The reason is that Tito was the first and only leader of a satellite country in the Communist orbit successfully to break away from the gravitational pull of Moscow. The event occurred unexpectedly in 1948. After a bitter feud between Tito and Stalin (centering on the Kremlin's disregard for Yugoslavia's national pride), Tito was finally expelled from the international Communist organization, the Cominform, for "insubordination."

The Kremlin apparently reasoned that this would shock Tito, the veteran Moscow-trained Communist, and that he would come crawling back asking to be forgiven for having been such a difficult, bad Communist. But Tito did not return to the international Communist fold. At the time, Moscow chose not to make the issue a cause for war or intervention. As a result, Yugoslavia has developed an independent, slightly more moderate strain of Communism.

A few basic points must be borne in mind, however, when considering the unique phenomenon, Titoism. Regardless of whether or not Tito is in favor with the leaders of "international" Communism, (1) Titoism is clearly a brand of Communism, (2) Tito fundamentally, is a ruthless Communist, and (3) Yugoslavia is still a Marxist-Leninist-oriented totalitarian country.

Why, then, does the United States Government continue to support Titoism with hundreds of millions of dollars of military and economic assistance?

Behind the answer is the fact that there are many nations in the world which we aid without necessarily approving of their governments. Examples are Generalissimo Franco's Spain, certain dictatorships in Latin America, and military regimes in Southeast Asia. In the case of Yugoslavia, there are some significant differences between Titoism, on the one hand, and Khrushchevism or Maoism on the other. These differences could prove extremely important to the outcome of the struggle between World Communism and the open, democratic societies.

First, even though Yugoslavia still calls itself a socialist (Com munist) state, a trend towards moderation, relaxation of some police controls, free enterprise, unrestricted travel, and limited co-operation with non-Communist countries is clearly in evidence. Foreign visitors agree that the atmosphere in Belgrade, the capital of Yugoslavia, is freer and more relaxed than in Moscow.

Secondly, Tito's break with Moscow shattered the "solid front" of "international" Communism. The resulting disunity, doubts, and confusion among leaders of the Iron Curtain countries clearly work to the disadvantage of World Communism.

Thirdly, Yugoslavia, while still not evidencing any real support of United States policies, often refuses to support the Kremlin or Peking on certain critical world issues, preferring to be classed as "one of the neutrals."

For these reasons the United States Government, beginning with the Truman administration and continuing under the Eisenhower and Kennedy administrations, has come to regard Titoism as a potentially significant "deviation," the first symptom of the disintegration of the Communist empire.

Critics of this point of view note that Tito is still a Communist, that despite "all our aid" Tito tends to be "neutral" *for Moscow,* and anti-American. He is a Communist, these critics say, and not a reliable ally.

It would be nice if our world were, like the typical "Westerns" on TV, very neatly divided into the "good guys" and the "bad guys." But this is not the case. In international affairs, very often, unhappily, we do not choose our friends — they are thrust upon us. Only time will demonstrate the wisdom of our calculated risk in supporting Titoism.

## 3. What is Maoism?

Maoism is Marxism-Leninism as developed in China by Mao Tse-tung, head of the Chinese Communist Party and absolute ruler of China. (See pages 57 to 58 for the story of his life.)

Authorities disagree as to the originality of Mao's contribution to Communist theory. Certainly, the Chinese Communists share with Communists throughout the world the basic Marxist-Leninist premises. Like Communists everywhere they are against

private property, capitalism, free enterprise, and the United
States. Chinese Communists believe in the "dictatorship of the
proletariat," that is, the importance of one-Party absolute control
over the daily lives and thoughts of China's 700 million people.

At the same time, Mao's claim to have adapted Marxism-
Leninism to Chinese conditions should not be entirely dismissed
as propaganda. Maoism usually claims credit for three innovations:

**1. The peasant base of Chinese Communism.** Because there
was no large group of city workers in China, Chinese Communism relied on the peasants for its chief support. Professor John
Fairbank of Harvard[2] puts it this way: "One seeming anomaly of
Chinese Marxism is its use of a peasant movement as the class
basis for revolution. . . . The Chinese Communists," he concludes,
"were obliged . . . to build their movement on a peasant base.
For fifteen years [to 1948] Chinese Communism has been a
peasant, not a proletarian, movement." In his book, *Chinese
Communism and the Rise of Mao*,[3] Professor Benjamin Schwartz,
also of Harvard, stresses the same point: "The Chinese Communist Party under the leadership of Mao Tse-tung has been . . . an
elite of professional revolutionaries which has risen to power by
basing itself on the dynamic of peasant discontent."

**2. The four-class, two-stage revolution.** Maoist strategy considers imperialism and feudalism its main enemies and prescribes
a two-stage revolution and a "united front from below," that is
a two-stage revolution and a united front with non-worker groups.
In this formula, called "New Democracy," Communists are represented as the champions not only of the proletariat (workers)
and the peasantry (farmers), but of the petty-bourgeois intellectuals (what we call white collar groups) and the small and
middle capitalists as well, although the latter two groups are
assigned an inferior and frankly temporary role.

The idea is to rally as many dissatisfied elements as possible
behind the Communist Party in its effort to overthrow the
"semi-feudal" government. When this first stage has been completed, the Communists will purge from the ranks of the revolu-
tionists all "unreliable" elements and "temporary" allies.

[2] *The United States and China* (Harvard University Press, Cambridge
Massachusetts, 1948), pp. 260–261.
[3] Harvard University Press, Cambridge, Massachusetts, 1951, p. 202

**3. Guerrilla warfare base.** The third innovation of Maoism concerns a plan, or formula, for armed struggle. This formula calls for the creation of a guerrilla force, drawn mainly from the peasantry, with a geographical base in the countryside from which it can operate and expand until strong enough to confront and defeat the enemy's main force.

Despite these innovations and differences in emphasis produced by the Chinese environment in which Maoism developed, it would be wrong to conclude that Maoism has broken with Marxism-Leninism. On the contrary, as Professor Schwartz points out,[4] essential core elements of Marxism-Leninism still remain integral, living elements of Chinese Communism. These may be identified as: (1) the Chinese Communists' own conviction that they are unswerving Marxist-Leninists; (2) the faith that they, the Chinese Communists, are the chosen instrument of history destined to lead China down a new path; (3) the basic Leninist theory and practice of Party organization; (4) the totalitarianism inherent in Marxism-Leninism; and (5) the Leninist doctrine of imperialism.

Mao's contribution lies in the application of Marxist-Leninist ideas to Chinese conditions, rather than in the formulation of any new basic concept. Thus, Maoism may be defined as *Chinese Marxist-Leninism* — not wholly the same but not radically different from its Soviet counterpart.

## Communism's Beliefs and Appeals

### . *What do Communists believe?*

Even though Communists in the Soviet Union, China, and the United States may differ on detail, they do share a number of assumptions and beliefs, an ideology of sorts. This ideology which we shall call Marxism-Leninism, or simply World Communism, demands uniformity and does not permit "deviationism" (unapproved thoughts). This makes it possible to

[4] *Chinese Communism and the Rise of Mao,* page 199.

answer rather precisely the question, "What do Communists believe?"

**Dedicated, active Communists believe:**

1. That life ends with the grave — that religion is an opiate [mind-dulling drug] of the people; that there is no God

2. That the State is more important than the individual; that the Communist Party is always right.

3. That the principal evils of world society are private property, capitalism (i.e. the free enterprise system), Western colonialism, and capitalist imperialism.

4. That the United States is imperialistic, aggressive, and deliberately hostile to the Soviet Union; that it is the United States Government that obstructs peace.

5. That a totally planned socialist economy is more efficient and more desirable than a competitive free enterprise system.

6. That Communism is inevitable, the "wave of the future."

7. That there is no real freedom in the United States (no anywhere under capitalism).

8. That because of unscrupulous "capitalists," the workers in the United States are oppressed and in constant economic distress.

9. That pledging allegiance to World Communism, to Moscow or to Peking, is more important than loyalty to one's own country.

10. That any act, even murder or informing on one's own parents, is justifiable if it serves the ends of World Communism.

These notions sound unbelievable and fantastic to most of us raised in the democratic atmosphere of the United States. They are, however, what a Communist must accept as his creed if he is to remain in the Communist Party.

## 10. *What are the appeals of Communism?*

Why would anyone want to be a Communist? To whom does Communism appeal and why?

Cleon Skousen, who served for sixteen years with the FBI, says

The influence of Marx and Engels has continued on the earth, not simply because they were against so many things, but primarily because they stood *for* something. In a word, they promised to satisfy humanity's two greatest needs: the need for universal peace and the need for universal prosperity.

The very fact that Communism offered a millennium for all the distracted, dissatisfied and unhappy people in the world assured it a hearing, not merely by under-privileged workers, but by many of the aristocracy, many of the wealthy, and many of the political and economic theorists.[5]

We may identify several hypothetical groups or kinds of people to whom Communism appeals. The purpose of this classification is to suggest why Communism may be attractive to widely different types of people.

(a) **The desperate.** Communism has an understandable appeal to the pitiful and the poor, especially the masses of uneducated and underprivileged of Asia, Africa, the Middle East, and Latin America. They think they have nothing to lose. In this sense, our society's failure to solve so many problems makes it easier for the Communists.

(b) **The misguided and the uninformed.** There are a great many such people throughout the world. They are easy targets for clever Communist propagandists. Who is not for peace? Who does not desire a better life for his fellow man?

(c) **The lazy.** Some people who are shiftless find Communism's promises attractive: "Divide up the riches; to each according to his need; a chicken in every pot."

(d) **The naive idealist.** Sometimes people with the very best intentions wind up serving Communist interests. Occasionally, even a few church members are found in the Communist ranks. But how can you both *believe* and *not believe* in God at the same time? Such an individual is naive and confused. He is an example of kindly ignorance in action.

(e) **Embittered members of minority races.** The Communists work very hard to capture for their cause members of the minority races in any country. When they are successful, it is usually among those few embittered members of minority races in countries where minorities are ill treated. These are people whose lives have been marred by tragic experiences with prejudice or

[5] Cleon Skousen, *The Naked Communist* (Ensign Publishing Company, Salt Lake City, 1958), p. 32.

poverty. Many of them, often too late, become disillusioned with
the false claims of Communism. (See "Is there racial discrimination in the Soviet Union?", page 117.)

**(f) The opportunist.** A few individuals join the Communist
party to "get ahead in politics," to feel the thrill of power and
leadership, to be able to give orders to Party flunkies. Their
life becomes involved with the game of politics for the game's
sake.

**(g) The frustrated individual.** Communism also may have
appeal for the frustrated man of action — the person who is a
crusader of sorts. He yearns for faith and for action. In the
Communist Party he hopes to find both.

**(h) The youthful adventurer.** A few young people of an ad-
venturous nature may join the Party out of curiosity, for a thrill.
After all, with passwords, codes, meetings at night, and couriers
from Hong Kong, life is exciting. Of course, as it turns out, there
are also endless, dull lectures on doctrine and duties. Eventually
such irresponsible youths come to realize that they have been
contributing to the destruction of their country.

**(i) Rich people with guilt feelings.** Why would a millionaire
join the Party or contribute to Communist causes? He may be at
the same time a member of one or several of the above groups.
Psychologists tell us that, in addition, he may have certain guilt
feelings about having so much money. By helping a group that
*claims* to be for the poor working class and for peace, he feels
better about it all.

**(j) The disillusioned.** Sometimes an individual beset with
problems, having lost faith in his religion or his political system
will turn to Communism. In the Party, for a time, he may find a
new faith and a new purpose. Human history is strewn with
tragic wreckage of the twice disillusioned, those children of the
god that failed.

**(k) The frustrated leader and fanatic follower.** Certain people
feel the need of discipline, leadership, and regimentation. You all
know the kind of person who isn't happy unless he takes or
gives orders, who wants to "belong" to a crowd and hates to think
for himself. Psychologists say he wants a "father image" to lead
him. This is the same kind of person as those who followed
Hitler. Communism attracts him too.

## 11. *Is Communism inevitable?*

Who has not heard of the old American adage that only two things in life are certain or inevitable: death and taxes! The facts certainly do not warrant adding Communism as a third item.

Naturally, the Communists insist that Communism is inevitable, the "wave of the future." That's perfectly good public relations, typical Soviet propaganda. One would scarcely expect them to say, "We're finished; we're through. Party membership is way down. Even the supply of sympathizers and dupes seems to be drying up." We wouldn't expect them to admit this, would we?

This is not to suggest that the crisis is past. Quite to the contrary! In an apparent effort to terrify the world, Khrushchev has tested more and bigger bombs than ever before. But two very hopeful signs do distinguish the resolute world of the early 1960's from the confused world of the late 1940's and early 1950's. The first is that we are strengthening our economy and defenses and accepting increased responsibilities overseas for the maintenance of peace. The second sign is that we are becoming better informed about the nature and scope of the Communist challenge. Other nations in the Free World have also learned much about Communism during the past, turbulent decade.

No, Communism is anything but inevitable — so long as we keep strong, have faith in ourselves and our system, learn all we can about the adversary, and work diligently for peace, freedom, and a better life for ourselves and for people throughout the world.

### Identifying a Communist

## 12. *How would I know a Communist if I met one?*

The Communist movement throughout its history has been secret and conspiratorial in nature — concealing the identity of

Party members. This behavior may be explained in two ways: (1) It is partly out of genuine fear of reprisal — the capitalists will destroy the Party. (2) It is due partly to the traditional attitude born of oppressive conditions in Russia under the tsars. This conspiratorial behavior has its unethical side — such as espionage and the infiltration of non-Communist organizations. Because a Communist's identity is concealed, it is not always easy to tell a Communist from a loyal American.

The difficulty of identifying a Communist may be illustrated by two short exercises in backward logic:

John often speaks against United States atomic testing.
The Communists often speak against United States atomic testing.
Therefore, John is a Communist.
*OR:*
The Communists are against United States atomic testing.
Bill is for United States atomic testing.
Therefore, Bill is a good, patriotic American and certainly not a Communist.

The first example illustrates the problem of guilt by association or by coincidence. John's reasons for being against atomic testing may have nothing to do with Communism.

In the second case, the fact that Bill does not openly support the Communists does not mean that he is a loyal American and not a Communist. Secret or concealed Communists usually pose as good loyal Americans.

At this point we seem to have reached an impossible situation. Is there, then, *no* way to be sure whether someone is or is not a Communist? In a sense, this is quite true. But two things are important to remember: (1) There are millions of loyal Americans and only a very few Communists; and (2) sowing the seeds of distrust and suspicion, American against American, is a standard Communist tactic.

This means we must beware of branding anyone with ideas different from our own as a Communist. At most, we can expect to identify only "open" Communists, that is, those who publicly acknowledge their political point of view or creed.

At the same time, the United States and its government must

be on guard against the activities of Communist Party members and their "dupes." It is never possible to separate with assurance a Communist Party member from a fellow-traveler or a sympathizer. The points in the Communist creed (listed on page 26) are useful in that they call attention to ideas accepted by Communists. It should be emphasized again that the purpose of this section is to help students develop standards for identifying and discounting *Communist propaganda*. Students should not take upon themselves the task of the FBI — to identify Communists and to bring them to justice.

## 13. What is a "fellow-traveler," a "sympathizer," a "dupe"?

A "fellow-traveler" is an individual who accepts Communist philosophy, shares Communist objectives, and approves of Communist organization and tactics; but who, for some personal reason, stops short of submitting himself to total Party discipline or joining the Communist Party.

To the Communist Party, a fellow-traveler can, on occasion, prove more valuable than an out-and-out Communist Party member. The fellow-traveler does the Party's work. At the same time, he can go into any court and, with a perfectly clear conscience, swear under oath that he is not and never was a member of the Communist Party. He can probably even pass a lie detector test on that question.

The record of Communist espionage and subversion from Austria to Australia, both ways round the world and especially in the United States, is sprinkled with the names of individuals who, though not formally members of the Communist Party, believed in the Communist cause. Such individuals have been willing to serve the Party's interest even when it meant betraying their own government.

The fellow-traveler thus poses special problems for the free, democratic societies of the world where the delicate distinction between liberty and license has become increasingly difficult to determine.

A "sympathizer" is one who goes along with many of the

Communist Party's objectives and programs but is not willing to go all the way. He is often confused, and even, on occasion, wonders whether the Party is not mistaken. This means he is likely to be somewhat less dedicated and less active than the "fellow-traveler," though at times he can be very useful to the Party.

A "dupe" is an individual who unconsciously or unknowingly lends his support to Communist causes. He is usually a good American trying to do the right thing. He is characteristically uninformed and usually politically naive.

Thus, the spectrum runs from indoctrinated-dedicated to uninformed-naive in this order: Party member, fellow-traveler, sympathizer, dupe.

# 3 The World Communist Movement

## Background and Purposes

**14.** *What is the background and the history of the World Communist movement?*

"Under the banner of workers' Soviets, under the banner of revolutionary struggle for power and the dictatorship of the proletariat, under the banner of the Third International [the Comintern] — proletarians of all countries unite. . . ."

With these words from the initial manifesto written by Trotsky, the Comintern or Communist Third International was established in Moscow in March of 1919. Trotsky (until his ousting), Lenin, Zinoviev, and Bukharin (whom Stalin later had executed) were its overseers. Control remained in Soviet hands (a Russian was always "elected" head). Communist Parties throughout the world belonged to the organization. Many of these Parties maintained a permanent representative in Moscow. All of them took their orders from Comintern headquarters.

The purposes of the Comintern were, in fact, twofold: (1) the communization of the world and (2) the promotion of Soviet foreign policy objectives.

The Communist Party in each country had to accept the Comintern's Twenty-one Conditions laid down by Lenin. These constituted the law, the rules which were to be observed by member Parties without question, on pain of expulsion.

The most significant of these "conditions" were:

(1) "All propaganda and agitation must be of a 'genuinely Communist character'," that is, made in Moscow. It must be systematically conducted within labor unions, among farm groups, in the city and countryside.

(2) The parties are ordered to conduct "both legal and *illegal* work."

(3) "The obligation to spread Communist ideas includes the special obligation to carry on systematic and energetic propaganda in the army."

(4) "Every party . . . is obliged to expose the tricks and dodges of its imperialists in the colonies, to support every colonial liberation movement not merely in words but in deeds, to demand the expulsion of their own imperialists from these colonies. . . ."

(5) "Every party [in] the Communist International is obliged to give unconditional support to any Soviet republic in its struggle against counter-revolutionary forces." Support Soviet Russia!

(6) "All the decisions of the Congresses of the Communist International, as well as the decisions of its Executive Committee, are binding on all parties belonging to the Communist International."

Since the Kremlin controlled the Comintern and the Comintern controlled active Communist Parties in most of the important nations of the world, the World Communist movement became in time a gigantic Soviet instrument for propaganda and subversion.

The history of the World Communist movement can be viewed meaningfully only in terms of the policies followed at various strategic periods. These changing policies have been called the Leninist Zig-Zag line. Decisions, personalities, attitudes, and events in Moscow have had a major impact on the policies and personnel of the member Communist Parties all around the world. The comrades and fellow-travelers from New York to Tokyo have for more than four decades taken their cue from the Kremlin. Should they be belligerent or friendly towards "cap italists" or the socialists? What should be their outward attitude towards Nazis? Should they pose as being for or against the United Nations? The precise line of a given moment on these and all other "controversial" issues is prescribed by Moscow — and it often changes drastically and suddenly.

Unless, therefore, we know something of these dramatic past shifts in the Kremlin-directed World Communist line, we cannot hope to understand the latest Communist line.

As it turns out, the zig-zag pattern of Communist policy, so far, has run back and forth seven times from *aggressive* to *"peaceful"* or *moderate*. The chart on page 36 shows the eight principal strategic periods. Notice the several abrupt Communist about-faces. Each was decided upon strictly in terms of the problems and requirements of Soviet policy at home and abroad. But loyal comrades everywhere, even in America, were obliged to fall in line, to parrot Soviet slogans, and to support the Kremlin's position. The classic case was the Nazi-Soviet agreement. When, in 1939, Stalin made a pact with Hitler, many Communists in other countries quit the Party in disgust.

## 15. *What are the goals and purposes of World Communism?*

When we speak of the goals and purposes of World Communism it is necessary to make two distinctions: the first is the distinction between immediate and long-range goals; the second is the distinction between the goals of one historical or strategic period as against another.

The long-range goals of World Communism have remained fairly constant. They may be summarized by the phrases: destruction of the capitalist system and the communization of the world. The emergence of Peking in 1949 as a second Communist power center, now rivaling Moscow, raises another angle. Is the World Communist movement still run by the Kremlin? What is Peking's role? (This aspect is discussed in Chapter 7.)

The World Communist movement also has displayed from time to time more limited, short-range goals. These may range from an attempt to wreck some political organization to a cam-

# The Zig-Zag of Soviet Policy and World Communism

| | Aggressive Line | More Moderate |
|---|---|---|
| **1917–1920** | Revolution, civil war; *war Communism;* foreign intervention. | |
| **1921–1927** | | *New Economic Policy;* encouragement of foreign economic relations, more cooperation with the West. |
| **1928–1934** | *First Five Year Plan;* collectivization of agriculture; militant policy at home; aggressive, hostile attitude abroad. | |
| **1935–1939** | | *United and Popular Fronts.* Cooperation between Comm and socialists, between the Soviet Union and the "capital ist" countries: "crush Nazi and Japanese fascism." |
| **1939–1941** | *Stalin-Hitler Pact.* Non-Aggression Pact with Japan; propaganda against U.S. and British war mongers; "Hitler's not so bad." | |
| **1941–1945** | | *Strange Wartime Alliances.* Germany attacks Soviet Unio Stalin appeals to U.S. and Bri for assistance. U.S. Lend-Lea to Russia; Pearl Harbor in eff makes U.S. and U.S.S.R. allie |
| **1946–1953** | *Postwar Readjustment.* Return to anti-Western policy on part of Stalin. Communist take-over of Eastern Europe. Communists conquer China, launch offensive in Asia; Korean War. | |
| **1953–** | *Khrushchev Era* | |
| | **Threats** Communist-inspired crises in Southeast Asia, Africa, Berlin; U.S. planes shot down; threats and nuclear testing in defiance of world opinion. | **Coexistence** Spirit of Geneva; talk of peac disarmament; end of fighting Korea; some relaxation at hot Spirit of Camp David. |

paign to ban United States nuclear testing. Short-range goals may appear on the surface confusing and quite contrary to the purposes of World Communism. Take for example the period of the Stalin-Hitler alliance, 1939–1941, which found the World Communist movement, in effect, supporting the previously hated Nazis. Such contradictory policies reflect the fact that the Communists are ready to use any means to achieve their goals.

It is important not to confuse objectives or aims with strategy and tactics. What you intend to do is one thing. How you go about doing it is another. At times the World Communist movement uses slogans such as "peace" and "coexistence" (see Chapter 7). But it regards these as temporary objectives. The great goal is to destroy the Free World's way of life.

## Strength and Organization

### 6. *How is the World Communist movement organized?*

The basis of World Communist activity is a complex of supposedly "international" organizations, which are in reality controlled or substantially influenced by the Soviet or Chinese Communist leaders. These interlocking organizations range from centralized political party directorates, such as the Comintern, to international labor organizations (for example, the World Federation of Trade Unions). Included also are cultural organizations, friendship societies, and certain World Peace Councils (not to be confused with genuine pacifist groups).

The pre-war Comintern is a classic example of the Kremlin-controlled "international" political organization dedicated to propaganda and subversion. From 1919 until its dissolution in 1943, it operated Communist Parties in Asia, Africa, the Middle East, Europe, and America. Some of the most prominent American Communists attended Comintern Schools in Moscow. There they studied Marxist theory, Communist political tactics, and military affairs. Through its Far Eastern Bureau in Shanghai, the Comintern organized the Chinese and Japanese Communist

Parties. Party leaders from around the world regularly made
trips to the Soviet Union for training and instructions. The
Comintern provided funds for the publication of propaganda in
dozens of languages. It also supplied secret radios, weapons, and
ammunition to its agents and Party members in many countries.
In these ways, it created and nourished a dangerous fifth column
wherever conditions permitted, wherever Communism was not
effectively checked.

The Cominform or Communist Information Bureau was created
in Eastern Europe in 1947. Until its dissolution in 1956, it carried
on many of the functions of the earlier Comintern.

At present there is no single, official "international" Communist
organization, although Communist Parties throughout the world
continue to take their guidance from Moscow and Peking. It
is possible that the Kremlin has decided that the world has
awakened to the nature and threat of World Communism and
that, therefore, all such organization and training activity must be
strictly *secret*. Front organizations have largely replaced official
"international" Communist organizations.

## 17. *What is a Communist Party?*

A Communist Party is a militant organization based on the
principles of Marxism-Leninism, and dedicated to the establishment of political and economic institutions that are a logical
outgrowth of this philosophy. The original or prototype is, of
course, the Communist Party of the Soviet Union.

The Communist Parties of the world today may be divided into
two main categories: (1) Those *in power* within the Sino-Soviet
bloc, and (2) Communist Parties operating in the nations of the
Free World. (Yugoslavia is a special case.) A further distinction
must be made: that between countries in the Free World where
the Communist Party is legal and countries where it is outlawed.

Perhaps the most direct way of introducing the concept of the
Communist Party is to ask how the Communists themselves
characterize the nature and function of their organization. Lenin,
Stalin, and Khrushchev are all surprisingly frank and informative.
Here are a few of their statements.

# COMMUNIST WORLD: WEST

Yugoslavia is Communist but follows an independent course. Albania seems to look to Peking rather than Moscow for leadership. Spain receives aid from the United States and has granted air bases to this country. Cuba (not shown on the map) has declared itself a Communist state.

A

Moscow, like other capital cities, has "something old; something new." Among the former are Red Square, the Spasskaya Tower (right), and St. Basil's Cathedral, completed in 1679. The Tower marks an entrance to the Kremlin, which is a national museum. The new buildings in the background loom over the older structures.

This photograph of Karl Marx was taken in the late 1870's when he was living in London and writing his chief work, *Das Kapital*.

A leader in the Bolshevik Revolution, Leon Trotsky became the first Soviet commissar of foreign affairs. Later he organized the Red Army which was victorious in the civil war, 1918–21. After Lenin's death, Trotsky was outmaneuvered by Stalin, expelled from the Party, and exiled.

In this statue at the 1955 Leipzig Fair, Stalin stands at the side of Lenin. His body was then resting beside Lenin's in the mausoleum in Moscow's Red Square. Khrushchev, in 1961, ordered the removal of Stalin's body from the tomb and the destruction of all statues of Stalin. This was the final act in the downgrading of Lenin's successor.

C

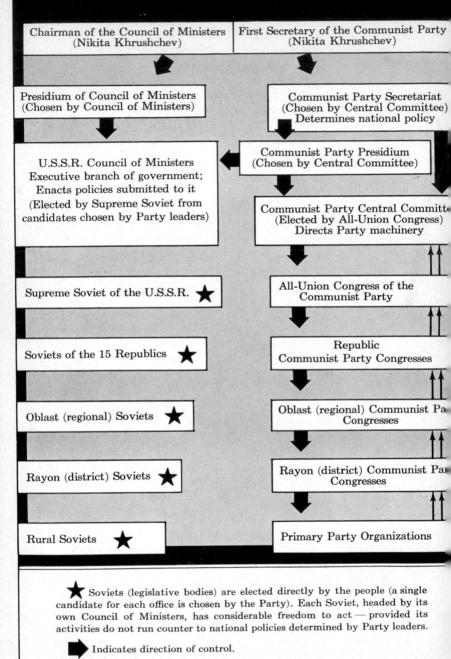

# POLITICAL SYSTEM OF THE SOVIET UNION

| Chairman of the Council of Ministers (Nikita Khrushchev) | First Secretary of the Communist Party (Nikita Khrushchev) |

Presidium of Council of Ministers
(Chosen by Council of Ministers)

Communist Party Secretariat
(Chosen by Central Committee)
Determines national policy

U.S.S.R. Council of Ministers
Executive branch of government;
Enacts policies submitted to it
(Elected by Supreme Soviet from
candidates chosen by Party leaders)

Communist Party Presidium
(Chosen by Central Committee)

Communist Party Central Committee
(Elected by All-Union Congress)
Directs Party machinery

Supreme Soviet of the U.S.S.R. ★

All-Union Congress of the
Communist Party

Soviets of the 15 Republics ★

Republic
Communist Party Congresses

Oblast (regional) Soviets ★

Oblast (regional) Communist Party
Congresses

Rayon (district) Soviets ★

Rayon (district) Communist Party
Congresses

Rural Soviets ★

Primary Party Organizations

★ Soviets (legislative bodies) are elected directly by the people (a single candidate for each office is chosen by the Party). Each Soviet, headed by its own Council of Ministers, has considerable freedom to act — provided its activities do not run counter to national policies determined by Party leaders.

► Indicates direction of control.

⇒ Indicates that the higher organization is made up of delegates from the lower.

D

**The Party is a "class" organ.** As early as 1904, Lenin said: "We are the Party of a class[1] and therefore almost the entire class [the "proletariat"] should act under the leadership of our Party, should adhere to our Party as closely as possible."

**The Party is an organizational weapon.** In 1920, after the Communist victory in Russia, Lenin said: "It was only because the Party was on the alert, it was only because the Party was strictly disciplined, because the authority of the Party was able to unite all governmental departments and institutions, because the slogans issued by the Central Committee were followed by tens, hundreds, thousands and finally millions of people as one man, and because incredible sacrifices were made — it was only because of all this that the miracle could take place which actually took place."

**The Party is authoritarian and not fundamentally concerned with democracy or elections.** Lenin said in 1921: "The class which took political power in its hands did so knowing that it took this power alone. This is contained in the concept dictatorship of the proletariat. This concept has meaning only when a single class knows that it alone is taking political power in its hands and does not deceive itself or others with talk about 'popular, elected' government 'sanctified by the whole people.'"

**The Party is centralized and demands iron discipline.** Lenin said in 1920: "the Communist Party will be able to perform its duty only if it is organized in the most centralized manner, only if iron discipline bordering on military discipline prevails in it."

**The Party becomes stronger by "purging" itself.** Stalin said in 1920: "In an epoch of bourgeois rule, a proletarian party can grow and gain strength only to the extent that it combats the opportunist, anti-revolutionary and anti-Party elements in its own midst and within the working class. Lassalle was right when he said: 'A Party becomes stronger by purging itself.'"

**The Party has no respect for the individual.** Lenin said in 1921: "If we really succeed . . . in purging our Party from top to bottom, 'without respect for persons,' the gains for the revolution will be really enormous."

**The Party is all-seeing, all-powerful and does not tolerate**

[1] We must keep in mind that the Communist claim to represent the workers, whether in the USSR or throughout the world, is false.

**organized opposition.** Stalin said in 1936: "In the USSR there is ground for only one party, the Communist Party. In the USSR only one party can exist." Khrushchev made the same point in an ominous, if colorful, way in 1956 when he said: "After the liquidation of the classes we have a monolithic society. Therefore, why found another Party? That would be like voluntarily letting someone put a flea in your shirt."

**The Party is ruthless in dealing with its enemies.** Khrushchev said in 1957: "Its entire history shows that the party could not have fulfilled its role . . . if it had not waged a ruthless struggle against the Mensheviks, the Social Revolutionaries, the Anarchists, the Trotskyites, the right wing deviationists, the bourgeois nationalists and other enemies of Marxism-Leninism. . . ."

We will search a long time before finding a more graphic, down-to-earth description of a Communist Party than this classic message translated from a Japanese Communist Handbook entitled *Cell Activities Made Easy:*

> When a number of individuals function as a group, they unite in some definite form. This is what is meant by organization. Members of labor unions, social groups, and cultural circles are organized appropriately. Similarly, members of a political party, whether they number several thousands or several million, must be organized. The bourgeois political parties and the Socialist Party . . . place greatest emphasis upon the vote at election time. In focusing their attention upon the election, these parties organize according to their member's place of residence, rather than according to his place of work. Our Communist Party is different. The Communist Party is not interested primarily in obtaining votes. To our Party, the working masses are more important. . . .
>
> The Communist Party must fight bravely for the needs of the working masses and, through this fight, develop within the masses a class consciousness. The Communist Party must be organized in a manner appropriate for such revolutionary activity. . . .
>
> The basic unit of the Party is called a Cell. Cells are created in shops, agrarian communities, schools, and residential areas. These Cells, each of which has a definite, independent character, serve as the nuclei of Party activity. The situation is exactly the same as in the case of the human body, where each cell functions as an independent organism, contributing at the same time to the function of the body as a whole.

These Cells are combined to form District Committees, Regional Committees, and a Central Committee. Through the Cell, the higher echelons activate the masses. Union of the Party and the masses is effected through the Cell. . . .

The Cell is the stronghold of the revolutionary movement.[2]

In a brilliant passage from his book, *The New Class*, former high-ranking Yugoslavian Communist Milovan Djilas summarizes the stark totalitarian reality of a Communist Party in power:

The mechanism of Communist power is perhaps the simplest which can be conceived, although it leads to the most refined tyranny and the most brutal exploitation. The simplicity of this mechanism originates from the fact that one party alone, The Communist Party, is the backbone of the entire political, economic, and ideological activity. The entire public life is at a standstill or moves ahead, falls behind or turns around according to what happens in the Party forums.

Under the Communist systems the people realize quickly what they are and what they are not permitted to do. Laws and regulations do not have an essential importance for them. The actual and unwritten rules concerning the relationship between the government and its subjects do. Regardless of laws, everyone knows that the government is in the hands of the Party committees and the secret police. Nowhere is 'the directing role' of the Party prescribed, but its authority is established in all organizations and sectors. No law provides that the secret police has the right to control citizens, but the police is all-powerful. No law prescribes that the judiciary and prosecutors should be controlled by the secret police and the Party committee, but they are. Most people know that this is the case. Everyone knows what can and what cannot be done, and what depends on whom. People adjust to the environment and to actual conditions, turning to Party forums or to organs under the Party's control in all important matters. . . .

Party ideological unity makes independent movements impossible within the Communist system and within society itself. Every action depends on the Party, which has total control over society; within it there is not the slightest freedom.[3]

[2] Rodger Swearingen and Paul Langer, *Red Flag in Japan: International Communism in Action 1919–1951,* (Harvard University Press, Cambridge, Massachusetts, 1952), pp. 96–97.
[3] Milovan Djilas, *The New Class, An Analysis of the Communist System,* (Frederick A. Praeger, Inc., New York, 1957), pages 70–71, 75.

## 18. *Do Communist Parties take orders from Moscow?*

The Twenty-one Conditions set up by the Soviet-controlled Comintern in 1920 specifically required Communist Parties throughout the world to follow the lead of Moscow. Several decades of experience have set the pattern and policy of World Communism from which to date there has been only occasional evidence of deviation. High-level defectors from Communist Parties in Japan, Germany, the Soviet Union, and America have all testified from personal experience that Communist Parties everywhere are directed, financed, and trained by Soviet agents (or perhaps now, in a few cases, by representatives of Peking).

A large percentage of the staffs of the important Communist Parties throughout the world have received training in Moscow or Peking. Many of them make regular pilgrimages to these capitals of Communism for conferences or refresher courses.

The "line" or editorial viewpoint of Communist Party publications all over the world tends to follow the policies and interpretations of the moment as issued from Moscow. Dr. Philip E. Mosely, formerly Professor of International Relations at Columbia University and Director of the University's Russian Institute, has cited 45 international questions of major importance, extending over the past 30 years, on which there has been no substantial difference in the position announced by the Soviet government and that taken by the Communist Party of the United States. It should be recognized, however, that neither Yugoslavia nor, at present, Communist China is taking orders from Moscow on all matters.

Nevertheless, there can be no question but that Communist Party organizations in the Free World are, in reality, agencies of World Communism and take their orders from Moscow and Peking. (See Chapter 8 on the United States Communist Party's ties with Moscow.)

## 19. *How strong is the World Communist movement?*

**Communist co-operation.** Often we hear the phrase "the World Communist movement" used as if we were facing some huge, popular, completely coordinated, and irresistible force. This is not the case. Such a view plays right into the Communist hands. Clearly, the Communist threat to America and to the Free World is serious, growing, and world-wide — but Communist strategy is not always effective, nor is the "international" movement these days characteristically well coordinated. World Communism today cannot be regarded as either popular or irresistible.

What does this mean? It means that while the Moscow and Peking military and economic challenges to our way of life have become more aggressive and more persistent with each passing year, the strength of "international" Communism — both as an ideology and as a political movement — has been waning.

The pattern of disintegration and disillusionment is clear. In 1948, Tito broke with Stalin, taking Yugoslavia out of the Moscow orbit (see page 22). Since the emergence of the Chinese People's Republic in 1949, Moscow-Peking relations have always been "proper" but rarely cordial, and there is mounting evidence of increasing friction. Poland has frequently shown clear and unmistakable signs of "deviation." East Germany and Hungary are "unreliable" on the record: In both, violent anti-Communist revolutions have occurred — revolutions which the Kremlin was obliged to suppress with tanks, first-line Soviet divisions, and subsequent widespread political purges. Little Albania, while not significant strategically, is symbolic. Khrushchev is opposed to the "Stalinist clique" in power there; Mao "supports the present Albanian regime," and so it goes.

Let us not, then, make the mistake of assuming that the enemy is better coordinated and more powerful than he is. This is what Moscow and Peking — whatever their family quarrel — would like us to think. The facts suggest that the Communist world has its problems too.

This is not to discount the very real, recent and serious Communist inroads in Africa, Southeast Asia, and Latin America. No American is likely to forget the shock he experienced when it became clear that Castro had established a Communist beachhead in Cuba. It is rather to indicate that "international" Communism is not always united with respect to either ideology or foreign policy.

**Party membership.** The total number of Communist Party

members in the world is estimated to be about 35 million, more than 5 million of whom are in non-Communist countries.

The largest Communist state Party is the Chinese with an estimated 17,000,000 members. The most formidable Parties outside the Soviet orbit remain the Indonesian with something like 1,500,000 members and the Italian with approximately 1,200,000 members.

Africa, which has been a recent target of intensive Communist action, still has not produced substantial Communist Party organizations. A recent State Department intelligence report brands the Soviet claim that there were "5,000 Communists in Africa 20 years ago, but there are 50,000 now," as "spurious," that is, unreliable.

Figures for current estimated Communist Party membership in ten representative countries of the Free World, outside of the United States, are as follows:

| | |
|---|---|
| France | 250,000 |
| Spain | 5,000 |
| West Germany | 40,000 |
| Sweden | 5,000 |
| Greece | 20,000 |
| India | 250,000 |
| Japan | 75,000 |
| Finland | 30,000 |
| Mexico | 5,000 |
| Brazil | 40,000 |

According to the most recent estimate of an authoritative source, there are presently 10,000 Communist Party members in the United States (see page 205 for more detail).

Several important points, however, must be kept in mind when considering these figures:

1. Party membership is no measure of the strength and effectiveness of Communism. When voters in France and Italy, for example, are dissatisfied, they may vote for candidates of the Communist Party even though they are not Communists.

2. "Front" organizations and mass organizations under Communist control increase Communist numerical strength many fold.

3. A Communist Party member is not like the average member of the Democratic or Republican party in the United States. The Communist works twenty-four hours a day for his "cause." He is dedicated, disciplined, and directed. His model is the Soviet Union. His goal is the destruction of our free way of life.

## Key Figures

## 20. *What kind of person was Karl Marx?*

Karl Marx is known as the father of modern Communism. He and his friend, Frederick Engels, produced a revolutionary theory that was to shake the world to its very foundations. Was Marx an underprivileged worker, one of the proletariat? He certainly was not. Was he a Russian? No, he had never even been to Russia. Who was he, then, and how did he come to develop the basic tenets of modern Communism?

Marx was born in 1818 in Trier, Germany, of bourgeois, or middle-class parents. His real family name was Levi. He was of Jewish descent, though his family was converted to Lutheran Christianity when Karl was but six years old. His grandfather was a rabbi, his father a lawyer. Marx's young life was full of disappointments, frustrations, and suffering — the life of a converted Jew in those days was not always a happy one.

Marx married, as they say, "above him." His wife, Jenny von Westphalen, came from an important family.

It was in 1842 while he was editing a liberal newspaper in Cologne, Germany (a position he later was forced to resign because of his radicalism) that Marx met Engels. A short time later, Marx went to Paris, where he co-edited the *German-French Annals,* a radical, socialist paper. When he was expelled from France for his radicalism, he moved on to Brussels. There he wrote *The Misery of Philosophy,* his first systematic exposition of Marxism (he and Engels had earlier published the *German Ideology,* setting forth the concept of historical materialism).

Finally, Marx moved to England, where he was to spend much of his life in poverty, writing the works that have made him famous: *The Communist Manifesto* (which he wrote with Engels) and *Das Kapital.* The first, written in an eloquent, popular style, begins: "A spectre is haunting Europe — the spectre of Communism." It sets forth the basic doctrine of Communism, the Marxist view of history, of society, and of man. The second is a heavier economic analysis of capitalism, to which Marx attributed all of the world's ills. The lot of the "worker" in mid-nineteenth century London — long hours, poor pay, child labor — left its mark on Marx. The middle class had not yet come into its own. The life of the working people was a difficult, unhappy one.

It is said that Marx became suspicious of everyone; he was quarrelsome; he developed an outward arrogance possibly due to his inner feelings of inferiority. Envy and bitterness were his constant companions. He seemed to know little of tolerance.

From such a perspective, Marx wrote of the world about him, of its present ills and its future prospects. Using the instruments of the dialectic, historical materialism, and his Marxist economic analysis, he would "scientifically" predict the future of the world. He made a number of predictions. Most of them have not materialized. Marx died in 1883, but the philosophy which he created lives on as a sort of misdirected faith.

## 21. *What were Lenin, Trotsky, and Stalin like?*

**Vladimir Lenin.** If you should go to Moscow today you could see Lenin for yourself. He is lying in state in a coffin in the Lenin mausoleum, a stone monument on Red Square just outside the walls of the Kremlin and right across from the Soviets' showplace department store, "Gum." Long lines of Russians and a few foreigners may be seen before the entrance to the tomb.

Lenin is known as the father of the Russian Revolution. He has even been called the George Washington of the Soviet Union, but the comparison is not entirely a happy one.

The son of a high school teacher, Lenin studied law, and joined the labor movement at an early age. He was dismissed from the university for his political activities. His brother was executed for plotting the assassination of the Tsar. Lenin devoted his life to the revolution. His was perhaps the most brilliant mind of all the Bolsheviks. His real name was Ulyanoff. (A revolutionary in those days usually adopted an alias.)

As early as 1897, after having been exiled to Siberia and then traveling abroad for a time, Lenin helped found the "Militant League for the Emancipation of the Working Class." This organization eventually grew into the Russian Social-Democratic Party. From the beginning, Lenin was the leader of that Party's militant left wing.

After ten years of wandering as an exile from one capital to another in Europe, Lenin returned to Russia when the Tsar's government was overthrown in the spring of 1917. In November he became the leader of the Bolshevik Revolution, which seized power from the Provisional Government. Among his important writings perhaps the most significant were *Imperialism* and *State and Revolution*. His collected works are today regarded among Communists with the reverence and interest usually reserved in the Western world for the Bible. Lenin died in 1924, after suggesting that perhaps Stalin was *not* the man to succeed him. Nonetheless, Stalin took over, but not until he had pushed Trotsky aside.

**Leon Trotsky.** The life of Trotsky was devoted to the cause of Communism. Trotsky was second only to Lenin in forming the Revolution. With the death of Lenin, Trotsky found himself at ideological odds with his former comrade-in-arms, Stalin. The ruthless Stalin had his way (see page 20). Trotsky is remembered by historians — but not by the Communists — as the father of the Red army.

Trotsky was born of peasant stock. He studied at Kiev University. His real name was Bronstein. Like Lenin, he was brilliant, and, for a Communist, he was an independent thinker. Neither of these qualities endeared him to Stalin.

Trotsky's ideas, his difficulties and disappointments — his life — he set down in 1938 in *The Revolution Betrayed*. He also wrote a *History of the Russian Revolution* and a biography of Stalin.

**Joseph Stalin.** Today Stalin, the leader of the USSR from 1927 to 1953, is no longer a Communist hero. Stalin, who fostered the belief that he was second only to Lenin among Communist leaders, was accused of fostering a "cult of the personality" by Khrushchev.

After attacking Stalin in 1956 for his "crimes against the Soviet people," Khrushchev in the fall of 1961 capped the anti-Stalin campaign by having the embalmed body of his former superior unceremoniously removed from the Lenin-Stalin mausoleum and buried in a common grave. This was the signal for a new and more thorough-going anti-Stalin campaign which included the removal and destruction of all statues of Stalin throughout the Soviet Union and Eastern Europe and even the change of the names of streets and cities, like Stalingrad, in order to erase the late dictator's name.

What had the absolute ruler and demi-god of the world of Communism for twenty-five years done to deserve such treatment? A great deal! But the strange part is that the attacker, Khrushchev, was Stalin's eager accomplice to most of the crimes.

Let us look very briefly at the man, Stalin. A small, usually quiet, unhandsome man, a habitual doodler who doodled wolves, girls, castles, and the word "Lenin" on scratch pads during important conferences and interviews, Stalin gave the impression of calm. *Time* Magazine reports that a Tito aide who once saw him angry recalls: "He trembled with rage, he shouted, his features distorted, he sharply motioned with his hand and poured invective into the face of his secretary who was trembling and paling as if struck by heart failure." Biographer Boris Souvarine called him a "repulsive character . . . cunning, crafty, treacherous but also brutal, violent, implacable. . . ." Said Churchill, now known for his sympathy for anything Soviet: "Stalin left upon me an impression of deep, cool wisdom and absence of illusions." Roosevelt found him "altogether, quite impressive. . . ."

Stalin was born on December 2, 1879 in a cottage (a shrine until the recent anti-Stalin campaign) in the small town of Gori in Georgia. He was one of four children; all of his brothers and sisters died in infancy. He was baptized Joseph Vissarionovich Djugashvili. His father was a shoemaker and an alcoholic. It is said that the father beat young Joseph unmercifully and finally deserted his family. Joseph's mother went to work as a laundress in order to be able to send her boy, whom she called Soso, to a parish school. She wanted him to become a priest. H did enter the Orthodox Theological Seminary in Tiflis, but was soon expelled for reading radical literature.

The next phase of his life began when he joined a clandestine socialist organization. He got a job at the Tiflis Geological Observatory. He and his young socialist friends began holding meetings in his room. Police raided the room and Joseph, "Soso," went underground, taking for himself still another nickname or "cover," Koba (meaning inconquerable). For agitation among Tiflis railroad workers, he was picked up by the tsarist police (who by this time had him sized up as a real trouble-maker). He was jailed and then deported to Siberia. There began the third phase of his life.

Since so many political prisoners who had been plotting revolution were exiled to Siberia, it became known as "The academy for revolutionaries." In Siberia Koba followed the ideological controversies between the right (Menshevik) and the left (Bolshevik) wings of the Social Democratic Party. He was clever enough not to commit himself to either side. He studied Marxist literature. He observed his fellow political exiles, their strengths and weaknesses. Finally, he escaped, and after traveling hundreds of miles by peasant cart and suffering hunger and frostbite, he arrived back in Tiflis. At this time he married Katerina Svanidze, a Georgian girl, who bore him a son.

The next phase of his life now began — active preparation for revolution. Koba began writing revolutionary tracts or pamphlets. Here is an example from one of them: "Russia is like a loaded gun, at full cock, ready to go off at the slightest concussion. Rally around the Party Committees. . . ." When the gun did go off, the first shot misfired. The revolutionary attempt was a failure.

Koba's pamphlets had caught the eye of Lenin in Europe, and he became Lenin's devoted disciple. The Party was without funds, so Koba stopped writing and talking and went into action. He directed fighting squads which robbed banks, government offices, and steamships. With his name on all police wanted lists, Koba spent a total of seven of the next ten years in prison.

World War I was the beginning of the end of tsarist power. It made possible the short-lived Kerensky government of 1917 and the Bolshevik take-over. Although Stalin had escaped from

Siberia, he did not take a very important part in the Revolution. Lenin and Trotsky were the main leaders. Stalin emerged as one of the seven members of the Party's political bureau, and was made Commissar of Nationalities. Lenin joked: "No intelligence is needed, that is why we've put Stalin there."

What Stalin lacked in intellectual capacity, he more than made up in organizational ability and political astuteness. He was a mixture of determination, shrewdness, and ruthlessness. He became Lenin's administrative assistant and "hatchet man." Early in 1922, the post of General Secretary of the Control Committee was created for him.

When Lenin died in January of 1924, Stalin was quick to consolidate his power. Within a year, most of Stalin's colleagues (including Trotsky) were on their way out. By 1929, all important contenders for power had been imprisoned, exiled to Siberia, or expelled from the country. Stalin was master of the USSR, head of the Party, and leader of World Communism. The record of his ruthless rule during the next decades is the story of the destruction of the Kulaks (middle-class farmers), forced collectivization of agriculture, the Great Purge Trials, the Soviet takeover of Eastern Europe, the emergence of China as a Communist power, the Korean War — in short it is the record of Soviet affairs at home and abroad until Stalin's death in March, 1953.

## 22. How much do we know about Khrushchev and his "inner cabinet"?

From the beginning, leadership of the World Communist movement has been in the hands of a few men in the Kremlin. But who are the key Soviet leaders today? Deciding who are the leaders in the Soviet Union is never easy for two reasons: (1) the secrecy which surrounds all events and all important Party members in Russia, and (2) the constant, unpredictable, sudden changes in the top leadership which have become characteristic of the Communist totalitarian state.

The heir-apparent of today may turn out to be the minor Party official of tomorrow. The old Bolshevik, Molotov, some years ago regarded as the number two or three man in the Soviet Union, was reduced in rank; assigned a minor post as a Soviet representative to an international organization in Vienna; and then, in the fall of 1961, brought back to the Soviet Union in disgrace, to face his accusers. Former chief of the secret police Beria, only a few years ago a contender for the top spot, was executed by his rivals in the struggle for power.

There seems little doubt that as of 1962 Khrushchev is the top man in Russia. He has surrounded himself with a small group of informal advisors known as his "inner cabinet." Let us, at least, become familiar with the names and backgrounds of these Soviet leaders. One of them could be Khrushchev's successor tomorrow. In any case, they all play key roles today.

**Nikita Sergeievich Khrushchev.** Khrushchev is Premier of the Soviet Union and First Secretary of the Communist Party. He is the single most powerful individual in the world of Communism.

Khrushchev's words and deeds add up to a rather frightening picture. He has been personally responsible for the purge and execution of countless of his countrymen. Whenever it has served his purposes, he has attacked friends, his former superiors, the old Bolsheviks. He was responsible for giving the order which resulted in the slaughter of thousands of Hungarians by Soviet tanks (in the 1956 Hungarian freedom revolt). He came to speak before the United Nations and then took off his shoe and pounded it on the desk, to the astonishment of the delegates.

Western statesmen, correspondents, businessmen, and researchers who have met with him, seen him in action, or studied his record characterize Khrushchev as "difficult," "a man of vigor and shrewdness," "tough," "opportunistic," "crude," "a second Stalin," "man of action," "ruthless," "at times relaxed and jovial," "not to be trusted."

But Khrushchev's evident qualities of dedicated ruthlessness and opportunism are augmented by certain other and quite different traits. He can be charming and jovial, and has responded warmly to the welcome given him in lands which he has visited. This Jekyll-and-Hyde character makes Khrushchev doubly dangerous.

Consider these personal evaluations by great leaders who can hardly be said to be pro-Communist:

Former Vice President Nixon:
A self-made man who worked his way up from the bottom . . .
He is an articulate spokesman for the economic system in which
he believes . . . He has immense drive; in sum, he is one of those
individuals who, whether you agree with him or not, is a born
leader of men.

President Kennedy:
Mr. Khrushchev is no fool . . . Americans traditionally like to
picture hostile dictators as unstable and irrational men, the almost
comic captives of their moods and manias . . . But the Khrushchev
I met was a tough minded, articulate, hard-reasoning spokesman
for a system in which he was thoroughly versed and in which he
thoroughly believed.

General De Gaulle:
Mr. Khrushchev seemed to me to be a strong personality. He is
a man who has fought all his life for his ideas, and that has necessarily left a mark on him.

Khrushchev was born in the small village of Kalinovka in the
Ukraine. As a boy he worked on his father's farm, then became
(in order) a shepherd, a miner, and a locksmith. Khrushchev
joined the Communist Party rather late (at the age of twenty-
four, a year after the Bolshevik Revolution of 1917). He studied
at the Workers' Faculty, Kharkov University, but abandoned his
studies in 1924. The year 1929, when Khrushchev was sent to
Moscow Industrial Academy, marks the beginning of his Party
career and ultimate rise to power.

In fights within the Party, Khrushchev never sided with either
right or left but always remained loyal to Stalin. He strongly
supported Stalin in the great purges of 1930's. At that time he
said: "Stalin is our hope. He is our expectation, . . . Stalin is our
banner! Stalin is our will! Stalin is our victory!"

The 1930's found Khrushchev in one important Party post after
another. As general secretary of the Ukraine Communist Party
Khrushchev was directly responsible for wiping out Stalin's opposition throughout that huge region of the Soviet Union. By
March, 1939, resistance had been eliminated, and Khrushchev
could report to the 18th Party Congress: "The love of Ukrainian

Bolsheviks for Comrade Stalin is reflected by the limitless confidence of the whole Ukrainian people in, and their love for, the great Stalin."

Khrushchev served on various military committees and Councils during World War II, mostly on the Ukrainian Front. With the war over, he again took over as First Secretary of the Ukraine Communist Party, a position he held until 1949 when he was again called to Moscow. Now, along with Molotov, Malenkov, Bulganin, and Beria, he became a contender for power. When Stalin died in March, 1953, Malenkov took over for a brief time. When Secret Police Chief Beria emerged as the most powerful leader, the "collective leadership" killed him. Khrushchev, in turn, was able to push Malenkov aside. For a time he had Marshal Bulganin, a figurehead, as his associate. Without resorting to the terror used by Stalin, Khrushchev has managed to get a firm grasp on power.

Khrushchev denounced the crimes of Stalin in 1956. Now he heads the government of the Soviet Union and also leads the Party. He will remain the most powerful figure in the USSR until a stronger combination emerges.

**Frol R. Kozlov (1908 — ).** Kozlov is one of the four party undersecretaries and is considered Khrushchev's closest party aide. Tactful and good looking, Koslov handles party appointments. He was born about 200 miles from Moscow into a peasant family. At the age of 15 he went to work in a factory where he subsequently became foreman. After serving on several Komsomol (Young Communist League) committees, he graduated from the Leningrad Polytechnical Institute as a metallurgical engineer. He supported Khrushchev during the Party anti-Stalin fight of 1957.

*Newsweek* recently said of Kozlov: "An amiable fellow with a taste for button-down shirts and jewel tie-pins, he is inclined to be somewhat stuffy. In the spring of 1961 he suffered a heart attack. 'But Kozlov,' says one top British Kremlinologist, 'has drive and ambition in his belly.'"

**Anastas I. Mikoyan (1895 — ).** Khrushchev said that if Mikoyan were an American he would undoubtedly be a successful businessman. Mikoyan is bright and clever with an unusual instinct for the politics of survival — an essential trait in the

Soviet Union. Stalin called him a "genius of trade." As Soviet First Deputy Premier, Mikoyan now runs Khrushchev's trade and economic warfare offensive. He is by training and inclination ideally suited to the task.

During the years of great unrest in the USSR, Mikoyan served as Secretary and "organizer" in various district and regional Party organizations. In this capacity he became an expert at the art of the "purge." In 1926, he "moved up" to Moscow, where he has been ever since.

In the 1930's he developed a system of supplying provisions through special stores to top Party, government, and army personnel. Then, during World War II, Mikoyan became a key member of the State Defense Committee in charge of trade and food. He is generally regarded as the one primarily responsible for stripping the satellite nations of some 30 billion dollars worth of goods and equipment after World War II.

Khrushchev was first to see Mikoyan's usefulness. Mikoyan was quick to recognize Khrushchev's rising star. So Mikoyan denounced his former boss Stalin and cast his lot with Khrushchev. As a result, Mikoyan, an Armenian, is today one of the few remaining "Old Bolsheviks" still "in favor" and in a position of power.

**Mikhail A. Suslov (1902 —     ).** Suslov is the Party theoretician and one of its tough undersecretaries. History will remember him as (1) the man responsible for the mass deportations from Lithuania during World War II; (2) the "butcher of Budapest" for his role in the suppression of the Hungarian revolt; and (3) as the leader of the Kremlin campaign against Tito's "revisionism" or "National Communism."

Trained as a political economist at various Moscow institutes, Suslov came up the familiar Party ladder, moving from district to region to "all-Union," from assistant to secretary to First Secretary. For a brief time he was editor of *Pravda*.

Within the Party, Suslov is considered as a specialist on foreign affairs, intelligence, and propaganda. He was chief editor of the 1961 Party program.

**Aleksei N. Kosygin (1904 —     ).** Kosygin, a Deputy Premier, is one of Khrushchev's key administrators and advisors on Soviet industry. He is an energetic Kremlin economic planner. Kosygin has been called, among other things, an efficiency expert. Clearly, he is one of the men most responsible for the upward surge in Soviet production. For example, Kosygin is thought to have played a major role in drafting the economic section of the 20-Year Plan adopted by the 22nd Communist Party Congress in the fall of 1961.

**Leonid I. Brezhnev (1906 — ).** Brezhnev is "President" of the Soviet Union by virtue of his ceremonial position as head of the Supreme Soviet ( see pp. 69 to 71 on Soviet Government organization). He is clearly one of the "new class." More importantly — at least for the moment — he is said to be one of Khrushchev's closest advisors.

He is a Ukrainian and a former agricultural technician. He joined the Party at the age of twenty-five, and quickly found that a career in politics offered more advantages than farming. During World War II, Brezhnev held a high position in the political administration of the Soviet Army — on the Ukrainian front.

Brezhnev worked for a time as an executive in the "virgin lands" experiment — the fairly unsuccessful attempt to turn waste land into agricultural ground. In 1957, Khrushchev made him a member of the Party Presidium.

**Dimitri S. Polyansky (1917 — ).** Polyansky is Premier of the huge and important Russian Republic and the youngest member of the Party Presidium. He is able, hard-working, and tough. At the same time he has been described as "breezy and relaxed." This is the combination of talent that brought him to the attention of Khrushchev. He has been a Party and Government workhorse: 1950–52, Secretary, Crimean Oblast (province) Committee; 1952–54, Chairman, Crimean Oblast Committee; elected Deputy, USSR Supreme Soviet; 1956, elected to Credentials Commission, 20th Party Congress; 1957, First Secretary Chkalov Oblast Party Committee, then First Secretary, Krasnodar Krai Party Committee; 1958 appointed Chairman, RSFSR Council of Ministers.

**Rodion Y. Malinovsky (1898 — ).** Malinovsky is Defense Minister and head of the Soviet Armed Forces. He was born in the Black Sea port of Odessa in a worker's family. Now 64, he is close to retirement.

His military career began in 1916, the year before the Russian Revolution, when young Malinovsky, then 18 years of age, was drafted into the tsar's forces. The next year his unit was sent to France. He was not in France very long before he was arrested by the French authorities for conducting Communist propaganda among Russian troops in France.

With the war over and the Revolution successful, Malinovsky returned to Russia where he immediately entered the Red army.

For the next two decades, as he climbed the officer's ladder, his military service alternated between troop command and various military schools and academies. By the eve of World War II, he had risen to the position of division commander. Malinovsky distinguished himself on several fronts as a strategist against the Germans and the Japanese.

In the official Soviet classification of military commanders, rated according to their prestige or standing, Malinovsky's name was in sixth place as of 1945. He holds five Orders of Lenin. He appears to be one of Khrushchev's present favorites for three reasons: (1) He served brilliantly on the Ukrainian fronts — Khrushchev's old stamping grounds. (2) He has considerable political sense. (3) He denounced his former superior, Marshal Georgi K. Zhukov, when the latter got into trouble with Khrushchev.

**Aleksei I. Adzhubei (1924 —     ).** Adzhubei is editor of the Soviet Government newspaper *Izvestia*. His more important distinction stems from the fact that he is Khrushchev's son-in-law. He met Khrushchev's attractive daughter Rada while studying journalism at Moscow University. Adzhubei, not really one of the leading figures in the USSR, came into the news when he interviewed President Kennedy — an interview which was published in large part in *Izvestia*. The Russian people rarely have an opportunity to read anything said by an American President.

**Mstislav V. Keldysh (1911 —     ).** Keldysh is President of the Soviet Academy of Sciences and an advisor on space and atomic research. He is really not a political figure. Born in 1911, he graduated from Moscow University in mathematics and physics in 1931.

His research has included special work on differential equations and the theory of function of complex variables. His research and writing have led to publications dealing with practical subjects. For example, one of his published papers has the title, "Vibrations of Wings with Suspended Attachments in Air Currents." Keldysh holds two Stalin Prizes and the Order of Lenin.

## 23. *What are the backgrounds of Mao Tse-tung and the other principal Chinese Communist leaders?*[4]

In orthodox style, China's Communist Party is organized on Leninist lines and operated on the principle of "democratic centralism." Practically speaking, this means that the vast Party machine in China (numbering over 17 million members by mid-1961) is a pyramidal structure, with power concentrated in the hands of a few professional Communist leaders. These men are linked by a common revolutionary doctrine and by years of association within the organization. The Party constitution adopted at the 8th National Party Congress (September, 1956) places ultimate decision-making authority in the Standing Committee of the Political Bureau. This group now comprises seven men:

| | |
|---|---|
| Mao Tse-tung | (pronounced mau dz-dung) |
| Liu Shao-ch'i | (lyou shao-chi) |
| Chou En-lai | (jo en-lai) |
| Chu Teh | (ju deh) |
| Ch'en Yun | (chen yun) |
| Lin Piao | (lin byau) |
| Teng Hsiao-p'ing | (deng syau-ping) |

**Mao Tse-tung (1893 — ).** Unlike Stalin, who inherited an operating regime from Lenin, Mao Tse-tung himself was the principal creator of the political-military machine which captured power in China in 1949. Leader of the most extensive Communist revolution in Asia, master of the Chinese Communist movement for the past quarter-century, Mao today dominates all policy decisions made at Peking. He also exerts great influence outside China, both within the Communist bloc and, increasingly, in sections of the Middle East, Africa, and Latin America. Born of peasant stock in Hunan, rich rice-bowl province of south-central China, Mao sprang from the World War I generation in China which, during the 1920's, turned to revolutionary Russia for the pattern and to Marxism for the key to modernize China. Delegate from Hunan to the founding meeting of the Chinese Communist Party (Shanghai, July, 1921), Mao rose to control

[4] Information provided by Howard Boorman, Research Project on Men and Politics in Modern China, Columbia University, New York.

the Party apparatus by 1935. Between 1935 and 1949, he shaped political-military tactics which expanded Communist power from minor pockets in the countryside to the entire mainland of China. He was chief of state (Chairman of the People's Republic of China) from 1949 to 1959, when he voluntarily relinquished the top government post to his deputy and fellow-Hunanese, Liu Shao-ch'i. Mao remains chairman of the Communist Party of China, top man in a hierarchy where position determines power. Mao's intellectual influence as a major theorist of Communist revolution is unquestioned. In practical terms, his power is related to the fact that he has linked Chinese national aspirations and the World Communist movement.

**Liu Shao-ch'i (1900 — ).** Deputy to Mao and the man most likely to succeed him in control of the Party, Liu Shao-ch'i is also a native of Hunan province. A Party member for forty years, Liu was a Communist agitator from 1922 to 1942, propagandizing and organizing miners, factory workers, and students in many parts of China for Communist political purposes. After this long period as an underground worker in areas controlled by the Kuomintang (Chinese Nationalist Party) and later by the Japanese, he moved in 1943 to Yenan, Communist capital during the Sino-Japanese war. Since then, he has worked at the top echelon of command in the Chinese Communist Party. Top-ranking (under Mao) vice chairman of the Central Committee and the Politburo, Liu has also been head of the government at Peking since April, 1959. He represented Mao Tse-tung as China's chief delegate at the important world meeting of 81 Communist Parties in Moscow (November-December, 1960). Often labeled as a doctrinaire theoretician, Liu Shao-ch'i is rather the veteran organization man. He is the person who has long been chiefly responsible for controlling organizational and ideological discipline in the Party in China.

**Chou En-lai (1898 — ).** Foreign affairs expert and chief Chinese Communist diplomat for many years, Chou En-lai has had more experience outside China in negotiations with non-Chinese than any other top leader in Peking. Though he was born into a scholar-official family in Kiangsu province, Chou early turned to radicalism. A Party member for forty years (he joined in France after World War I) and a major figure in the Party leadership for almost as long, Chou has proven both competent and durable. He was prominent as negotiator with the Kuomintang and with United States officials during the post-war mediation efforts. Chou En-lai has served since 1949 as premier of the Peking regime, chief administrator of Communist China's enormous government bureaucracy. In addition to this key role, Chou was foreign minister at Peking from 1949 to 1958, when Ch'en Yi succeeded him. Within the party, he is vice chairman of both the Central Committee and the Politburo, ranking only after Mao and Liu Shao-ch'i. Trim, intelligent, supple, and cosmopolitan, Chou En-lai is nevertheless a thoroughly disciplined man whose adult career has been entirely devoted to expanding Communist authority within China and Chinese Communist influence internationally.

**Chu Teh (1886 —  ).** Broad, brown-faced, and solid, Chu Teh is the father of the Chinese Communist army. He has been closely associated with Mao Tse-tung since their initial rendezvous in the hinterland of Kiangsi in 1928. A native of Szechwan, the populous land-locked province of southwest China, Chu had a minor career there as a local military officer prior to World War I. He then went to Europe, espoused Communism, and joined the Party in 1922. During the 1930's and early 1940's, the Chu-Mao team developed the guerrilla military tactics which established and gradually extended Communist power in the countryside during the Chinese-Japanese conflict. Commander-in-chief of the Chinese Communist military forces for many years, Chu Teh has not actually been a field commander since about 1938. Vice chairman of the government at Peking during its first decade, Chu Teh gave up this post in 1959 to become chairman of the Standing Committee of the National People's Congress (Communist China's parliament). This post had been held till then by Liu Shao-ch'i. Now fourth-ranking (and eldest) member of the party elite, Marshal Chu Teh has in 75 years witnessed drastic changes in China from the final decline of the imperial dynasty to the present, Communist-directed drive toward national industrialization and military modernization.

**Ch'en Yun (1900 —  ).** Now fifth-ranking member of the Peking Politburo, Ch'en Yun began life as a manual worker in Shanghai. He joined the Communist Party there, and became prominent as a labor organizer in Shanghai during the 1920's. Rising slowly but steadily through the Party hierarchy during the following years, Ch'en made his first trip to the USSR in 1935, remaining there until 1937. Member of the Political Bureau by 1940, he held key responsibilities at the Yenan base during the Chinese-Japanese war. Then he moved to Manchuria in 1945 as senior Chinese Communist official in that critical area during the civil war with the Nationalists. Since the establishment of the Central People's Government at Peking in 1949, Ch'en Yun has been prominent as an economic planner and an advocate of policies designed to spur national economic development and industrialization. Vice chairman of the Central Committee and the Politburo, Ch'en Yun possesses both disciplined practical ability and a record of consistent loyalty to Party authority.

**Lin Piao (1907 —     ).** Vice chairman of the Central Committee and the Politburo of the Party since 1958, Minister of Defense in the government since 1959, Lin Piao has been a professional soldier throughout his career. A top student at the Moscow-financed Whampoa Military Academy headed by Chiang Kai-shek in the 1920's, Lin defected to the Communists in 1927. He was a member of the first group of military officers who joined the Chu-Mao camp in Kiangsi in 1928. During the next twenty years, he became the outstanding Communist field commander in China. He headed vanguard forces on the Long March in 1934–35 and won an impressive early victory against the Japanese invaders in 1937. Following V-J day, he moved to Manchuria. There he re-grouped guerrilla forces and built them into the crack Fourth Field Army, which defeated the Nationalists in the northeast in 1948. Then he swept southward through China to occupy Canton a year later, and spearheaded the Chinese offensive in Korea in late 1950. Peking's leading strategist and tactician, Marshal Lin Piao is short, slight in build, pale in complexion. A soldier to the core, the core is that of a tough, professional Communist: a man close to Mao, Chu Teh, and the inner circle of the party for over three decades, and now the sixth-ranking (and youngest) individual in the top command.

**Teng Hsiao-p'ing (1900 —     ).** A native of Szechwan and a Party veteran, Teng Hsiao-p'ing has risen rapidly since 1950 to the top level of political authority in Peking. Though he joined the Communist Party in France in the early 1920's, he was not prominent during the formative years of the Communist movement in China. During the Chinese-Japanese conflict and after, Teng served as political commissar in the Communist military forces. He worked for several years in units commanded by his fellow-Szechwanese, Liu Po-ch'eng (the "one-eyed Dragon"). Member of the Central Committee of the Party since 1945 and of the Politburo since 1955, Teng has since 1956 held the key post of General Secretary of the Party. As such, he is the top executive officer responsible for coordinating policies and programs. He has had no training or experience in the Soviet Union, but since 1956 he has made three trips to Moscow to attend highly important Communist meetings. Western observers have characterized Teng as an able and intelligent man, both aggressive and articulate.

# 4 The Soviet Union – Its Political, Economic, and Military System

## The History of Communism in Russia

**24.** *What were the causes of the Revolution and of the Communist victory in Russia?*

The causes of the Revolution and the Communist victory in Russia are many and complicated. They relate to the traditions of Russia, to the ideology of Marxism, to conditions in Russia and in the world in 1917, and to the superior organization, propaganda, and leadership of the Bolshevik party under Lenin. Many books have been written on this subject. In this chapter it is possible only to summarize what happened and why.

The Communists were able to take over Russia because they were the only group with a unified organization, a common purpose, and effective leadership at a time when revolution was in the air and when all other political forces had collapsed or were suffering from paralysis of will.

**The Russian scene.** Russia had been ripe for revolution for some time. Economic and social conditions were deplorable and getting worse. The common people were hungry, but the Tsar seemed unable to cope with the situation. In March, 1917, the government, which had proved unequal to dealing with unrest and the problems of World War I, disintegrated. Nicholas II was imprisoned, and very few thought the monarchy could be revived or wished to revive it. The new Provisional Government, publicly committed to a democratic reconstruction of Russia, was led by men (such as Prince George Lvov and Alexander Kerensky) who had some governmental experience in the old Duma (Russian Parliament). But they lacked the ability to assume effective authority themselves.

**Indecision of the moderates.** The moderate leaders of the Provisional Government were hampered by lack of agreement on a political program. They had limited understanding of the problems of government, and were uncertain whether they ought to continue the war. They were under constant pressure from other political forces, above all the Soviets (Councils) of Workers' Deputies that had been spontaneously created in most Russian cities. Because the moderate Mensheviks and Socialist Revolutionaries provided weak leadership, the Bolsheviks (Communists) soon gained a foothold in the Soviets and control of the key Petrograd (now Leningrad) Soviet.

**Practical consequences.** The army fell apart when it became clear that the war was to continue despite lack of supplies and staggering losses, and without intelligent direction from the new government. The peasantry, sensing the weakness of the new government, began to seize lands owned by the state and the big landlords. The German and Austrian armies pushed farther eastward. A politically unsophisticated general, Kornilov, tried to reorganize the government by a *coup d'etat*, but failed. Kerensky, now prime minister, was unable to restore order. Meanwhile Lenin, long committed to bringing about a Communist revolution, risked everything on using trained Bolshevik armed units to seize power in the capital. Lenin won. His victory in November, 1917 was made possible in large part by the fact that his enemies had not taken him seriously. Although there was widespread opposition to the Bolshevik (later Communist) government, jealousy and rivalry among leaders nullified those efforts. Brutal treatment of the peasants by the White Armies and foreign intervention increased popular support for the new government. By 1921 a Communist regime was firmly established.

## 25. *What are the important milestones in the history of the Soviet Union under Communism?*

In this book we can discuss only a few of the milestones in the history of Communist Russia. Students interested in a more detailed account will enjoy reading these two authoritative books:

Sir Bernard Pares, *A History of Russia* (New York: Knopf, 1953). First published in 1926, this well-written book by the English scholar is generally regarded as a standard in the field.

Jesse D. Clarkson, *A History of Russia* (New York: Random House, 1961). This new work by an American professor brings the fascinating story up very close to the present.

Other equally useful and stimulating books and articles are suggested in the selected readings for each chapter. These range from research monographs, useful as reference, to more readable popular accounts from such magazines as *Life*, *U.S. News and World Report*, *Time*, *Newsweek*, and the *Reader's Digest*.

For the moment, however, we must be satisfied with some broad strokes of the pen, the major milestones along the path of Soviet history. Let us look very briefly at the eight more or less standard periods in Soviet history already noted in connection with our study of World Communism:

**The first period: War Communism, 1917–1921.** This was the period of the Bolshevik consolidation of power and of the spirit of world revolution. Lenin and Trotsky still regarded the world as on the brink of Communism. Of course, they were wrong. The civil war continued within Russia. This also was the era of Allied intervention, when United States, Japanese, and other forces actually landed on Russian soil "to protect Allied interests." The Bolsheviks fought the invaders and took extreme measures to consolidate their power. They began the nationalization of industry (June 3, 1918), the forcible collection of grain, the elimination of the Kulaks (prosperous farmers), and the creation of labor armies. In other words, this period provided a practical demonstration of what Communism was to be like — and it was only the beginning.

**The second period: New Economic Policy, 1921–1928.** With the consolidation of Bolshevik political and military gains at home and the ebbing of the revolutionary tide abroad, Soviet leaders turned their attention to the economic front. Here, things were definitely not going well. What to do? Taking a slogan from his own writing, "One step forward, two steps backward," Lenin decided on a tactical retreat. This was known as the New Economic Policy (NEP). It was somewhat more moderate than the previous line. Lenin engineered the policy of resuming relations with the "capitalist states." This was, we might say, the first period of coexistence. It was like all periods of coexistence, designed with a specific purpose in mind: in this case, to gain time and to seek much-needed economic assistance abroad.

Lenin died in 1924. His death brought on a struggle between the two major contenders for leadership, Trotsky and Stalin, over proper Soviet strategy. Stalin wanted to concentrate on building up the Soviet Union as a citadel of Communism. Trotsky advocated pushing the world revolution immediately. (For further details see pages 20 to 21). Stalin, as you know, won the struggle.

Between 1927 and 1930, Stalin effectively destroyed much of his opposition. Lenin was dead. Trotsky was banished in 1929. He was murdered in Mexico, presumably by a Soviet agent, in 1940.) Stalin had become absolute dictator of the Soviet Union. He had arrested and executed virtually all of his former colleagues and many of his "friends."

**The third period: First Five Year Plan, 1928–1934.** At this point, the Soviets launched the first of their celebrated plans designed to industrialize the country. The period saw a shift from the moderate line of the NEP period to a more militant posture. The Soviets sought both to build up the Soviet Union at home and to push revolution abroad. Capitalism was violently attacked everywhere.

It was during these years that Soviet agriculture was forcibly collectivized (see pp. 86–88). Peasant resistance to collectivization led to man-made famine. Millions of peasants perished; slave labor assumed huge proportions.

**The fourth period: "United" and "Popular Fronts", 1934–1939.** Nazi Germany and militant Japan had grown strong and were expanding. They now threatened the Soviet borders — East and West. Both were violently and actively anti-Communist. The time had come for another shift in policy. The result: another coexistence period. The Soviet hate campaign against both "capitalist countries" and socialist parties was suddenly turned off. In its place the Communists raised a new slogan: a United Front against Nazi and Japanese militarism and aggression. The Soviet Union even joined the League of Nations, which Lenin had denounced as an "imperialists-thieves kitchen."

The moderate line in foreign policy was matched by a ruthless line at home. The *Yezhovshchina,* the Stalin purges of 1935–39 (named for police chief Yezhov, who himself was purged eventually), cut down the greater part of the generation of Bolsheviks who had made the revolution, fought the civil war and launched the great experiment.

In 1939, the Kremlin became alarmed by Hitler's 1938 Munich victory in dismembering Czechoslovakia and by the Japanese advances into China. Accordingly, Stalin undertook simultaneous negotiations with England for an alliance directed against Germany and with Germany for an alliance against France and England. (The Kremlin had meanwhile attempted to hold off the Japanese by selling them the Soviet-controlled railway through North Manchuria.) The outcome of these negotiations was the Hitler-Stalin, or Nazi-Soviet Pact of August, 1939.

**The fifth period: Nazi-Soviet Pact, 1939–1941.** With the Pact in August between Stalin and Hitler, Communist hypocrisy came out into the open for all to see. This agreement set the stage for the Nazi invasion of Poland, September 1, 1939. On October 9 the Soviet government newspaper *Izvestia* declared: "One may respect or hate Hitlerism just as any other system of political views. This is a matter of taste." The official Soviet view of Churchill left less to choice: On January 26, 1940, *Izvestia* attacked Winston Churchill as the "greatest enemy of the Soviet Union."

Meanwhile Hitler and Stalin had divided helpless Poland

between them. Soviet forces had also invaded Finland; and in August of 1940, Stalin had annexed the Baltic States and part of Romania.

This was the period of the third Five-Year Plan (see p. 84), and the Soviets used the time to build. In April, 1941, to secure the Eastern borders and to gain additional time, the Soviets signed a Five-Year Neutrality Pact with Japan.

On June 21, 1941, without warning, 160 German divisions attacked the Soviet Union. Through no fault of its own, the Soviet Union was back on the Allied side!

**The sixth period: strange wartime alliances, 1941–1945.** This period the Soviets refer to as "the Great Patriotic War" and "the National War of Liberation." It was also the era of "strange wartime alliances;" of the Soviet-American-British coalition against the Fascist powers.

German forces overran European Russia and penetrated as far east as Stalingrad. The advancing Nazi armies devastated the Ukraine and destroyed many of the cities of the Soviet Union. What the German armies did not demolish the retreating Russian forces earlier had burned, as part of a "scorched earth" policy to keep the enemy from making use of resources.

Three things saved the Soviets: (1) "General Winter" — that is, the sub-zero cold for which the German forces were ill-prepared and badly equipped, (2) the vast expanses of territory through which the over-extended Germans were obliged to supply their beleaguered forces, and (3) lend-lease aid from the United States in the form of billions of dollars worth of equipment and supplies sent to the USSR and other Allies to help defeat the then common enemy.

Soviet losses were staggering. Industrial and agricultural production was cut in half. Fifteen million Russians lost their lives. But the USSR also profited from the war. After driving out the Germans, Soviet forces occupied adjacent lands. In violation of wartime agreements, the Soviet Union used all the resources of Communist intrigue to establish Communist regimes in these countries and to prevent elections in which the people might freely vote for governments of their own choice.

**The seventh period: postwar readjustment, 1946–1953.** The complicated period of readjustment from the end of the war to

Stalin's death can scarcely be summarized. Some of the more striking or significant events of the era may be noted:

1. Soviet reconstruction at home. The re-building of the shattered Russian countryside. The Soviet stripping of Manchuria and Eastern Europe of industrial equipment in order to assist in development at home.

2. The consolidation of the Communist control in Eastern Europe, particularly the Communist take-over of such countries as Czechoslovakia (see pp. 175–177).

3. The Soviet shift back to a militant aggressive posture, especially Soviet-directed uprisings and rebellions by Communist guerrillas in Greece, Iran, Indo-china, the Philippines, and elsewhere.

4. Soviet membership in the "nuclear club" with the explosion in 1949 of a small atomic bomb, several years ahead of Western estimates of their ability to do so.

5. The emergence, the same year (October, 1949), of a Communist regime in China — tied politically, militarily, and economically to the Soviet Union.

6. The Communist-created Korean War, launched June 25 1950, with the Soviet trained and equipped North Korean army attacking south across the 38th parallel (for additional detail see pp. 167–168).

7. Soviet propaganda for peace without readiness to negotiate seriously for the effective control of nuclear armaments and the limitation of conventional forces.

**The eighth period: the Khrushchev era, 1954 —** . Stalin died in March, 1953. It is not clear whether or not preparation had already been made for a smooth transfer of power to a sort of *troika* — a three-man leadership consisting of Malenkov, Molotov, and Beria. In any case, none of them lasted long. The "collective leadership" arranged to have Secret Police Chief Beria killed — apparently with the knowledge and support of Khrushchev and the Soviet Army. Then Khrushchev maneuvered Malenkov into resigning in favor of Bulganin — a Khrushchev "yes-man." Molotov appears never to have been a serious contestant in the deadly race for power. Khrushchev had little trouble removing Bulganin. Once in the top spot, Khrushchev set about consolidating his power by cleverly removing, one after another, all of the real or imagined contenders for power. At the 22nd Party Congress in the fall of 1961, Khrushchev stood before the assembled delegates as the undisputed leader of the USSR.

The Khrushchev years have seen many strking developments at home and abroad. Most of these are discussed in the following pages.

## Political System of the Soviet Union

### 26. *How does the Soviet one-Party system of government operate?*

In theory, the Union of Soviet Socialist Republics is a federally organized constitutional democracy. In practice, the constitution is relatively unimportant. Decisions are made by the Presidium and/or the Secretariat of the Central Committee (see chart, "The Political System of the Soviet Union") of the Communist Party and implemented by a hierarchy of governmental organizations backed by the authority of the Party. The system of checks and balances and the concept of separation of powers, so important to the functioning of the government of the United States, are absent in the Soviet Union.

What gives the Communist Party this privileged all-powerful position? Authority derives from the presumed superior understanding of the "science" of Marxism-Leninism enjoyed by the Communists. No other political parties are deemed necessary — and none is allowed.

**Territorial-administrative structure.** The Soviet Union is a federation of 15 theoretically independent Republics, the largest of these being Russia proper, which is called the Russian Soviet Federated Socialist Republic (RSFSR). This Republic alone occupies a land area almost twice the size of the continental United States (not including Alaska).

The other 14 Republics grouped around the RSFSR are formed primarily on the basis of nationality.

Each of the 15 Republics, like our American states, has its own constitution and government — plus a parallel Communist Party structure. Each is allowed to manage its own affairs as long as they do not run counter to central policy. The catch is that all important decisions on all significant matters are made in Moscow. To be sure, those powers not delegated to the central government are reserved for the Republics — but these are relatively unimportant.

The 15 Republics (states) are divided into 116 oblasts or regions (provinces). Oblasts are divided into rayons or districts, and these, in turn, are divided into the smallest territorial-administrative unit — the rural soviet. This pattern varies slightly in the seven smaller Soviet Republics.

**The Government hierarchy.** The top command, the executive branch of the Soviet Government, is the USSR Council of Ministers (see chart, "The Political System of the Soviet Union") It is something like the President's cabinet in the United States Each Soviet Republic also has its own Council of Ministers.

The Supreme Soviet, the legislative body, and similar bodies in the various Republics have little actual power. Their main function appears to be to "rubber stamp" (give automatic approval to) decisions, laws, and appointments made by the Party Known as soviets of working people's deputies at the *oblast* level and below, these "legislatures" are theoretically elected by direct, universal, and secret suffrage. In practice, candidates are actually chosen carefully and in advance by the Party. That is why, when questioned as to why only one candidate appears for each office in any election in the Soviet Union, the official Communist guide in Moscow can reply to an American tourist: "Why put up the second best man?" A few top Party officials decide *for the people* who is best for the job — he is rarely the people choice. Here again the system differs fundamentally from democracy.

**The Party hierarchy.** Membership in the Soviet Communist Party (almost 10 million) is about 8 per cent of the total adult population of the country. Consider what this means. This small but tightly organized and highly disciplined group controls the destiny of 210,000,000 Russians.

At the top of the Party structure are the Presidium, the

Secretariat, the Central Committee, and the various staff departments of the central apparatus in Moscow. These exist also at the republic level.

This organizational structure is shown in the chart on "The Political System of the Soviet Union."

The two central points, the keys to the system, are: (1) Supreme authority in both Party and government is vested in the same man — currently Nikita Khrushchev, Chairman of the Government's Council of Ministers *and* First Secretary of the Central Committee of the Communist Party; and (2) The Party's organizational structure, authority, and activity reach into every corner of the country.

## 27. *What is the significance of the term "Iron Curtain"?*

The expression "Iron Curtain" first received currency in the Western world after Winston Churchill used it in 1946. It refers to the Soviet policy of regulating communication and information entering or leaving a country controlled by the Communists. It also refers to the fact that Russians lack the right to travel freely within the Soviet Union and to leave the country if they wish. Secrecy, censorship, strict control of travel into or out of the Soviet Union: these are all part of the pattern of the Iron Curtain. The purpose of this system of controls is to help the Communists stay in power.

How does the Iron Curtain serve the purposes of the Communist power? For one thing, it makes it easier for the Communist propagandists and agitators to put into the minds of the people under Communist rule whatever the Communists leaders want them to believe. Without the Iron Curtain it might be difficult to maintain the Communist system. The system is based on an image of Communist purposes and of life inside and outside of the Soviet Union that the Communists apparently believe cannot stand the free competition of ideas or comparison. The Soviet leadership does not allow information to reach Soviet citizens by which the people can check on what their leaders tell them.

The whole machinery of teaching, communications, and information, from the schools through the press, radio, and tele·

vision, is pressed into the service of the propaganda campaigns of the Communist rulers. The various devices of censorship and strict border controls that we generally describe under the heading of the Iron Curtain are used to keep the Soviet people from learning of events and institutions that might make them question the Communist regime's official story of life.

This effort is not completely successful. Enough information about the outside does get in, in spite of the Iron Curtain, to raise doubts in the minds of at least some Soviet people. However, it is obvious that the kind of information control to which the Soviet citizenry is subjected gives rise to a great deal of ignorance and distortion. To the extent that this whole effort is successful, the Soviet people can be made to support the Kremlin's policies. Since these policies are opposed to those of non-Communist governments, the Iron Curtain is obviously a source of friction and tension in international relations. The Curtain also helps the Soviet rulers to spread throughout the world the false picture of conditions in the USSR that they wish to disseminate.

But it would be a mistake to think that the Iron Curtain is entirely an advantage to the Soviet leaders. When people outside of Russia learn the truth about Soviet policies, including the policy of maintaining the Iron Curtain, the Soviet secrecy, propaganda, and misinformation arouse mistrust of Soviet motives and disillusionment with the Communist system. Such repressive policies are out of place in the modern world.

In the fall of 1961, the Soviets began to erect a wall dividing Communist Berlin from free Berlin. The Communists drew tanks up behind this wall and placed machine guns at critical spots, to keep the captive peoples of Eastern Europe from fleeing to safety through the one escape hatch in Berlin. What an eloquent comment on the world of Communism — a prison wall to keep people from fleeing their beloved country!

## 28. *Do the Russians vote?*

The 1936 Soviet Constitution, in force today, guarantees universal, direct, equal, and secret suffrage. More than 120,000,000 Soviet citizens, or 99 per cent of the eligible voters in the USSR, voted in the last election. Considering the fact that only 60 to 65 per cent of the eligible voters in the United States usually turn out at the polls, does this mean that the Soviet Union is more democratic than America? The answer is no. The nature of the Communist system makes voting in the Soviet Union a meaningless gesture, an exercise in rubber stamping the Party's choice.

The name of a single candidate for each office appears on the ballot — *the* candidate put forward by the Communist Party. Before the Russian even goes to the voting place, he knows that he really has no choice. He is simply expected to approve the Party's man. If he doesn't like the system, why doesn't he stay home? He can't do that either. Every Soviet citizen over eighteen years of age is required to go through the motions of voting, and both the government and Party authorities see to it that every citizen records his vote in his electoral district. But if he votes in a booth, secretly, why doesn't he leave his ballot blank or "write in" his own choice? This, in fact, would be possible, but it would serve little purpose and could be very dangerous. Still fresh are memories of the days when the Ministry of Internal Affairs, the secret police, checked voting slips on a mass scale to find out who had crossed out the name of a single candidate for the Supreme Soviet or some other position. Such an "enemy of the regime" got into more trouble than it was worth. The attitude of the average Russian today is, "Why ask for trouble?" Thus the Russian people go to the polls, make their mark after *the* candidate's name, and come home to await the inevitable Government announcement that Comrade Khrushchev has been elected by the greatest "popular" majority in the history of the Soviet Union.

## 9. Why don't people in Communist countries rebel against the system, or leave, if it's as bad as we hear it is?

Rebellion is never an easy task. It is especially difficult in a totalitarian police state where "dangerous thoughts" are rooted out before they can lead to action. Even those who might wish to get rid of Communist tyranny tend to feel that there is little

point in trying to resist. This situation makes the revolutions
that have been made against Communism all the more significant

The spectacle of millions of Russians, Eastern Europeans, and
Chinese fleeing from their homelands to escape Communism is a
sober reminder of the true nature of the system. Where else in
human history have people by the millions found life in their own
countries so intolerable that they were willing to give up friends
family, and all their earthly possessions in exchange for a breath
of freedom beyond the wall? So they have rebelled and they con
tinue to flee — by the millions. Let us look briefly at the record

In the USSR uprisings against the Soviets began immediately
after the Bolsheviks seized power. From 1918 to 1921 a civil wa
was waged over almost the whole extent of the USSR. In 192
all Central Asia rose in revolt against the Communists, and peas
ant revolts flared in West Siberia from the Urals to the Altai, in
the Volga regions, and in central Russia. The same thing happened
in the Ukraine, Byelorussia, and some parts of northern Russia
At the same time the famous mutiny of the Kronstadt sailors took
place. These uprisings were only put down by the use of th
severest repressive measures, together with the introduction o
the New Economic Policy, which permitted the peasant to dis
pose of his agricultural produce as he wished.

In Central Asia the so-called Basmachi insurrection against th
Sovietization of this part of the USSR lasted intermittently fo
almost 20 years. There were also uprisings in Georgia and in th
North Caucasus, and in 1929 there were constant acts of resist
ance on the part of the peasants when forced collectivization o
agriculture began. These risings went on for two or three years
The Communist answer was to remove millions of peasants an
their families from their homes. It is said that more than 5 mi
lion people were sent to Siberia and other parts of the USSR. Th
artificial famine brought about by Communist agricultural polic
in 1932–1933 cost the lives of at least 6 to 7 million people an
broke the back of peasant resistance to collectivization. The ove
all number of political prisoners began to rise steeply in 1929 an
by the mid-1930's it reached a figure of from 5 to 7 million; th
figure did not drop until the early 1950's.

During the terror of 1936–1938 several hundreds of thousand
of persons were shot and at least 4 or 5 million sent to concentra
tion camps. This and the all-embracing network of secret polic

agents destroyed at the roots any large-scale attempts to resist the Party dictatorship. A number of attempted uprisings did, however, take place within the USSR after World War II.

Two other examples of revolts within Communist countries are the uprising in East Berlin in 1953 and the tragic Hungarian Revolution of 1956 (pp. 169–171).

Despite this record it would be wrong to conclude that the USSR is today on the verge of revolution. Most specialists on the subject agree that while dissatisfaction within the Soviet Union remains widespread, an organized revolution against the powerful Communist regime seems extremely remote.

## 30. *How important are the secret police?*

Hitler had his Gestapo. Tojo had his Special Higher Police. The tsar in pre-Communist Russia had his *Okhrana*, or hated secret police. Stalin had his OGPU and NKVD. Khrushchev maintains a huge secret police apparatus as part of the Committee on State Security. Terror and fear are to the totalitarian state what incentive is to our free societies.

Lenin said: "Violence when it is committed by the toiling and exploited masses is the kind of violence of which we approve." Stalin added that the secret police were absolutely necessary to the maintenance of the Soviet regime. In the early days of the revolution the Soviets evolved a theory of "preventive terror" — the shooting of innocent persons to frighten those who might otherwise harbor thoughts of opposing the regime — and "reprisal terror" such as the Nazis later also used.

The terror, arrests, mass murder, liquidation, and purges on which the Soviet Union has been built reached their peak with the Great Purge of 1935–1938, when millions of Russians were rounded up, shot, imprisoned, or sent to forced labor camps.

While the more obvious forms of terror on a mass scale are no longer generally employed, they have been replaced by more effective and subtle means of control. Economic and social pressures are now the favored means of enforcing the Party's demands for strict conformity with its dictates and public approbation of all its projects. For example, punitive unemployment can be equivalent to a death sentence in the Soviet Union today. Not

only does the individual lose his job and housing; no one will
hire him. His friends are hesitant to assist his family, for they
fear they will be considered guilty by association. With such
treatment an individual's behavior often becomes so strange and
anti-social that he is a definite threat to the survival of his neighbors and friends. At this point, they welcome the victim's arrest
or elimination as a common criminal. We call this "blacklisting."

Coupled with drastic social and economic pressures for enforcing discipline, we find an extensive system of surveillance
which is certainly not limited to foreigners. All Soviet citizens
must carry identification papers and are frequently required to
explain the reason for, or to present authority to, travel in military areas or regions not close to home. No phone books are
available to the public except in a few Black Sea resorts and in
Moscow. All long-distance phone calls and international mail
and telegraph are subject to censorship. Contact with a foreigner
or a loose remark in public immediately subjects one to an investigation. Conformity is required of all. Every Soviet citizen is
acutely aware that even such a distinguished and popular person
as Marshal Zhukov can disappear from public view. The Russian
is careful of what he says, even to his friends. The "friend" may
turn out to be a secret police agent.

The secret police, informers, and other agents of the KGB
(Committee on State Security) provide the Party with the information and means to instill fear throughout the USSR and its
satellites. The fact that people who conform get ahead and live
more happily also promotes acceptance of the Soviet system.

### 31. *What do we know about forced labor camps in the Soviet Union?*

Total planning means total government control. Forced labor
camps have been one of the means employed by the Kremlin to
"cleanse" society and to carry out its plans. A new sawmill in
eastern Siberia, a new mine in Central Asia — where do the
workers come from? They are often "political prisoners" transported, or transplanted, from some other region of the Soviet
Union.

Former Soviet official Victor Kravchenko reported that "in official circles, twenty millions became the accepted estimate of this (prisoner) labor reservoir. . . ."[1] More conservative estimates range from 5 to 15 million.

Information on the location and nature of these huge concentration camps has been gathered from a variety of sources, including a number of former inmates who have escaped and made their way through the Iron Curtain.

One of the most comprehensive reports on the camps was put out in 1955 by the Munich Institute for the Study of the History and Culture of the USSR. In a partial listing, it pinpoints more than 200 camps, giving the name and location of each.

What are these camps like? Here is a description of one of the camps in the late 1930's by a person who himself was an inmate:

> I was brought to the Labor Camp on the Onega River. There I found about 35,000 prisoners. Like all other camps this camp is a purely economic institution. The prisoners work on undertakings and are supposed to be paid for their work. Bread is the basis of their food. The size of the bread rations depends on the output of their work. They get a hot meal twice daily; between four and five in the morning and between eight and nine in the evening. During the day you don't get anything but hot water. Sugar is unknown. No fruit or vegetables were ever given to us. Up to the outbreak of the war the bread ration amounted to 900 grams (as a maximum during the war the ration was reduced to 650 grams). No clothing was provided for the work, no mattresses, no blankets or pillows. We used to sleep on the floor in barracks or on dirty bunks.
>
> Our work was in the forests near Archangel. We had to cut trees. In our camp there were several hundred women, to whom the same rules applied. . . .
>
> We had to work in our own clothing. After two or three weeks our suits were torn to pieces: the prisoners were half naked. The temperature was very low: even in June we had up to twenty-five degrees of Celsius below zero (−13° Fahrenheit). After twelve to thirteen hours of work in the snow-covered forests, we used to return to the barracks thoroughly drenched. In the same rags we went to sleep: there was nothing to cover ourselves with. Very often these rags were stolen. And after such nights we had to get up in the mornings in the same rags, cold, frozen, half dead.

[1] *I Chose Justice,* (Charles Scribner's Sons, New York, 1950).

The prisoners could not wash. Men did not shave. There was no time for it; there was no need for it. We used to work without respite. Sunday was also a working day. Even May 1 was a working day. The majority of brigades in my camp had no rest during the entire period I spent there.

The great majority of the inmates were political prisoners, divided into two groups: one of them was 'spies,' the other 'socially dangerous elements.' The first group consisted mainly of people from national minorities. In my camp, for instance, there were 400 Greeks, old inhabitants of the Kerch region in the Crimea, who had suddenly been arrested in 1937–38 — they were sentenced to five to eight years in labor camp. Russians and Ukrainians used to get ten years as dangerous elements. The reason for their arrests was usually the occupation of their parents (middle-class people, rich peasants, civil servants, intelligentsia, and . . . Communist-oppositionists).

The work is being done promiscuously — in day and night shifts: in subpolar conditions it makes no difference, as during the winter the day is only two to three hours long. Almost all prisoners are suffering from scurvy, loss of teeth.

The penal labor camps are places of the greatest moral degradation: prostitution, thievery, swindles mark this struggle for existence.[2]

It is thought that since Stalin's death the Communists have reduced the number of camps and improved conditions within them. Forced labor is no longer as important to Soviet society as it used to be. Other means of control are now regarded as more effective and economically advantageous.

## The Soviet Economic System

### 32. *How is the Soviet economy organized?*

The economy of the Soviet Union may be characterized as totally planned and completely government controlled and operated. Emphasis is placed on heavy industry and military production rather than on consumer goods. The basic units of the

[2] David J. Dallin, *The Changing World of Soviet Russia,* (Yale University Press, New Haven, 1956), pp. 155–157.

Soviet economic organization are the factory, the state farm, and the collective farm.

The "profit motive," "free choice of one's career," "going into business for one's self," "taking over dad's store," "a wonderful little farm in the country," "the stock market," "a drive-in" — all of these items and many more which are commonplace in America are meaningless in terms of the Soviet economy. They are either unacceptable ideologically or simply nonexistent. That is not to say, however, that a man or woman who has technical competence cannot get ahead in the Soviet Union.

How *is* the economy organized? What makes it tick? The Soviet economy is run according to a master blueprint called *The Plan.* Actually improvisation, major errors, and revision of the plan have characterized the system. The current version is a Twenty-Year Plan which was announced in 1961. (See page 85 for details.) Until 1957 operational control of the Soviet economy was in Moscow with responsibility divided among some forty economic ministries. This highly centralized economic structure was largely dismantled in 1957. The Soviet economy was decentralized and reorganized into 105 economic regions. With some changes, this is the situation today. In each region, a regional economic council, or *sovnarkhoz,* operates as the planning and operational authority for virtually all industrial and construction enterprises.

The Gosplan (centralized planning agency) is still responsible for long-range planning and for over-all supervision.

What are the purposes, advantages, and disadvantages of the planned, decentralized system? How has it been working?

While it has been suggested that a political power struggle behind the scenes may have prompted Khrushchev's decision to make such a drastic reform in 1957, some very real economic considerations also appear to have been involved. The problems were essentially: (1) how to reconcile the aim of maximum growth with the desire for consumer goods, (2) how to assure both efficient planning and central direction and local or individual initiative, and (3) how to eliminate top-heavy bureaucracy with the duplication and competition on the regional level that this inspired.

The decentralized pattern may have solved certain problems. It is said to have produced more efficient use and organization of local resources. Some of the red tape of "having to go through Moscow" to obtain even a box of pencils has been eliminated. Local arrangements can probably solve more quickly certain supply and transportation questions.

At the same time, a whole new set of problems has been created. One of the most acute is the problem of regionalism. Where previously overcentralized planning caused bureaucracy, inefficiency, and disregard of local needs, now the regional administrators are accused of a different kind of inefficiency — trying to get things for their own region at the expense of shipments required in other regions.

British economist Alec Nove[3] sums up the situation this way:

> The imperfections and stresses inherent in the Soviet system of central planning are still there. Many Soviet economists are urging a major recasting of the system, to permit wider scope for free contract based on rational prices, to reduce the area of administrative decision and increase the importance of "automatic" forces in economic life . . . Voices are advocating the use of linear programming methods which would necessitate theoretical and practical changes of the first magnitude. None of this the actual reforms so far adopted have realized. The Party leadership is, by tradition and self interest, averse to automatic economic forces and will probably resist reforms on these lines. Yet this same Party leadership is actively searching for new ways of achieving efficiency in its self-imposed task of "overtaking America." Thus, there will be more hesitation, more experiments, and perhaps conflict as the search for a more rational basis of economic organization continues.

## 33. Is the United States ahead of the Soviet Union economically?

Any attempt to compare the economies of the United States and the USSR is a difficult, dangerous business. This is especially true if a short, concise treatment is desired. We must pay attention to at least three points: (1) present levels of economic development (steel production, oil, and electric power), (2

[3] "Post-Stalin Reorganization of Industry," in Alex Inkeles and Ken Geiger, eds., Soviet Society: A Book of Readings, (Houghton Mifflin Company, Boston, 1961), pp. 328–329.

differences in systems, purposes, and emphasis of the two economies (To what use is a given ton of steel put? Why are there
relatively fewer TV sets and automobiles in the Soviet Union
than in the United States?), and (3) pace of development, rate
of growth (Is the Soviet economy gaining on us?).

**Levels of the two economies.** In terms of a comparison of the
two economies, across the board the United States is clearly
ahead in almost all areas. Here are some comparative production statistics for the first six months of 1961:

|  | USSR | USA |
|---|---|---|
| Iron | 25,000,000 tons | 28,500,000 tons |
| Steel | 34,900,000 tons | 44,859,000 tons |
| Oil | 79,700,000 tons | 188,700,000 tons |
| Electric power | 157,000,000,000 kwh | 422,766,000,000 kwh |
| Motor vehicles (buses, trucks, cars) | 275,000 | 3,331,332 |
| Television sets | 934,000 | 2,801,000 |
| Washing machines | 583,000 | 2,523,700 |
| Shoes | 220,000,000 pairs | 304,304,000 pairs |

Two critical points must always be kept in mind when comparing these statistics and before drawing any conclusions:

**Point 1** — The Soviet Union is operating at full capacity, with
the throttle wide open. The economy of the United States is not
operating at full capacity. In steel production, for example, the
United States regularly operates at something like 70 to 80 per
cent of capacity (1961 capacity was nearly 150 million tons).
This means that the Soviet Union is considerably weaker and the
United States substantially stronger in production facilities than
the comparison of present statistics would suggest.

**Point 2** — The Soviet Union emphasizes heavy industry and
military production — coal, steel, and aircraft industries. This is
done deliberately at the expense of the average Soviet consumer
who is asked to wait indefinitely for most luxuries and many items
that we would regard as daily necessities. Automobiles, stoves,
refrigerators, color film, or mechanical toys are as scarce in the
Soviet Union as they are expensive. This means that when
economic development and production are compared, across the
board, the United States shows up substantially stronger, more
fully developed and prosperous than the USSR.

**Difference in system and emphasis.** The difference in the approach and emphasis of the two systems thus makes it necessary

to evaluate these comparative statistics very cautiously. For two reasons, it would be wrong to jump to the conclusion that the United States is so far ahead of the Soviet Union economically that the Kremlin will never catch up. Here are the two reasons:

First, the difference in systems or emphasis means that one ton of Soviet steel produces for the Soviet planners as much heavy industry or war material as a ton and a half or two tons of steel in America. The Soviets do not bother with a great many automobiles, washing machines, dryers, refrigerators, and similar items. Soviet steel is used primarily for heavy industry, not for luxury, consumer goods. In terms of national economic or military strength, this difference in purpose and system has the effect of equalizing the differences in present production levels of the two economies.

Secondly, we dare not think only about today. This has been an unfortunate American habit. As important as current comparisons are trends, i.e., what the situation is likely to be ten or twenty years from now. This is where pace of development or rate of growth comes in.

**Rate of growth of the economies.** Before World War I, the Russian economy was sixth or seventh among countries of the world. The Soviet economy is today second only to the United States. In terms of the economic yardstick which economists call the Gross National Product (GNP: the national total output of industry, agriculture, and services), the Soviet Union trails far behind the United States. The Soviet GNP is roughly one-half that of the United States, but since 1950 the Soviet GNP has been expanding at a rate of 6 or 7 per cent as compared with a mere 3.5 per cent for this country. This means that if the Soviet Union can maintain or increase this rate of growth (assuming that the rate for the United States remains constant) the Russians could eventually catch up. However, as the size of an economy increases, the rate of growth usually slows down.

Speaking before the St. Louis Junior Chamber of Commerce in June of 1960, Vice President Nixon suggested that the problem had been exaggerated: "Mr. Khrushchev boasts," Nixon said, "that he will catch and pass us in seven years. By any projection that can be applied, there is no possibility tha the Soviet economy will overtake our own at any time in this century."

At the same time a report issued by our Central Intelligence Agency (CIA) in May, 1960 estimated the Soviet GNP at $120 billion in 1950, $225 billion in 1960, and projected a figure of $420 billion in 1970. (The United States GNP in 1958 was $440 billion.)

Both Mr. Nixon and the CIA report have a point, and we would do well to pay serious attention to each. On one hand, we should avoid the mistake of overestimating what the Soviets can do. At the same time, we dare not underestimate Soviet industrial and military power.

## 34. What is a Five-Year Plan, and how does it operate?

The objective of Soviet planning has been to industrialize the country, to create a workable "socialist" system, and to collectivize agriculture. (See page 86 on the collective farm. This has meant, in practice, total planning and total control of every aspect of the nation's life — economic, political, and social.

What kinds of factories? Where? How many of them? Levels of production? Priorities? How many tractors? Shall we build a few bicycles? — Or, perhaps the steel could be put to better use elsewhere? How much emphasis on housing and consumer goods? All these things and many more are decided by the Government and Party planners. This approach is likely to be used by any country when it faces an emergency.

The Five-Year Plan was the standard planning unit of Soviet industrial development and agrarian re-organization until the Sixth Plan ran into real trouble early in 1957. Then a new Seven-Year Plan was suddenly announced for the years 1958–65. At the 22nd Party Congress in the fall of 1961 still another Plan, this time a Twenty-Year Plan, was announced.

*The First Five-Year Plan* was launched in 1928 following a period called The New Economic Policy (1921–1927). It represented a gradual shift from the more moderate line of the previous years to a hard-hitting policy designed to build the Soviet Union first, fast, and at whatever the cost in human suffering or individual freedom. Emphasis was on industrialization — more and bigger industries, shipyards, and steel mills. The people would have to wait for luxury items — and even for many necessities. This is why sacrifice and suffering resulted.

According to Soviet claims, 93 per cent of the Plan was achieved in four years, not five. Industrial output increased more than 100 per cent. Steel production rose 40 per cent. Pig iron jumped 80 per cent. If we ignore the ruthlessness and regimentation with which the Plan was pushed to completion, this represented a substantial achievement.

But in evaluating such figures we must remember that the high percentage of increase must be related to the low base from which it started. It would be possible to increase steel output in Ghana 100 per cent by building a single small plant. Adding two more small plants the next year would bring about a 200 per cent increase, and so on. This is why Soviet statistics for so long were presented as "per cent of increase" and not in absolute figures.

*The Second Five-Year Plan* (1933–37) took form even before the first Five-Year Plan had been declared completed. Its aim was the same as the first Plan, but the rate of industrial development was now slower (a yearly increase of 16 rather than 21 per cent). Emphasis on expansion of industry and mining in the Soviet Far East and in Western Siberia was intensified. Collectivization of agriculture, begun during the first Plan, was completed by the end of the second. Some 93.5 per cent of all peasant households were included in collective farms as of July 1938.

*The Third Plan* (1938–42) became a war casualty, that is, it became largely inoperative as a result of World War II. For the same reason the *Fourth Plan* could not be put into effect until 1946. The latter was largely concerned with rebuilding the industries and cities destroyed by the war. *The Fifth Plan* (1951–55) emphasized heavy industry and military preparations. At the same time, some modest concessions to the Soviet consumer were made as Soviet leadership moved from Stalin (who died in March, 1953) to Khrushchev.

*The Sixth Five-Year Plan* (1956–1960) was designed to give special attention to hydroelectric plants, mines, fuel, textiles, automation, and atomic energy. Huge capital investment and thousands of new industrial plants rounded out the impressive scheme. Because this plan did not work out, the Sixth Plan early in 1957 was drastically revised downward. Then, amid hints of failure, it was abandoned in the fall of the same year in favor of a brand new *Seven-Year Plan* (1958–1965).

This Seven-Year Plan was designed to correct inadequacies in the Sixth Plan. Part of the trouble with the Sixth Five-Year Plan was simply bad planning and management. Khrushchev's program of decentralizing industrial management sought to correct this. Another shortcoming was the weak agricultural underpinning for the expanded heavy-industry and military structure. As a partial solution, Khrushchev took a risky gamble. He brought extensive new lands under cultivation, which yielded quick returns for a while, but are now in danger of turning into a dust bowl. He also introduced reforms in agriculture, such as selling state-owned tractors to the farms.

Another reason for the failure of the Sixth Plan was that the goals had been set too high. The Seven-Year Plan moderated these slightly. Incidentally, the satellite states had been running their economies on a complicated timetable, with five-year plans which did not coincide with those of the Russians. By tearing up the Sixth Plan and starting afresh with a Seven-Year Plan, Khrushchev was able to coordinate the satellite economies with the Russian. There was also the issue of long-range planning, sadly neglected until the Seven-Year Plan was introduced.

A new *Twenty-Year Plan* (1961–1981) was projected at the 22nd Congress of the Communist Party of the Soviet Union in the fall of 1961. It promised complete electrification of the country, as well as vast improvement in industry, agriculture, and the daily life of the people. The plan calls for a 500 per cent increase in the total Soviet industrial output, thus "leaving the present over-all industrial output of the United States far behind."

To placate the neglected Soviet consumer and the disgruntled housewife, the Plan proposes to "concentrate its efforts on insuring a rapid increase in the output of consumer goods. The growing resources of industry," we read, "must be used more and more fully meet all the requirements of the Soviet people and to build and equip enterprises and establishments catering to the household and cultural needs of the population."

This ambitious scheme calls for automation, development of atomic power, a network of modern highways, more cars, and

"abundance of agricultural production." In short, the new Sovie
Plan promises the Soviet people that if they will but wait anothe
twenty years they may confidently look forward to having some o
the things which people in the Free World have long enjoyed
The Soviet consumer is now doing slightly better than he di
some years ago. This makes the Soviet citizen hope that perhap
the system may one day pay off some of its promises.

## 35. What is a collective farm? a state farm? How d they work?

Farmers in the Soviet Union live a different life from the:
American counterparts. Land tenure differs radically from th;
in non-Communist countries. In the Soviet Union, private owne:
ship of land and agricultural implements has been eliminate(
All land is state property. Virtually all arable land has bee
turned over to the *kolkhozes* (collective farms), the *sovkhoz(*
(state farms), and research and experimental farms which, i
most cases, are comparable to sovkhozes. A small number of su!
sidiary farms, whose agricultural output is insignificant, are ru
by industrial enterprises, sanatoria, and welfare agencies.

**Kolkhoz (collective farm).** According to Soviet definition,
*kolkhoz* is a voluntary union of working peasants, organized f(
the purpose of collective farming. The kolkhoz charter indicat
that all property, including land, belongs to the kolkhoz. Kol
hozes are given title to the land "in perpetuity." by the stat
However, it must be added that the kolkhozes were not orga
ized in keeping with the principle of voluntary participation b
were the result of state coercion. Nor is it true that the kolkhoz
have title to the land, since, without regard for the wishes
kolkhoz members, the government can merge several kolkhoz
into one or convert the kolkhoz into a sovkhoz, with all the pub
property acquired through the labor and funds of the kolkh
members transferred without compensation.

On January 1, 1961, there were 44,000 kolkhozes (collecti
farms) in the USSR. They included 17,300,000 peasant hou;
holds. The kolkhozes had 36,200,000 head of cattle (includi
12,800,000 cows), 27,300,000 hogs, and 71,200,000 sheep. Th

At the opening ceremonies of the World Youth Forum, held in Moscow in July 1961, delegates on the platform (left to right) were from U.S.S.R., Brazil, Guinea, Italy, Cuba.

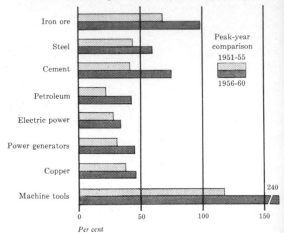

## U.S.S.R. Output as a Percentage of U.S.

The comparison, in units of output rather than dollars, charts Soviet production against the *best* year's U.S. production for each five-year period. Had U.S. economy operated at full capacity the comparison would look different.

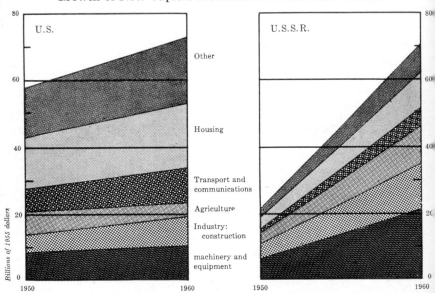

## Growth of New Capital Investment in U.S. and U.S.S.R.

Soviet investment policy favors capital (calculated in dollars) for producers' goods, e.g. machinery and industrial construction. The Soviet Union's investment in that category was well ahead of this country's in 1960.

F

The Soviet government neglects no opportunity to bring its message to the people. This outdoor display is near Moscow's Red Square.

This park in Leningrad has a statue of Peter the Great, who founded the city. Seeing men and women working side by side at the same job is commonplace in the Soviet Union.

The sign reads, "Management of Agricultural Works." Woman: "Dear me! There must be a fire somewhere!" Man: "Don't get panicky, aunty! This is just our management looking to see how the field work is progressing."

— Батюшки! Где-то пожар!
— Не наводи панику, тетя! Это наше правление смотрит, как идут полевые работы.

The collective farm pictured is in Kazakhstan. It is one of many which have brought 50 million acres of virgin land under cultivation in an effort to increase agricultural production.

owned 611,000 tractors, 272,000 grain combines, and 408,000 trucks.

The farm members are allowed to use tiny plots and to own a limited number of livestock as a means of livelihood in addition to their work for the collectives. Khrushchev has announced that gradually the kolkhozes will buy up all privately owned livestock — thus eliminating the last vestige of private farming.

**Sovkhoz (state farm).** The *sovkhoz* is a state enterprise whose property — land, produce, livestock and implements, and service and farm buildings — belongs to the state. All persons working in the sovkhozes receive wages for their labor like factory workers and have no share in the farm profits. The sovkhozes are considered to be the highest form of socialist land tenure.

On January 1, 1961, there were 7,368 sovkhozes (state farms) in the Soviet Union. The sowing area in the sovkhozes amounted to 67,200,000 hectares (about 678,000,000 acres). The number of workers in the sovkhozes averaged 5,560,000 annually.

The number of farm animals in the sovkhozes was as follows: 4,460,000 head of cattle (including 5,000,000 cows), 12,670,000 hogs, and 31,429,000 sheep. The number of agricultural machines was: 397,000 tractors, 221,000 grain combines, and 236,000 trucks.

**Life and work on a collective farm.** What do collective farms look like? How do they function? Let us look at a *kolkhoz*. The collective farm is essentially an oversized farm village, a planned semi- self-sufficient community with its own shops, schools, library, bath house, hospital, and theater. Anywhere from several hundred to three thousand families may live in this rural unit.

Half of the Soviet population presently lives on these huge government-run enterprises, which average in size about 25 or 30 square miles. Together these collectives account for more than 80 per cent of Soviet farm production. They are very important to the Soviet planned economy.

Collectivization was carried through by force in the early 1930's by combining more than 25,000,000 individual farms. In the process, some 5 million *Kulaks* (well-to-do or middle class land-owning farmers) were shot, sent to forced labor camps, or deprived of their property and forced into collectives.

All the peasants' land, with the exception of a few very small private plots (called kitchen gardens), has been collectivized.

Boundaries have been done away with. All agricultural machinery is the property of the collective farm, as are all buildings.

Every able-bodied collective farmer is required to do work on the farm, and if he refuses to do so, or shirks his duties, he is liable to be expelled from the collective and have his small private plot confiscated.

Wage-payment for work on the collective farm is made on the basis of the amount of time worked. The value of the labor-day (paid partly in money and partly in products) is figured at the end of the year, on the basis of the income and expenditure of the collective farm. Average payment for a labor-day in the USSR varies between one and one-and-a-half rubles — a maximum of about a dollar and a half per day.

How does the collective farm system compare with individual farming in the United States? Lazar Volin,[4] a specialist on the subject, makes this evaluation:

> There is . . . a general tendency . . . to have two or more persons doing a job on a collective farm that is usually performed by one person in the United States . . . Russian agriculture also has less technical equipment than is found in America and it is often inferior in quality. The inferiority, coupled with a lack of know-how, results in frequent breakdown of equipment, which slows farm operations. The situation is often aggravated by poor supply organization — shortages of fuel and spare parts for tractors and machinery, and inadequate repair facilities. The lower educational and, especially, living standards of the Russian collective farmer adversely affect his efficiency. . . .

## 36. *Do workers in the USSR have labor unions?*

There have been labor unions in the USSR since the first days of the Soviet regime. But the Soviet labor unions are not voluntary associations of workers dedicated to higher pay, shorter hours, and better working conditions. They are instruments of the state.

Lenin called the trade unions "schools of Communism." Their job is as much to police the workers on the job, enforce "labor

[4] "The Collective Farm," in Inkeles and Geiger, eds., *Soviet Society*, pp. 339–340.

discipline," and encourage extra effort as it is to negotiate contracts with management. Long before the Russians asked for a "troika" to direct the UN, they instituted "troikas" in their factories — where the "troika" includes: the factory's Communist Party leader, its manager, and its trade union executive, acting as one. Pay rates in Soviet industry, under the labor-management contracts sponsored by the unions, are piece rates, i.e. so much per item produced rather than a given amount per hour. "Progressive pay rates" are the practice — that is, the unions encourage higher output and when it rises they reduce the piece rate and increase the "norm," or required standard. The unions operate clubhouses for factory workers which provide entertainment and social activities — but also serve as propaganda institutions for the Communist Party.

The Soviet labor union is wholly centralized and entirely government controlled. Officers are Communist Party members. Provincial (oblast) organizations are subordinated to the republic organizations, and every union comes under its particular all-union council. These all-union councils of the individual unions are, in turn, combined in the All-Union Central Council of Trade Unions (AUCCTU). The AUCCTU is the national governing body for all the Soviet labor unions. Its word is law.

While in name and organizational structure labor unions in the Soviet Union bear some resemblance to labor unions in the Free World, in function and practice they are entirely different. Theoretically, membership in one of these unions is voluntary. Actually, there is no opportunity to vote on the issue of open versus closed shop — to join or not to join, that is *not* the question. The worker in the Soviet Union finds he must join the union to survive, let alone to prosper.

Accordingly, more than 90 per cent of the workers in the Soviet Union belong to one of these government-run unions. What is their function? They are maintained for the purpose of instilling labor discipline, ensuring that labor legislation is observed by all, and issuing interpretations of various aspects of labor laws. The Soviet labor union also administers the social insurance system, and fulfills many of the other functions normally performed in the non-Communist society by a department of labor or health and welfare, by social security agencies, or by other governmental bodies. The critical point to remember is that the Soviet government runs both the industries and the unions, represents both management and labor.

This all means, of course, that there are no strikes in the Soviet Union. Since the labor union, the Communist Party, and the government are in reality one and the same, a strike by a government union against a government owned and operated enterprise does not make sense. Why strike against yourself?

The Communist argument that there are no strikes in the Soviet Union because the workers are entirely satisfied with their conditions is amusing to anyone with even a rudimentary knowledge of life behind the Iron Curtain.

## Soviet War Potential and Science

### 37. Is the USSR stronger than the United States militarily?

Soviet strategy is based on one essential factor — power. The USSR depends on its armed forces for protection in the event other policies fail, for intimidation to achieve political objectives, and for direct expansion if a safe opportunity can be created.

The total strength of the armed forces charged with carrying out these missions, as of January 1, 1960, was approximately 3,600,000 men. This strength permitted the USSR to maintain some 100 army divisions with the necessary support units; the second largest navy in the world (no aircraft carriers; some 45 submarines); and army air forces which exceed those of the United States in total number of combat aircraft (but not in heavy bombers).

Early in 1960, Khrushchev announced that these forces would be reduced by one third within two years. At the same time, he stated that their fire power and overall capabilities would be greatly increased by the introduction of powerful new rocket forces. In other words, this reduction was designed as a reorgan ization to meet the demands of modern war. It was not to be construed as disarmament. In July of 1961, Khrushchev stated that the reduction was being suspended in view of the Berlin situation; he later announced a 50 per cent increase in the Soviet budget for the armed forces.

While we cannot hope to assess in depth the capabilities and limitations of the Soviet armed forces, the following quotation from an unclassified United States Army publication[5] suggests that these forces represent the greatest threat to the security of the West since Hitler:

> The Soviet armed forces have achieved a balance, a maturity, and an excellence of performance which considerably enhance their traditional quality of large size.

> Although shortcomings still exist, the Soviet military establishment of today ranks, qualitatively as well as quantitatively, among the best in the world, and constitutes a greater menace to the West than ever before.

The Soviet Union is known to have a substantial arsenal of nuclear weapons and a large number of bombers capable of carrying such weapons, as well as "operational" Intercontinental Ballistic Missiles.

Reduced to the lowest common denominator this means that the Soviet Union and the United States have the military capacity to inflict tremendous damage on each other.

## 38. *Does every young man in the USSR have to serve in the armed forces?*

All young men are expected to serve in the armed forces. In accordance with the Constitution of 1936, the length of service of Soviet draftees is established by the law on universal military service. The present law, enacted September 1, 1939, covers all men in active service, as well as in the reserves. A young man is inducted upon reaching age 19. Graduates of secondary schools or the equivalent are drafted at 18. The induction dates are between September 19 and October 15 of every year.

[5] *Handbook on the Soviet Army,* Department of the Army Pamphlet No. 30–50–1, July 31, 1959, pp. 5 and 6.

The term of active service for non-commissioned officers and privates is from two to four years, depending on the branch of service.

At the termination of active service, the draftee becomes a reservist of the first category. Persons not called to active service because of physical disabilities or various exemption privileges are put in the second category reserve. Reserve categories I and II, in turn, are divided into three classes according to age. The first category goes up to the age of 35, the second to 45, and the third to 50.

Conscientious objectors are not recognized, nor given an opportunity for non-combatant duty.

## 39. *Is Soviet science superior to that in the West?*

The world is well aware of the extremely rapid recent developments in the fields of science in the Soviet Union. Soviet space achievements and the explosion of the 50 megaton bomb are the most dramatic evidences of Soviet scientific progress. In the fields on which the Communists have chosen to concentrate they have made startling progress. These have been, it may be noted (a) fields of major military and strategic importance, and (b) projects designed to produce maximum propaganda impact on the world. The rocket to the moon was designed to dramatize Soviet progress; the big bomb to intimidate the world. It may be noted further that in both of these achievements the Soviets have been assisted by captured German scientists and perhaps by stolen American secrets.

At the same time it should be recognized that the Russian have a great tradition of science which pre-dates the Russian Revolution and has nothing to do with Communism. Who has not heard, for example, of Mendeleev's periodic law of matter or Pavlov's famous experiments with dogs?

Nonetheless, if we compare Soviet and American science *in all fields,* the Soviets appear to be considerably behind the West.

In a report to the National Science Foundation, Professor John Turkevich of Princeton University, who served until 1960 a United States scientific attaché at the American Embassy in Mos cow, makes this assessment with respect to basic scientific research:

"Soviet science is far behind that of the United States, despite Russian achievements in space . . . the United States has the most powerful and aggressive group of scientists and science programs and the best-equipped laboratories in the world. . . ." Further emphasizing that neither Soviet equipment nor talent matches ours, Professor Turkevich adds: "For every good man they have, we have ten."

Professor Turkevich concludes that even Khrushchev recognizes American superiority: in 1959 he suggested to Khrushchev that eventually the United States would surpass the USSR even in the space field. Khrushchev responded: "America is powerful and strong. If Americans put their mind to beating us, they can do it."

## 40. *Is the USSR ahead in the space race?*

"Space race" is a term used to describe the competition between the United States and the Soviet Union in the development of rockets and satellites to penetrate space. The gun opening the race was fired in Moscow in 1957 when the Soviet Union launched its first satellite, Sputnik I. Training for the race had been going on for years in both the USSR and the United States.

Since 1957 the two competing countries have fired many satellites around the earth and into outer space. Who will be the first man to land on the moon — a Russian or an American?

The real difference between the two programs is that Russians seem more anxious just to get men out into space — whereas the United States is more interested in the scientific knowledge that can be gathered by space shots. The Soviet Union, consequently, earlier developed bigger and more powerful rocket engines than the United States. This made it possible for them to blast off with larger vehicles, some of them weighing several tons. The Communists are apparently willing to spend less time in safety tests, and they do not announce their failures. One of the most spectacular Soviet "firsts" has been the 1961 flight of Yuri Gagarin, who circled the earth in a Soviet space craft.

The Soviet space program has been conducted in great secrecy. Reporters have been barred from launchings. When the Soviet press announced that 7,027 persons were awarded medals and decorations for the work on Gagarin's flight into outer space, only one of the 7,027 names was announced: Nikita Khrushchev's.

The United States, on the other hand, has been moving systematically ahead with a program focused on the scientific and technical aspects of the satellite. Our satellites have been more numerous, and they are designed to do more things; weather satellites, communication satellites carrying TV cameras, and satellites designed to detect missile launchings anywhere on earth are among this country's achievements to date.

The record of United States "firsts" in this exciting field is impressive. During the year 1960 alone, our "firsts" included:

| | |
|---|---|
| Pioneer V | messages from 22.5 million miles out in space (March 11) |
| Tiros I | first weather satellite; 22,000 photos; helped spot storms (April 1) |
| Transit I-B | first navigation test satellite (April 13) |
| Midas II | first heat-sensing satellite; to detect missile launchings anywhere on earth (May 24) |
| Transit II-B | first to carry another satellite into space; to study solar effects (June 22) |
| Discoverer XIII | first satellite capsule to be recovered after having been in orbit (August 10) |
| Echo I | first reflector communications satellite (August 12) |
| Discoverer XIV | first satellite to be recovered in mid-air after being in orbit (August 18) |
| Courier I-B | first "repeater" comunications satellite received and transmitted more than 100 million words (October 4) |
| Explorer VIII | first satellite to investigate the ionosphere for methods of improving radio communication (November 3) |
| Discoverer XVII | first to record effect of solar storm radiation on human tissue after prolonged space flight (November 12) |

Thus, when we hear someone say "the Russians are ahead of us in the space race," we should ask him: "In what way?"

## 41. How does the USSR compare with the United States in the nuclear weapons field?

Any consideration of the number of bombs, the relative amount of missile thrust, or the diversity and effectiveness of delivery systems becomes somewhat academic in the light of one crucial point on which the experts appear to agree: The Soviet Union and the United States have the nuclear capability to wreak frightful destruction on each other!

It is, of course, possible to imagine situations, certain types of crises, where the relative amount of total power or the sophistication or diversity of the delivery system might prove decisive.

The most reliable recent statement on this topic comes in answer to two questions asked of our Defense Secretary, Mr. Robert S. McNamara.

"Q. — If we have to go to war in Europe, are we committed to a nuclear war or could it be limited to conventional weapons?

"A. — Let me say to start with that our nuclear strength is several times that of the Soviet Union. We will utilize our nuclear weapons wherever and whenever it proves necessary to protect our national interest. However, to increase the range of military options open to us we have increased both our nuclear and our conventional capabilities.

"Q. — Mr. Secretary, how do you think we stand relative to Russia on the anti-missile missile?

"A. — We have known for some time that the Soviet Union has been working on anti-missiles. However, our contractor, the Bell Laboratories, is outstandingly competent and has had years of experience in the development of ground-to-air missiles. It is my personal belief that we are ahead of the Soviet Union in the development of the anti-missile missile."

Some interesting statistics are included on the insert chart which compares the US and the USSR in terms of numbers of nuclear weapons as well as delivery systems.

# 5 Daily Life in the Soviet Union

## Impressions: Contrasts and Similarities

### 42. *What are the most striking impressions of a visitor to Russia?*

In his interesting book, *The Russians as People*,[1] the English author Wright Miller speaks eloquently for most foreign visitors to Russia when he says:

> One is baffled again and again by a subdued or characterless exterior, of scenery, of people, of buildings, and of behaviour, which one must suspect conceals a life to which one cannot find the key. The great grey blocks of modern flats [apartments], the endless broad streets of older two-storey houses with their unpointed brickwork and steaming double windows, the wooden villages which seem dumped rather than rooted in the forest or ravine or steppe — they defeat interpretation, unless after long acquaintance, as completely as the streets of South London or Leeds. The people seem neither particularly friendly nor particularly hostile but somewhat expressionless for the most part, like the scenery which wanders away

[1] Wright Miller, *The Russians as People* (E. P. Dutton and Company, New York, 1961), pp. 12–13.

in all directions with little to catch the eye. And if occasionally the scene is redeemed by a bright new edifice, a quiet canal, pillared façade, or the gilded bulbs of some fantastic church, or if one meets, as one is sure to do, a Russian who lights up with hospitable warmth, one feels at a loss to know whether these are accidents or whether they are at last the typical Russia for which one is trying to probe.

Russia is strange but perhaps it is not strange enough. It might be easier if one had to adapt oneself to a total strangeness, as of the desert or the tropical forest, yet Russia is not altogether unlike other countries of Northern Europe. So one finds it all the harder to believe that the generally unpicturesque and unkempt appearance is not accidental and somehow not the "real" Russia. Even the national smell is unpicturesque. It is a weary smell composed, one comes to realize, of the stale dust and sweat of heavy clothing, the reek of native green tobacco, the bitter smell of black bread, the stink of Soviet soap and hair-oil, and the tarry odour of imperfectly refined petrol. There are stale damp dishwater smells and crude oil for people's hair but never anything sharp or pungent — except vodka, and the burning cold in winter, and a certain amount of raw onion on the breath.

When one adds to all these impressions the discomforts of the average Soviet hotel and that instrument of torture the Soviet telephone, the paucity of maps, guidebooks, and directories of every kind, the continual waiting for chits and for service, and the maddening combination of red tape and inefficiency with personal willingness to help, the total effect on a free tourist could well seem the result of a deliberate conspiracy to prevent him from getting to know Russia.

Over the past five or six years, thousands of Americans have gone to Russia to see for themselves. Let us sample the impressions of one or two of these Americans — whose names you are sure to know. As it turns out, less well-known visitors — professors, engineers, educators, or just plain tourists — come away with precisely these same impressions.

**Adlai E. Stevenson's impressions.** Governor (now Ambassador to the UN) Adlai E. Stevenson, in 1958, traveled 8,000 miles through Russia. Some of his impressions recorded in *Look* Magazine[2] are typical of those made by other American visitors:

[2] Adlai E. Stevenson, "Our Enemy's Two Faces — The Soviet Smiles Surprised Me," *Look,* Vol. 22, No. 24 (November 25, 1958), pp. 32 and 35.

This was my first trip to the Soviet Union in 32 years. So there were surprises aplenty in store for me . . . what surprised me most was the friendliness I found on all sides. Like most Americans who visit the Soviet Union these days, I came away both exhilarated and depressed. I was cheered by the warmth of my welcome (so friendly at times that I felt as if I were campaigning again!) and also by the energy and enthusiasm of people eager to show us how rapidly they are developing their enormous country. But I was depressed by the success of the Soviet system in regimenting a nation of 200,000,000 people and keeping them in ignorance of what is going on in the outside world.

**Vice President Nixon's observations.** In 1959, Vice President Nixon also made a tour of the Soviet Union. As in the case of Governor Stevenson, the Soviets naturally were anxious to make an impression on so important a visitor. They did, but not always the one intended. Mr. Nixon reports:[3]

Now, nothing I saw during my 11 days in the Soviet Union — and let me say at once that I don't believe this makes me, overnight, a "Russian expert" — none of the sharp impressions I carried away leads me to believe that they will equal our standard of living in seven years — or in 70, if only we remain true to the traditions that have made possible our fabulous growth up to now. . . .

I was especially curious about our reception in the so-called "closed cities" of Siberia, next on the schedule, where few Americans have ever been seen. Certainly, as we headed into Novosibirsk airport, there was nothing in the air view to remind us of our traditional notion of Siberia as arid and barren and forbidding. The countryside was lush and flat, a typical checkerboard of green and yellow and the black of freshly turned fields.

The crowd at the airport was easily the largest we had yet seen. And the city officials who greeeted us pointed out with considerable pride that theirs was a new and young and vigorous city, comparable to the cities of our own American West. It certainly could boast of the same tradition of warm hospitality.

It was interesting to note that these officials themselves repeatedly referred to Novosibirsk as the "Chicago of the Soviet Union" . . .

Novosibirsk is especially proud of its growing industry, and our hosts took us directly to their largest machine-tool plant, the Yefre-

[3] Richard M. Nixon, "Russia as I Saw It," *National Geographic*, Vol. CXVI, No. 6 (December, 1959), pp. 715, 730–735.

mov factory. We were told that its products are exported principally to China and the European satellites.

I was surprised to note that roughly half the machines in the factory were American-made. Many of the rest bore German markings. One of the correspondents with us, who had spent the postwar years in China, noticed that one of the Cincinnati-made machines carried an instruction plate in Japanese.

Knowing that the Soviets had sacked the Manchurian factories during their "caretaker" occupation of that Chinese province, he asked the foreman if the machine had in fact come from Manchuria.

"No." he was told. "It was one of the machines we bought from you during the war."

"How does it happen to have this Japanese plate?" the reporter persisted.

The foreman shrugged and laughed, "Who knows why Americans do anything?"

The correspondent gave up on that one, but the remark about the "machines we bought from you during the war" started him off on a further line of questioning. He asked, in all, seven sub-foremen and twelve workers if they know the approximate value of American lend-lease aid to Russia during the war. Not only did none of them know the amount — in round figures, eleven billion dollars — none of them had even heard of lend-lease! These machines had all been "bought" from the United States during the war!

Contrasts, curiosity, energy, fear, regimentation, ignorance of the outside world — these are the most striking impressions of most foreign visitors to the Soviet Union.

## 43. How does Moscow differ from say, New York. Chicago, or Los Angeles?

New York is like no other city in America — or for that matter in the world. But if we were to picture in our mind's eye Chicago, San Francisco, Los Angeles, Minneapolis, Houston, Boston, Denver, New Orleans or Orlando, we could certainly identify some very typical, characteristic features of American cities. Here are six features common to most *American* cities:

(1) Streets jammed with automobiles and taxicabs; in the fashionable shopping districts (5th Avenue, New York; Wilshire

Boulevard, Los Angeles), sidewalks bustling with smartly dressed women shoppers.

(2) Row after row, street after street, of plain or fancy downtown stores and shops each exhibiting conspicuous signs reading "Saks Fifth Avenue," "Sears," "J.C. Penney," or "Max's Cut-rate Clothing!"

(3) The bright lights of the theater and entertainment section. Flashing neon signs, theater marquees, and brightly illuminated, glassed-in sandwich shops.

(4) Miles upon miles of residential areas within or just outside the city limits ranging from modest land developments to areas of more expensive homes. Whatever the income level, these attractive, individual homes are likely to have trees, lawns, gardens, and — in the middle-class range and above — not infrequently in the west, private swimming pools.

(5) The neighborhood shopping center featuring a department store, a supermarket, and a host of satellite shops ranging from ice cream parlors to trading stamp marts.

(6) Corner gas stations, golf courses, drug stores, motels, drive-in sandwich stands; plus — (a purely American phenomen) — the drive-in theater.

What is the point of this recitation of Americana? The point is that *none of these familiar American features are to be found in the average Soviet city*. Moscow, it may be added, like New York, is not typical. The Soviet leaders have recently been attempting to dress up Moscow so that obvious contrasts are less evident, but the fact remains that the Soviet cities compared to their American, European, or Asian (Tokyo, Hong Kong, Singapore) counterparts are drab affairs indeed.

The Soviet city basically is composed of new and not-so-new official government buildings, apartment buildings (usually resembling housing developments in the United States), the older residential portions of the cities (semi-slum areas), government-run factories and shops, and one or two large department stores. The streets in the newer cities and those rebuilt since the war are very wide; but, except in Moscow, few automobiles are in evidence. Visitors are struck by the absence of children, bicycles, and dogs. Women's attire is a bit brighter and the shops display a greater variety, at least in Moscow, than a few years ago, but still the differences are vastly greater than the similarities.

There are a few things which the American or European city does have in common with its Soviet counterpart: slums, unattractive manufacturing areas, and some sub-standard housing. In comparing the American and Soviet city, we may say that the differences are *striking* and the similarities are, mostly, *unfortunate*.

It remains only to note that many Soviet cities do have some very attractive aspects, and some of them are features worth copying: the wide clean streets, the elegant subways of Moscow and Leningrad, many beautiful parks, and the absence of gaudy advertisements on every corner and building.

## Home Life and Standards of Living

## 44. *What is the situation of the average Russian family?*

Compared to the standard of living of the average American family — which is the highest in the world — the standard of living in the USSR today is very low. Nor is the average Russian family as well off as its French, German, or Scandinavian counterpart in the Free World. Ninety-nine per cent of Russian workers and employees have monthly incomes below 200 rubles (approximately one ruble equals one dollar). The minimum wage rate is 30–40 rubles a month. (For a more detailed discussion of salaries and prices, see page 103.) At the same time, there is a shortage of housing; and food and clothing are very expensive, by any standards.

The standard of living in the Soviet Union depends very much on who you are, what you do, where you work, and whom you know. In short, the Communists have developed in Russia not a "class-less society," but a nation of "haves" (Party and Government functionaries, artists, great scientists), "have nots" (the average worker and peasant), and "in betweens" (members of the professions, minor bureaucrats and Party officials.)

Milovan Djilas, a high-ranking Yugoslav Communist who broke with the "international" Communist movement, makes the point in eloquent terms.[4]

[4] *The New Class*, p. 46.

. . . There are fundamental differences between professional politicians in other systems and in the Communist system. In extreme cases, politicians in other systems use the government to secure privileges for themselves and their cohorts, or to favor the economic interests of one social stratum or another. The situation is different with the Communist system where the power and the government are identical with the use, enjoyment, and disposition of almost all the nation's goods. He who grabs power grabs privileges and indirectly grabs property. Consequently, in Communism, power or politics as a profession is the ideal of those who have the desire or the prospect of living as parasites at the expense of others.

There are few private homes in the Soviet Union. A visitor will encounter no new neighborhoods of modest one-family houses. There are no districts of fine homes such as Bel Air in California or Scarsdale, New York. But there are "dacha" settlements (summer villas), like the writers' colony at Peredelkino, and some of the Government dacha clusters around Moscow are fairly exclusive. Except for artists, professional people, and high-ranking Government and Party functionaries, however, most families live in overcrowded, inadequate facilities.

Let us compare a typical "lower middle class" family in the Soviet Union and the United States. We'll call them the Joneses and the Dimitrovs.

The Joneses are as American as apple pie. Mr. Jones is a mechanic. He works at one of the large aircraft plants, just outside a major industrial city. His base salary is $500 a month. Mrs. Jones is a homemaker. She spends her time running their modest 6-room home and taking care of their two children, Betty, age 13, and Bob, age 9. The Joneses are buying their home, which is in a nice residential neighborhood about twenty-five minutes from where Mr. Jones works. The Joneses still have another ten years to pay on their home; then it will be theirs. It cost them $11,500. Their payments, including interest, are $90 per month. With overtime pay saved up for several months, the Joneses have just purchased a five-year old second-hand car for which they paid $400. While not everyone in America is as well off as these Joneses, the fact is that there are millions of middle-class Joneses in the United States.

What about the Dimitrovs? He has Jones' job in Moscow.

He is also a mechanic. For twenty years he has worked in the First National Ball-Bearing and Roller-Bearing Plant in Moscow (formerly known as the Kaganovich Plant). Mrs. Dimitrov also works. She drives a bus. They live in one of the rare, newer 4-room apartments in Moscow, which they and their 11-year-old son Ivan share with another family. It has a living room (partitioned to make two rooms), two bedrooms, a small bath, and a tiny kitchen. Mr. Dimitrov makes 150 rubles per month; Mrs. Dimitrov makes 80 rubles. They pay a small monthly rental fee and little income tax (see page 105 on Soviet income taxes). Medical services are inadequate — but free. By Russian standards, the Dimitrovs are well off, though Dimitrov has no automobile, no home of his own (not even a private apartment), and his wife works. But with eggs at the equivalent of two dollars a dozen and an average man's suit priced at over $100, the standard of living of this "middle-class" Russian family is terribly low by American standards, or even Western European standards.

We may sum up the difference by saying that salaries at all levels in the Soviet Union are roughly half those for the same jobs in this country, whereas prices for most items are approximately double United States prices. There are, of course, exceptions to this rule. With relatively lower rent, the Russian standard of living is roughly one-third that enjoyed by the average American family. But beyond this, making the average Russian's life even more difficult, is the matter of the poor quality and constant shortages of almost everything.

In recent speeches Khrushchev himself has commented on shortages of food in some cities, and on the "window dressing" put on for his benefit when he has toured the country. Khrushchev quoted women who told him how wonderful it was that he visited their towns because suddenly the stores were filled with goods they didn't normally have.

## 45. *How do salaries and prices in the Soviet Union compare with those in the United States?*

Prices, of course, have meaning only in terms of wages. In the United States, during the 1930's, you could get a hamburger or a malt for ten cents, a shoeshine for a nickel, a gallon of gasoline for fifteen cents, and a haircut for a quarter. *But,* the monthly salaries or weekly wages of the school teacher, the painter, the office worker, and the mechanic during those "good old days" were roughly one third what they are today. On the other hand, if a worker today makes 100 dollars a month, he could not possibly afford to pay two or three dollars for a pound of butter or a dozen eggs or a hundred and fifty dollars for an overcoat. This is, however, precisely the position in which the average Soviet citizen presently finds himself. And the fact that he pays comparatively small rent and little income tax does not make up the difference.

Study this representative list of average monthly salaries in the Soviet Union. Figures are based on information from the *Monthly Labor Review* of April, 1960 as modified by more recent information. (At the current official exchange rate one ruble is worth $1.10.)

| *Position or Job* | *Monthly Salary Range* (in rubles) |
|---|---|
| Scientist | 800–1,500 |
| Professor | 500–1,000 |
| Docent (Assistant Professor) | 300– 500 |
| Plant manager | 100– 300 |
| Engineer | 100– 200 |
| Physician | 100– 200 |
| High school teacher | 85– 150 |
| Primary school teacher | 60– 100 |
| Skilled worker | 100– 250 |
| (tool maker, lathe operator, accountant) | |
| Semi-skilled worker | 60– 90 |
| (bus driver, store keeper) | |
| Unskilled worker | 40– 60 |
| (street repair man, janitor, maid) | |

Here is a price list showing the cost in the Soviet Union today of some typical items. (A kopeck roughly equals a penny.)

Food

| | | |
|---|---|---|
| small loaf of bread | 12 | kopecks |
| pound of butter | 3 | rubles |
| medium sized chicken | 3–4 | rubles |
| dozen eggs | 2½ | rubles |
| pound of sugar | 1 | ruble |
| pound of apples | 2 | rubles |

Clothing

| | |
|---|---|
| man's suit | 110 rubles and above |
| man's overcoat | 150 rubles and above |
| | |
| Leica-type camera | 160 rubles |
| fountain pen | 2 rubles |
| television set | 250 rubles |
| automobile | 2,500–4,000 rubles |

Try this experiment. Make your own comparison. Take this price list to various stores in your community. Write down after each item the price for which it is being sold here in America. Then, find out what is the current average salary of a teacher, a painter, an office worker, a mechanic in the United States. When you have done this, make your own comparisons. You will be surprised at the results.

## 46. Do the Russians pay income tax?

Soviet propaganda makes much of the point that the Russians pay very low income taxes. The promise is that they will eventually be eliminated altogether. Their highest bracket is 13 per cent. The average Russian pays about 5 per cent. When we compare this with the United States top bracket of 91 per cent or even with the 10 to 40 per cent paid by the vast majority of Americans, the Kremlin would seem to have a point.

But wait! Before we start packing to move to the Soviet Union, it might be well to examine the case a bit more closely.

Numbers, percentages, and statistics can be misleading. They are only meaningful in context, that is, when seen as a part of the whole picture. The Soviet boast about low income taxes is an excellent example of the old story of trying to depict what an elephant looks like by describing only its trunk: An elephant is a long, thin, rough-skinned, flexible animal, like a hose.

As we know, everyone in the Soviet Union works for the government. This means that the government sets both the level of salaries and the rates of income tax. Consider this:

> What does it matter whether the government pays the worker a $200 monthly salary and charges him 50 per cent income tax, thus leaving him $100 in take-home pay
>
> or
>
> pays him a salary of just over $100 per month and charges him a mere 5 per cent in income tax, also leaving him a take-home pay of $100?
>
> *In either case, he still has only $100.*

Instead of direct taxation (which is low and is scheduled to be abolished eventually) the Soviet state supports itself and its economic expansion out of a hidden sales tax, the "turnover tax." The price of every item includes a turnover tax which is never specified on the price tag. Half of the price of a product sold in a government store may be tax. This is, in effect, the profit — which goes to the state. This is one reason why some critics of Communism call it "state capitalism."

From an economic point of view, the whole argument about low income taxes in the Soviet Union is rather meaningless. But it is important psychologically and politically for the Communists to claim that "in the Soviet Union, as compared to the capitalist world, income tax is extremely low!"

## 47. *Is it true that in the Soviet Union women work at men's jobs?*

Many of the jobs customarily held by men in America are done by women in the Soviet Union. These include bricklaying housepainting, driving trucks and buses, sweeping the street (with twig brooms), construction work, and just plain ditch digging and road repair.

It comes as something of a shock to the traveler from the West to encounter a large group of Russian women in the hot sun pouring concrete for a new apartment building in Moscow or a sidewalk in Leningrad.

But the official Soviet Intourist travel guide will soon set the visitor straight: "These are the democratic women of the Soviet Union," she explains. "You see, in the Soviet Union we have eliminated discrimination based on sex."

From the Soviet Government's point of view it is, in fact, essential that as many women as possible work, for two reasons: First, without their contribution to the labor force, the Soviet economy could not possibly develop at the forced pace planned for it. Secondly, the great majority of families in the Soviet Union would find it difficult to exist on the wages of the husband alone. Salaries are too low; prices, too high.

The big complaint from the women is that they have to work to make ends meet and still do all the work of housewives (including standing in line for many scarce items), and there are not enough places for the children in the nurseries and kindergartens. So the working women often have to be mothers, housewives, and workers, all in one — and most of them without washing machines and vacuum cleaners, many without even a private kitchen or private bathroom.

## Education, "Culture," and Recreation

### 48. *What are schools like in the Soviet Union?*

There has been a great deal of discussion in recent years about education and schools in the Soviet Union. More than once we have heard it suggested that Soviet education is superior to American education. Can this possibly be true? How do the two systems compare?

**Educational goals.** The first question we must ask is "education for what?" As Americans, most of us believe that education should prepare us for life, by providing skills or preparing us for a chosen profession, by giving us a broad knowledge of history, society, and human nature, by teaching us to use our leisure time more wisely and enjoyably. In short, education in the United States is focused on the development of the individual. The fulfillment of *his* potential, the achievement of *his* hopes and dreams — these are the traditional goals of education in a democratic society.

In the Soviet totalitarian society no such "bourgeois" notions stand in the way of the Communist's emphasis on education for service to the State: To the Communist, the individual is not important. The only meaningful question is how many engineers or doctors are needed next year to fulfill the Plan.

Those who would be inclined to agree that perhaps this Communist approach is not such a bad one must also agree that the search for genuine truth has *no* place in Communist education. Students are *not* allowed to hear both sides of a question in courses in the social sciences and the humanities.

**The Soviet educational system.** Until quite recently only seven years of education were compulsory in the Soviet Union. After the seven-year school, the student might: (1) take a job requiring practically no skill, (2) be drafted into a labor-reserve school providing up to two years training for occupations of moderate skill, (3) enter a technical school for several years of training or (4) go on to the upper grades of a ten-year school for "academic" college preparatory education.

The 19th and 20th Party Congresses, the latter in February 1956, made the decision to require a ten-year compulsory education. The practical effect of this was easier courses and less homework in the (junior) 9th and (senior) 10th years, since no longer could all students be regarded as college preparatory material. "Practical studies" now became the theme. This experiment did not prove satisfactory. Everyone wanted to go on to higher education — an office job.

Khrushchev, therefore, reversed his course. He suddenly rejected the ten-year principle to proclaim that eight years of education would be quite enough. "All students," he said, "must prepare for useful work" and take a full-time job upon comple tion of the eighth grade. Thus, in contrast to the twelve years of education (through high school) which has become the standard in America, school for the average Soviet boy or girl ends at the eighth grade.

**Good points of the Soviet system.** Doesn't the Soviet educational system have any good features? It has a number, and they are very important. Most important is the greater seriousness with which the average Soviet student approaches his studies. Also significant is the early and continuing emphasis of Soviet education on mathematics, foreign languages, science, and classical literature.

**Conclusion — the balance sheet.** The conclusion writes itself. The student in the Soviet Union is exposed to more basic subject matter earlier. He is likely to be better in mathematics and foreign languages than his American counterpart. At the same time, much of his education turns out to be indoctrination and propaganda. He is likely to know much less than his American counterpart about world history, economics and philosophy (except Marxist), religion, psychology, and many other fields. In a word, his education is specialized, limited, and slanted. If he is bright, he will have been well prepared to be a cog in the Soviet machine.

## 19. *Does the Soviet Union have freedom of the press?*

Freedom of the press is sacred to our democratic tradition. It is the essential right to disagree, to be heard. It is the privilege of publishing what one thinks and feels, regardless of politics or religion. It is the right to read what we like. The press of the Free World represents a wide range of differing political viewpoints and purposes — and sometimes none at all.

The Soviet press is different. It has no freedom, no life of its own. There are 10,000 newspapers in the Soviet Union, but not one dares express an opinion which differs in the slightest degree from the official Party view on any major issue. The "facts" to be printed are carefully selected. In the USSR today, all printed matter, down to wrapping labels, is censored. The Communist Party leadership appoints or approves the appointment of all editors, removes them at will, and tells them what to publish. There are no privately owned or individually operated Russian newspapers. Nor can one buy a copy of *Life, Look, The New York Times, The Reader's Digest,* or *Popular Mechanics* at any bookstand or magazine counter anywhere in the Soviet Union. A few foreign Communist papers are for sale, but even these are censored before being made available.

The major Soviet libraries supposedly have certain Western newspapers, but these are not accessible to the general public, only to a very few persons holding special cards entitling them to this privilege. Under the circumstances very few Russians ever have a chance to read a London or New York newspaper.

This situation is no recent development. It is fundamental to the Soviet approach and essential to the Communist system. Lenin wrote:

> The role of a newspaper is not confined solely to the spreading of ideas, to political education, and to attracting political allies. A newspaper is not only a collective propaganda vehicle and collective agitator. It is also a collective organizer.

Thus, the role of the press in Communist countries is entirely different from the role of the press in the Free World. With us, the focus is news and information, "all the news that's fit to print" as *The New York Times* puts it. With the Communists, propaganda and "socialist education" are the avowed purposes and daily diet, and the Government is both teacher and dietitian. The Kremlin regards "objectivity" as a capitalist notion. "Truth" is what the Party says it is. "Truth" is what serves the interests of Communism. There is no "objective truth."

## 50. *What do the Russians do for recreation?*

As we have seen, both husband and wife normally are employed in the Soviet Union. The daily routine of living (standing in line at the food-store, for example) is tiresome and time consuming. Sunday is almost always taken up by shopping, with stores open on Sunday and closed on Monday. Because Russia workers have to devote much more of their time to shopping and household duties than do Americans, they have much less free time. Therefore, recreation in leisure time, as we know it in the United States, is not a part of the average Soviet citizen's daily life. Reading, however, is important to the Russians, and they do a lot of it. (See pp. 113–115.)

In addition to reading, recreation for the average Russian may be divided into six kinds: (1) sports, (2) dining and dancing, (3) plays, movies and concerts, (4) TV, (5) outings or vacations (beach and mountains), and (6) compulsory meetings and lectures.

**Sports.** Soccer, swimming, ice skating, track and field sports, volleyball, and tennis are all popular in the Soviet Union. Golf is unknown. Group gymnastics are stressed. Outstanding athletes are subsidized by the government, and they devote full time to this occupation. This is one reason why the Soviet athletes have, in recent years, made such an impressive showing in the Olympic Games and other athletic meets. Some twenty million Russians participate in physical culture clubs. These are directed by official supervisors. They include a series of tests, or merit badges, which culminate in the coveted Communist award, "Ready for Labor and Defense."

**Dining and dancing.** Russians do not "go out for dinner" as much as Americans do. For one thing, there are few restaurants in any of the cities and these are quite expensive. In Moscow, one of the world's largest cities, for example, there are only thirty restaurants. There are, however, some 130,000 public catering establishments which remind one of army mess halls. After 12:30 A.M. only a few bars or restaurants remain open in all of Moscow.

Dancing is popular with the young people of Russia. Group dances are organized by the Komsomol (Communist youth organization). Rock and roll and other Western dances, although very popular, are discouraged and sometimes prohibited by the authorities, who regard such recreation as "capitalistic" and bourgeois. Western jazz is very popular with Soviet youth — so much so that jazz recordings and tapes bring fancy prices on the active black market.

At the good hotels in the cities — whether the Soviet city is

large or small — Western style dancing may accompany dinner
in the fashion of an American dinner dance. The small orchestra
normally sounds not unlike a mediocre American hotel band
playing one of the hits of the 1930's.

In the countryside, particularly among the non-Russian nationalities, traditional folk dances are popular. Americans who saw
the Moiseyev dancers on television will remember the spirited
dances of the Ukraine, the Caucasus, and Asiatic Russia.

**Plays, movies, concerts, and the ballet.** Soviet plays and
movies are often, though not always, loaded with Communist
propaganda. They usually have, as we say, a message. This
effect is more difficult to achieve in the case of music. Consequently, concerts and the ballet are great favorites. The Russian
ballet, a traditional art perfected long before the Communists
took over, is still regarded as the finest in the world. Tickets
are at a premium and they are not inexpensive. They are usually
sold by factories and offices to the "worker of the week."

**Television.** There are about 90 TV stations and 4 or 5 million
TV sets in the Soviet Union. (Figures for the United States are
550 stations and 55 million sets.) Television in Russia is very
popular even though screens are small, only one channel is
normally available, and broadcast hours are limited to certain
periods in the daytime or evening. Drama, the ballet, and
the dance appear to be the Russian favorites. There is no color
TV in the Soviet Union. A recent cartoon in the official Soviet
humor magazine *Krokodil* shows a Russian family at home sitting
before a TV set. Every member of the family, including the
dog (rare in the Soviet Union) has on a pair of red and blue
glasses. The caption: "Color TV."

**Outings and vacations.** Vacations at official resorts are provided by the Government for the Party "faithful" and for the
worker who has exceeded the production norm. High Party officials are likely to be accompanied by their families. Sons and
daughters of such families manage to have a good time both at
home and on vacation.

The lovely scenery of such sub-tropical Black Sea beaches as
Yalta and Sochi entitles them to a high rank among the world's
most beautiful beaches. But at these beaches one does not find
a cross-section of the population of the Soviet Union as one
could at the well-known beaches of this country. There is still

another difference between life at an official resort area in the USSR and life at a typical American resort. The vacations of the lucky ones at a Soviet resort are organized to include lectures, calisthenics, and guided tours. The Party makes sure that even on holiday people get what is good for them.

For the average Russian, vacation is spent at home. He has no car. Moreover, it often is hard for the working husband and wife to arrange their vacations at the same time.

**Compulsory meetings and lectures.** Certain forms of indoctrination are also regarded as recreation by the Komsomol or Young Communist League — but not by the young people themselves. Who wants to hear about dialectical materialism when the rest of the gang is at the beach? Nevertheless, the young Communist must attend one of these supposedly recreational activities at least once a week.

## 51. *What do the Russians read?*

Except for the Japanese, the Russians probably read more than any people on earth. At best, we Americans rank a poor third. In Russia, people on buses, taxi drivers waiting for a fare, workers on lunch hours, boys and girls in parks or at the library — everyone, everywhere seems to be reading a book or magazine.

One wonders why the Russians read so much, and what they are reading.

**Why they read so much.** *Why* is very often a big question. In this case we cannot hope to answer it completely and satisfactorily. But several points would seem worth noting. First of all, for more than forty years the Communist one-Party Government in Soviet Russia has encouraged people to read more. Competition is keen. Knowledge is power; knowledge is money — in the Soviet Union perhaps even more than in the United States. What Russians read, of course, the Party tries to control. Secondly, the Russians as a people have built-in curiosity. In this sense, they are much like Americans. But unlike Americans, they have little or no opportunity to satisfy their curiosity. They do the best they can on their skimpy and controlled literary diet. They even learn to read between the lines of the official press. Politically, then, the average Russian is probably more sophisticated than the average American. This hunger for truth is why the few copies of *Amerika* (this country's Russian-language magazine, distributed in the Soviet Union on an exchange basis) are snapped up by the Russians and circulated throughout the Soviet Union. Thirdly, life in Russia is drab and difficult. Recreational choices on a Sunday afternoon are much more limited than in America. A good novel, a spy story, or a science-fiction article helps Ivan and Natasha escape for a refreshing while from the realities of daily life in present-day Russia.

**What they read.** What do the Russians read? At the outset, it must be stressed that all books, magazines and newspapers in the Soviet Union are selected and censored by the one-Party Communist Government. Thus, what the Russian can buy in a book store, or a newsstand, or borrow from a library — every single item — bears the Communist Party's stamp of approval.

What does this mean in practical terms? It means that although the Russians may read more than we do, with pitifully few exceptions they read only three types of material: (1) Communist Party publications, (2) Pro-Communist books and magazines, or (3) Non-political material (Shakespeare translated into Russian is very popular with students in Russia).

If we were permitted to take a poll of readers in Russia — both students and adults — Russian reading preferences would probably come out something like this:

**First:** Russian classical literature. Tolstoy, Pushkin, Gogol, Chekhov, and other great writers in the Russian liberal tradition are favorites. Modern Soviet works are much less popular.

**Second:** Translations of Western literature. Shakespeare, Hemingway, and Cronin are among the favorites. Cooper, Mark Twain, and Edgar Allan Poe are also well known to most students. How many Russian authors have you read?

**Third:** Modern Russian literature. Those authors whose works tend to be the least political are the most popular. Russian readers are clearly unimpressed with the worker who abandons his sweetheart to return to Kharkov to meet the factory norm and thus becomes an "unselfish hero of the State."

**Fourth:** Spy stories and science fiction. These are the Russian versions of American "Whodunits" and "Westerns." They are extremely popular, but, of course, not in the same sense as the great classics.

One final comment should be added on what the Russians do not read: They do not read foreign magazines and newspapers. Young people in this country might well spend more time reading good literature and books on serious subjects. Because our books and publications are not censored, Americans have the great advantage of being free to seek the truth in all fields of learning.

## Religion

## 52. Do the Soviets permit freedom of religion?

Lenin called religion an "opiate of the people," a drug designed to make misery easier to endure. As we know, Communists are materialists; they do not believe in God. From time to time atheist propaganda has been toned down and zealots have been warned against antagonizing religious persons. The current phase, however, is one of rampant propaganda against religion.

Why, then, does the Soviet Government permit some churches to remain open? Isn't this freedom of religion?

Religious freedom is more than an open church building. It has to do with attitudes, laws, policies and goals. True, there are a number of Protestant, Catholic, and Russian Orthodox churches open throughout Russia. Some synagogues are also functioning. But before we conclude that there is, in fact, freedom of religion in the Soviet Union today, we should consider a few additional facts:

1. While the churches which remain are often crowded with older people, one seldom sees any of the younger generation. Few children may be found in any church or synagogue. One reason why the few churches in Russia are so crowded is that many other churches have been shut down, torn down, or converted into anti-religious museums.

2. Sunday schools, Bible schools, church-operated schools of any kind (day, night, or weekends) are expressly forbidden by the Soviet Government. Some Protestant groups (par-

ticularly Seventh Day Adventists, Jehovah's Witnesses, and Pentecostalists) have been particularly the victims of repression.

3. It is not possible to buy a Bible or even a religious book anywhere in the Soviet Union. According to information from the American Bible Society, no Bibles have been published in the Soviet Union since 1926. In 1947, Metropolitan Gregory of Leningrad and Novgorod, in New York for a visit, accepted an offer from the American Bible Society of a proposed gift of over a million and a half Gospels, Russian Testaments, and Russian Bibles. After a small shipment including only 5,000 Bibles had been made, on July 6, 1948 the Society received a cable from Metropolitan Gregory in Moscow saying "to avoid misunderstanding don't send the offered things." That was the last heard of the matter.

4. The Soviet eight-year school, which every Russian boy and girl must attend, teaches Marxism and atheism as a regular part of the program. From the first grade, the child learns that "there is no God," that Lenin was right.

5. Further, the government (Communist Party) controlled press maintains a constant campaign against religion. This usually takes the form of stressing the "uselessness" of religion or of making jokes about the "old-fashioned people" who still believe in "the nonsense about God." A typical, recent cartoon in the official Soviet humor magazine *Krokodil* shows two priests talking. One says, "But, Father, the Holy Water has stopped running." The other replies: "Call a plumber!"

6. A Communist Party member will seldom run the risk of attending church services. It might be thought that he had fallen prey to old, bourgeois ideas.

Why does the Soviet Government tolerate any religion at all? Why doesn't it stamp it out? Probably for three reasons: First Communist Eastern Europe is predominantly Catholic. The Kremlin has enough problems. It does not wish further to antagonize whole populations. In Russia, itself, the state church under the tsars was the Greek Orthodox, and many people were deeply religious. Secondly, Khrushchev reasons that to attempt to stamp out religion might create a huge religious underground

Thirdly, so long as some churches remain open, the men in Moscow can use this fact in their propaganda to convince the uninformed throughout the world that there is religious freedom in the Soviet Union today: "After all, the churches are open!"

The Kremlin is, thus, banking on the belief that as the present, older generation passes from the scene, religion, too, will fade away. In this case, the Soviet policy-makers have chosen slow death rather than liquidation or murder.

## 53. Is there racial discrimination in the Soviet Union?

Communists claim that Soviet society is free from discrimination. What are the facts? There is clear national discrimination practiced against minority groups in the Soviet Union. The Jews have long been discriminated against by the Soviet regime, and there is mounting evidence of increasing unofficial discrimination against African students in the Soviet Union.

Of the total population of the Soviet Union of 210,000,000, some 90,000,000 are non-Russian nationalities (Ukrainians, White Russians, Uzbeks, and Tatars). Leadership is firmly in the hands of the Russians. Russian history and Russian culture are extolled at the expense of the minorities. Everyone must learn the Russian language. Resentment by these minority groups goes back to the Russification attempted by the tsars. This, in fact, led many non-Russians to support the Revolution.

At first, the Communists gave recognition to the minorities. This policy gained support for Communist ideology in other countries, though discrimination was by no means absent in Russia even at this time. Gradually, the Communists shifted back to many of the Russification policies of the tsars, such as rewriting the history of minor nationalities to glorify Russian conquests of lesser peoples "in their own interest." Five nationalities were actually exiled en masse to Siberia because large numbers of them co-operated with the Germans during the Nazi occupation. Khrushchev modified some of the excesses of Russification, but the basic policy stands. It is, in fact, a most extreme form of discrimination, and is bitterly resented by many of the non-Russian nationalities in the USSR.

Discrimination against the Jews in the Soviet Union takes the form of religious, cultural, national, and economic suppression. The teaching of Hebrew is expressly forbidden by the authorities. Jewish organizations have been dissolved, and Jewish periodicals as well as publications dealing with Jewish problems have been suppressed. Jews are not allowed to visit Israel. They may not even write to Jewish communities in other parts of the world. Zionism is regarded as a "counter-revolutionary movement of the Jewish bourgeoisie," and, therefore, is seen as a potential threat to Soviet life. Jews who once occupied a most important place in the economic life of the Eastern European satellites have been systematically removed from positions of influence. The clearest evidence of official Soviet discrimination is the passport, or identification card, which all persons in the Soviet Union are required to carry with them at all times and which lists the person's nationality.

Soviet discrimination against the colored races is not a new thing. Chinese and Japanese students who studied in Moscow and Leningrad during the 1920's and 1930's regularly complained of the "second-class" treatment they received. The situation is no different today.

The following are extracts from an interview with Mr. S. Omor Okullo, a 26-year-old African student.[5] Mr. Okullo spent two years studying at the University of Moscow on a United Nations scholarship. He was expelled by the Soviet Government after he protested against the way Russians treated African students in Moscow.

Q. Mr. Okullo, you have written a letter to Soviet Premier Khrushchev protesting the treatment of African students at the University of Moscow. Why?

A. We informed the Soviet Government about a Somali student who was attacked and beaten up and left unconscious by four Russian students.

Q. Why was he beaten?

A. His crime consisted of dancing with a Russian girl.

Q. Were there other incidents of this sort?

A. Well, one day the Russian students distributed a typed circular in the Russian language saying that the African students were

[5] From a copyrighted article in *U.S. News & World Report*, Vol. XLIX No. 5 (August 1, 1960), pp. 59–60.

getting too big for their boots in Moscow. What they meant really was that we came from poor homes and were getting big in Moscow and becoming an anti-Soviet group.

And one day one of the African students was insulted and called a "monkey." He was going in a lift (elevator), and had merely asked them to stop for him on a certain floor. . . .

Q. Why are so many African students so unhappy in Moscow?

A. One problem is that living conditions are very unsatisfactory. Also there is not any relationship between the Soviet students and the African students. Many times, when Russian students are discovered in the company of African students, the Russians are summoned and reprimanded by the Komsomol (Russian youth organization).

In an open letter to African governments, another African student, A. R. Amar of Uganda, member of the Executive Committee of the African Student Union in the USSR, summed up the situation this way:

In the name of all loyal Africans, the Executive Committee of the African Student Union in Moscow wishes respectfully to call the attention of all African governments to the deceit, the threats, the pressure, the brutality, and the discrimination with which Soviet administrators and strategists have so often handled African and other foreign students in the U.S.S.R. We further wish to stress the great danger Communism is to true Africanism. We hate colonialism and racial discrimination in any form, wherever it may appear. New and dangerous forms of colonialism and discrimination are being fostered by the Communist system and by Soviet strategists and are a grave threat to the future of Africa.

## Social Problems

**4.** *Does delinquency exist among teen-agers in the USSR?*

In the Soviet Union as in the United States, juvenile delinquency is a problem. Material on the following pages suggests

the standards Communist society has set for youth and make
clear that these are not always met.

*Komsomolskaya Pravda's* (literally: "Youth Truth") Publi
Opinion Institute in Moscow recently asked a number of Sovie
young people to comment on the younger generation in Russi
today. Here are some of their answers:

**From a girl student** (Penza): "Some of our young people . .
go by the slogan: 'Life is given to you only once, so you shoul
get everything out of it you can.'"

**From a working woman** (Moscow): ". . . young people some
times have nothing to do. . . . There is one movie house in ou
borough. The big building that goes by the name of Construc
tion Workers' House of Culture is almost always closed; no on
but the people who work there knows what goes on in i
Motion pictures are rarely shown there, and consequently it
hard to get in to see a film. Hardly any parties for young peopl
are held. There was not even a New Year's Eve party. Just wha
do they do there?

If you happen to be standing near that House of Culture on
Saturday evening in the hope of getting in to see a movie pictur
you're asked: "Miss, would you like to come with us to celebrat
somebody's birthday?" It is not hard to imagine what kind c
'birthday' it is. But to people just starting out in life everythin
is interesting. So instead of the movies they land in a 'coz
crowd.' This is where it all starts: the indifference, the pessimisn
the mistrust of people. And the most terrible thing is to sto
trusting people."

**From a carpenter** (Uryupinsk, Stalingrad Province): "I kno
several young people in my city who are 'satisfied' with the
way of life, with not working or studying anywhere, with spon
ing off mamas and papas. They dress ridiculously. They wea
their hair long and grow sideburns and beards, as though the
were inhabitants of a desert island. In the daytime they go in
hiding somewhere, like moles, and in the evening they are
be encountered in the movie houses and theaters and at you
people's parties in the clubs. If they try to demonstrate a 'clas
dance' they are warned that this is not a [place] for such pe
formance. But if they fail to understand friendly advice, the doo
of the club frequently have to be closed to them."

**From a militiaman** (Moscow): "Among the negative traits that exist among young people are: unseemly conduct in the relations between men and women, lack of modesty and pride, and abuse of alcohol to create artificial gaiety or to embolden the drinker into committing hooligan acts."

**From a newspaper correspondent** (*Pravda*, July 6, 1961): There are many drunks and rowdies in the streets here (in Krasnoyarsk). At the delicatessen next door to the House of Soviets, young people buy vodka and drink it right on the spot. When they are drunk, these insolent young people loiter on the sidewalks, push women and children out of their way and board streetcars and buses out of turn. The hooligans are completely out of hand in the Park of Culture and Rest — they create disturbances, molest passersby, and start brawls. There have been cases of crime as well."

**Measures to combat juvenile delinquency.** Since 1935 the Soviet statute book has contained punishments for minors from 2 to 14 years of age. A law was passed in 1935 which made children criminally responsible from the age of twelve in the case of murder, theft, acts of violence, and infliction of grievous bodily harm. Juvenile criminals were sent to so-called "labor and education" colonies in which trained staffs attempted to reform them. In the 1940's more severe penalties were laid down for juvenile offenders. It was decreed that from the age of 14 a delinquent was subject to the same punishments as were meted out to adults, with the exception of the death penalty, which could only be imposed on persons over the age of 18.

Juveniles guilty not of any specific criminal or political offense but of "anti-social" behavior are also brought to court. The label "anti-social element" is attached to anyone in the Soviet Union who deviates from the standards of public conduct laid down by the Communist Party. The young "good citizens" in the Soviet Union belong to the Young Pioneers and the Komsomol and engage in activities sponsored by these groups. Soviet juvenile "stilyagi" or beatniks are bitterly attacked in the Soviet press as "anti-social elements," and the term is stretched to cover all young people who show great interest in anything American or Western, enjoy abstract art, jazz and rock and roll, and wear tight trousers, loud shirts and beards, or even chew gum!

Any young person who declines to take up a job or course of study to which he has been assigned after leaving school, regardless of his tastes or aptitude, is condemned as someone who "despised labor discipline," a "self-seeker" or a "parasite." There are many cases in the USSR of juveniles who embark on a career of theft and hooliganism because they cannot find an outlet for their ambitions, have been forced to break off their studies, or have been denied entry to institutions of higher education of their choice. These young people constitute something of a danger to the Soviet regime, since they develop a nihilistic attitude to life (some of them have been given the name "nibnicho" — literally, those who believe in "neither God nor the Devil"). Recently the Soviet press has been referring to a type of young person often to be met with nowadays in the Soviet Union — who goes around in a semi-drunken condition, unkempt . . . and indulges in insulting behavior towards girls.

Komsomol (Young Communist) brigades have been formed in the Soviet Union to combat these "anti-social elements," and factory workers are also required to set up patrols to catch hooligans and bring them before so-called "people's courts, which mete out summary punishments, and try to reintegrate the culprit into society. The hooligans are armed and often put up a fight against the "model" Komsomols who are sent out to police the streets. Occasionally members of this amateur Komsomol militia are murdered in the course of their duties.

One of the frequent Soviet press complaints is that the volunteer Komsomol police aides and the police themselves frequently turn their backs on "hooligans" to avoid a showdown with them. The volunteer militia also abuse their office to settle personal scores on occasion. In Sochi, one of the most elegant resort towns on the Black Sea, they slashed and ripped the clothing of young men and women whom they considered to be wearing "daring" styles. The "daring" styles turned out to be slacks for women regarded in many parts of the country as "bold"; and bright colored sport shirts, considered "Western."

Although we know little about juvenile delinquency in the Soviet Union, it is apparent from the quotations on these pages that the problem does exist and that it is of concern to people in the USSR.

## 55. *Is divorce common in the Soviet Union?*

It would be difficult to improve on John Gunther's brief, comprehensive treatment of this basic problem. The following excerpt from *Inside Russia Today* suggests the nature and scope of the problem in Russia today.

> Another illustration of the prevailing mood of conservatism in social relations is divorce. This, as everybody knows, was in the old days granted automatically in the USSR. The old quip was, "Just marriage is grounds for divorce in Russia." The early revolutionaries prided themselves on the contempt with which they held the marriage relationship. In 1928 I knew a Russian girl, in her early thirties, who had been married seven times. Not only was divorce (in those days) granted at the simple request of either party, without notice having to be given and in a procedure that did not take more than three minutes, but a husband or wife could get a divorce without even informing the partner. All this has long since been supplanted, and the divorce rate in the Soviet Union is substantially lower than that in the United States. Marx predicted that the bourgeois family would "vanish as a matter of course," but nowadays the whole emphasis of Soviet legal and other procedure is to protect marriage and the family.
>
> The situation at present is that, if a man or woman wants a divorce, he or she must go to a people's court (not merely a registration bureau) and make application in person. *Both* parties must appear; the procedure is laborious and expensive, with a sizable fee attached. This court has no power to grant a divorce, but only hears the preliminaries of the case; the usual practice, especially if children are involved, is for the judges to insist that the estranged husband and wife go through a "cooling-off period," during which time they will be expected to adjust their differences. If, however, reconciliation fails, the case may then be brought to another, higher court, and divorce will be granted, but only if the cause of dissatisfaction is adjudged to be "real" enough. Alimony may be substantial. Casual infidelity is not grounds for divorce, nor is mental cruelty. This procedure is so stringent that many Soviet sociologists and jurists are urging its relaxation, largely out of consideration for children. . . .[6]

[6] John Gunther, *Inside Russia Today* (Harper & Brothers, New York, 957), pp. 330–331.

It may be added that there have been frequent complaints o the discriminatory attitude toward illegitimate children. In Russian a person's name always includes a middle name composed of his father's name with an ending (-ich or -ovich for boys, -na or -ovna for girls). This appears in all documents, including the passport everyone must carry, and is used in all polite conversation. What happens when a child is born out of wedlock, even if his parents later marry? The child is stigmatized by lack of the middle name. Even if the father wants to give the child his name, he cannot. A Leningrad school teacher estimated that a fifth of the children she has taught were illegitimate and suffered social discrimination. Why so many "illegitimate" children? The answer is partly that legal divorce is so hard to obtain that in many cases the man or woman seeking divorce remarries without benefit of the law — then, when a child is born, an illegitimat child, this establishes legal grounds for claiming dissolution o the first marriage and recognition of the new one. But the chil is legally illegitimate, however much loved and desired by th parents, who may be now married.

## 56. *What about crime?*

The crime rate in the Soviet Union, like that in the Unite States, appears to have risen steadily during the years since World War II. Statistics on crime, as in the case of juvenil delinquency, are confined to percentages.

In May of 1961, the death penalty (abolished in 1947 and the reinstated) was extended to include three crimes previously punished by imprisonment. They are: embezzling state or public property, counterfeiting, and terrorizing prison inmates or attack ing prison personnel. The other crimes now punishable under Soviet law by death are treason, espionage, sabotage, terroristi acts, banditry, and murder. Whatever the crime, punishment i the Soviet Union is apt to be considerably more severe than fo the same crime in the United States.

The Soviet press reports a stepped-up drive against "anti social, parasitic elements" in Soviet society. If a man's neighbor should decide that he is a parasite — that he is "going throug the motions of work," but actually securing his income from some private, unauthorized source — such an individual could be sent into exile for from two to five years.

According to a report on "Crime in the Soviet Union," published by the Institute for the Study of the USSR in Munich, this law is "designed to frustrate the attempts of the Soviet citizen to escape from the clutches of the Soviet economic system. Any attempt to live on one's own," the report concludes, "is a crime and must be punished."

The Soviet press reports the existence of a definite class of professional criminals who do not work and have no permanent homes. This group is particularly embarrassing to the Soviet regime since its members became adults after the Soviets seized power, and thus must be regarded as "products of the system."

## 7. Is alcoholism a problem?

There are no statistics on the number of alcoholics in the Soviet Union today. But drunkenness and other social problems exist in the Soviet Union, as they do elsewhere. The point to be remembered, however, is that the Communist regime has claimed that "socialism" would eliminate such evils. Nevertheless, the Russians, traditionally fond of vodka, appear to be drinking more than ever before.

The Party and Government have been attempting to meet the problem by legislation and lecturing, by constant stories in the Soviet press stressing the seriousness of the problem, and by a nation-wide program of "sobering-up stations."

A few years ago, the Soviet Government passed a liquor-control ordinance. It stipulated, among other things, that henceforth Russians would be limited to "one drink per customer at all hotels, restaurants, and bars." No ration card; nothing to sign; just one drink per customer. One Muscovite was heard to comment: "We are presently engaged in one of the greatest games of alcoholic musical chairs in history." Naturally, Ivan went from bar to bar.

Some of the comrades eventually got tired of such nonsense. Since the law did not apply to stores selling bottled liquor, the answer was obvious. Any Russian so inclined simply bought a bottle of vodka, took it home or to a friend's apartment, and drank as much as he wished.

The sobering-up station program, in existence for some time, apparently has not solved the problem either. In an article entitled "Subsidized Drunkards," the government newspaper *Izvestia* (March 29, 1961) trains its editorial guns on the sobering-up station:

> In the morning Docent Nikolai Leonidovich Kuzmin delivered a lecture at the Moscow Construction Engineering Institute. And in the evening? In the evening he ended up in a sobering-up station. Under the cold jets of the shower the docent shook his head and giggled, as though something tickled him.
>
> "He's an old acquaintance," the doctor on duty said confidentially. "This is not the first time he has 'registered' here."
>
> A sobering-up station. Possibly many people imagine this to be a stark, murky establishment. Far from it. A sobering-up station is rather like a hospital. The "guests," after taking a pre-slumber bath or shower, snore serenely on beds with puffed up pillows and snow-white linen in large spacious rooms. Some of them sleep through the night and some right through the following day. When they have sobered up, they reclaim their possessions, wearing sheepish grins; then, after paying four rubles — not a fine but a "medical service fee" — they go home.
>
> When one looks at this picture, the question automatically arises. Cannot the sobering-up stations function without special comfort and charge not the four rubles for "medical services" but an obligatory fine for violating public order?
>
> Let us note that four rubles falls far short of covering the total expense of the service. Drunkards are being maintained on a state subsidy!

What is most significant about this story is that the Soviet Government newspaper in no way suggests that the sobering-up stations be done away with. The question is only how they should be run, who should foot the bill.

Further, it may be noted that the problem of illegal liquor in the Soviet Union has almost all of the aspects familiar to us here in America. Indeed, the situation in the Soviet Union had become serious enough by the spring of 1961 that the Presidium of the Russian Republic Supreme Soviet issued a Decree bearing the title, "On Increasing the Penalty for the Home Manufacture of Vodka and Other Alcoholic Beverages." This decree provides stiff fines and from one to three years in prision for "the manufacture or possession for purposes of sale of vodka, chach, arrack, mulberry vodka, beer or other strong alcoholic beverages of home distillation." If the Russian can prove that the home-brew is strictly for home consumption, and not for sale, then the prison sentence is only one year.

One of the problems of controlling liquor sales is that for years managers of restaurants and delicatessens met their sales quotas by selling relatively expensive liquor in large quantities. Although they may have had only a few sandwiches on the menu, they always met their sales quota. In short, they had a vested interest in pushing liquor sales. Restaurants and delicatessens are still expected to meet a sales quota in rubles, and liquor sales are still the easiest way, especially when there are shortages of some foodstuffs. That this situation continues is evident from frequent denunciations of it in the press.

## Popular Attitudes

## 58. How does the Russian "man on the street" feel about the United States?

It is important at the outset to make a distinction between the official attitudes of the Party members and Government officials and the feelings of the Russian people. Official Soviet attitudes range from proper to hostile. Unofficial Russian feelings about the United States range from proper to friendly.

Most American travelers to Russia and all of the experts agree that the feelings of the average Russian about America and Americans can be summed up in three words: ignorance, curiosity, friendliness.

John Gunther sums up Soviet ignorance of our country, which he says is formidable, in this way:[7]

[7] *Inside Russia Today*, p. 74.

Russians by and large think that only rich American boys go to college, and that the United States is totally run by big business. They honestly cannot believe it when you tell them that President Eisenhower's father was a railway worker, or that the brother of Harlow H. Curtice, the president of General Motors, is a paint and metal inspector, whose pension will be $63 a month when he retires. They cannot believe it that the *New York Times* prints verbatim the full texts of speeches by Soviet leaders, that the United States has an advanced and comprehensive social security system, and that you can buy a chocolate bar for a nickel. It stuns them to hear that Americans do not need permission to travel from city to city, or that you do not need to submit a passport at a hotel. They cannot believe it that city police have no connection with the national government, or that Yale and Princeton are not operated by the state. I have heard a Russian boy ask quite seriously, "Are there mountains in America?" and "Do you have oranges?"

In spite of the Iron Curtain, Russians have continued to be surprisingly friendly to Americans. Certainly their main motive concerning America and Americans is curiosity. The censorship and rigid information control practiced by the Communists arouses curiosity. To be sure, most Soviet citizens probably believe a good deal of the anti-American propaganda to which they are constantly subjected. They are most likely to believe things that fit into their past experience, such as charges that a foreign (in this case American) government is planning actions leading to war. At the same time, the persistent Soviet propaganda stressing the aim of catching up to and overtaking America naturally makes the man on the street in Russia wonder what America is really like — if it's so bad, why are we trying to catch up with it? Their experience with foreign invaders in two World Wars has made them mistrustful of the intentions of foreign countries. Moreover, they have been indoctrinated in Marxist concepts according to which all governments that are not "socialist" are controlled by profit-seeking men who will stop at nothing to achieve their selfish and evil objectives.

On the other hand, the Russian people know that the United States is not all bad.

The Russians remember many good things that Americans have done for them. Herbert Hoover's early relief mission to Russia, regardless of politics, in the period after the Revolution when starvation and typhus swept parts of the country, is still remembered warmly by many Russians under its initials, "ARA" — American Relief Administration. Relief supplies contributed by Americans during World War II are recalled by the people, even though the Soviet government gave them almost no publicity or recognition. The quality of American machinery acquired by Russia under wartime lend-lease was self-evident to Russians who used it. Most of all, there is tremendous curiosity about our country: copies of *Amerika* (an official government magazine which is allowed to circulate in very limited quantities under an exchange agreement with the Russians) are passed from hand to hand and eagerly read — when Russians can get them. This curiosity and latent feeling of friendship is a reason why the regime tries to keep the Russians from access to all the facts about the United States.

## 59. Why are the Russians always so serious? Don't they have a sense of humor?

The Russians have a good sense of humor. It's the Communists who are the bores. The tradition of Russian humor is much like that in America. While a certain melancholy strain runs through Slavic culture, Russian literature up to 1917 nevertheless sparkled with wit and humor.

Even the characteristically drab and boring Communist culture and dull life in Russia today have, here and there, a few bright patches of humor — if one knows where to look for them. No one can be serious all the time!

Many of the best jokes in Russia never see the light of the printed page — not because they are "off color" in our sense of the word, but because they are off color *politically*. Jokes about Khrushchev, the Communist Party, the Red Army, Communist China, the Eastern European satellites, and Soviet missile failures are simply not permitted by the Communist-controlled press. This has resulted in an active "humor underground" in Russia. A tourist who knows Russian well does not have to be in the Soviet Union very long before encountering this spirit of the real Russia.

Here is a story that is circulating by word of mouth in Kiev.

One Communist Party member says to another: "Isn't it wonderful, Comrade, the Party is going to provide every loyal Party member with his own helicopter."

The other Communist, looking puzzled, asks: "What do we need them for?" His friend replies: "To get to Moscow to stand in line for shoes!"

Or, how about this pointed story from the Moscow "humor underground:"

An American traveling in Russia says to his Intourist guide, "America is a free country. I can stand on the steps of the Capitol building in Washington and shout, 'President Kennedy is an idiot,' and I won't be arrested. Nothing will happen to me."

The Intourist guide replies, "It's no different here. I can stand on the steps of the Kremlin and shout, 'President Kennedy is an idiot,' and not only will I not be arrested, but I will receive the Order of Lenin for meritorious service."

The Party does permit the people a brief escape from the hum-drum of daily life in the form of a bi-weekly humor magazine of stories and cartoons called *Krokodil* (our word crocodile). This magazine, published in Moscow, is in Russian; it is in color and it is very popular with Ivan and Natasha. Like all publications in the Soviet Union today, it is issued under the auspices of the Communist Party. While topics such as Khrushchev are strictly taboo (as noted above), a surprising amount of devastating self-criticism is permitted, and some of it is extremely funny.

# 6 China Under Communism

## The Background of Communism in China

**60.** *What is the history of the Communists' rise to power in China?*

The story of the Communists' rise to power in China may be told briefly in four acts:

**Act 1 — The birth and early development of Communism, 1918–1923.** In 1911, the Nationalist Revolution began. Led by Dr. Sun Yat-sen, it aimed to convert China from a monarchy into a constitutional state. Coming just at this time, the Russian Revolution had a tremendous impact on China, particularly among the student class. Marxist study groups sprang up in cities and on campuses everywhere.

To organize and channel discontent, the Comintern dispatched an agent from Moscow to China. The year was 1920. The man was Voitinski. In 1921 he gathered together a couple of Chinese professors from Peking National University and some students and workers for an important secret meeting in Shanghai. The group decided to call itself the Communist Party of China. Its purpose, it was agreed, would be "the capture of political power."

By 1922, the young Party had officially joined the Comintern and had sent representatives to Moscow. The years 1922–23

131

were spent in recruiting members, expanding Party work, and training. This was all done secretly.

Meanwhile, the Nationalist Revolution continued. But it had not met with the immediate success expected, especially in northern China. Dr. Sun sent his young lieutenant Chiang Kai-shek to Moscow to seek Soviet assistance.

**Act 2 — Soviet advisors and the Nationalist-Communist alliance, 1923–1927.** Soviet political and military advisors began arriving in China "to aid the Nationalist Revolution." A Soviet agent, Michael Borodin, headed the advisory group. The Chinese Nationalist Revolution now moved into high gear. A military academy financed by the Kremlin and staffed with Russian officers was set up. Political propaganda corps were created within Nationalist military units. But perhaps most important of all, Borodin succeeded in getting the Chinese Communists accepted in the Kuomintang, or Nationalist Party. This made it possible for the Communists to use the vehicle of the *Nationalist* Revolution to promote *Communist* ideas and objectives throughout China. The Communist Party, of course, kept its own separate organization and maintained its secret ties with Moscow.

This technique worked so well that in 1925, within a year after the death of Dr. Sun, Borodin, his Soviet staff, and left-wing or Communist Chinese were in virtual control of the Revolution, which by this time had engulfed most of South China.

Chiang Kai-shek (and other Chinese conservatives and moderates), who had been watching this process with alarm, seized a favorable moment; sent the Russian advisors home; and outlawed the Communist Party. The Kuomintang now had two enemies to worry about before the Revolution could succeed: the Northern Militarists *and* the Communists.

**Act 3 — The emergence of Mao Tse-tung and the development of a base in the countryside, 1927–1945.** Outlawed and pursued, the Communists found operations in the cities of China increasingly difficult. A young Communist, Mao Tse-tung, then only 33 (see page 57 for a sketch of his life), developed a Communist base in the countryside. This agrarian base expanded into a substantial area in south-central China controlled by the Communists in defiance of the Nationalists, who now had become the government of China.

Under pressure from Nationalist military forces in the south, the Communists in 1935 decided to move their base north. Over 300,000 Communists started the long march which took them 6,000 miles to Yenan in North China. Here they established the headquarters from which at the end of the war with Japan in 1945 they launched a political and military offensive designed to take over all of China.

Curiously, in 1936–1937, in the face of expanding aggressive Japanese forces, the Nationalists and the Communists once more formed a united front. The Nationalists hoped, thereby, to increase China's power to resist Japan. For the Communists, the arrangement followed the Comintern 1935 united front line and was in accordance with the best Leninist tradition which sanctioned *temporary* alliances with Nationalist groups when it would serve the ends of Communism. As was to be expected, this "marriage of convenience" did not last.

During the years 1940–1945, both *Kuomintang* and Communist forces spent as much time fighting each other as they did resisting Japan. It is not surprising, then, that these two traditional foes found it impossible to get together when the war was over.

**Act 4 — Communist expansion and takeover, 1945–1949.** Years of war with Japan had destroyed China's industry, produced widespread dislocation of families, interrupted schooling and jobs, and caused untold suffering. Inflation mounted. China in 1945 was in a bad way.

In accordance with the 1945 Yalta agreement between Premier Stalin and President Roosevelt, Soviet armies swept over Japanese-controlled Manchuria in the two weeks before Japan's surrender. This helped finish Japan. It also put Soviet forces in a position to give aid to the Chinese Communists who were close by. When these Soviet forces finally withdrew, they turned over or allowed to fall into Chinese Communist hands some 3,000,000 pieces of military equipment and weapons captured from the Japanese.

For a variety of reasons, during these critical years United States support of the Nationalist government of China proved inadequate and ineffective. Some critics of American policy say we did too little too late. Others insist that nothing we might have done would have prevented the Chinese Communists from

turning the tragic economic and political situation of those decisive years into a Red victory. Many persons in touch with the
situation also hold that the Nationalist government was ineffec-
tual in meeting its problems.

In any case, with the war over, the Chinese Communists were
able to combine skillful, if deceitful, political maneuvers with
propaganda and increasing military power to push the discouraged and disintegrating Nationalists off the mainland and
onto the island of Taiwan or Formosa.

### 61. *How can we explain the Communist victory in China?*

Hundreds of books and articles, thousands of pages, millions
of words have been written in an effort to explain why the Communists conquered China. This material, whether scholarly or
popular, one page or a thousand, characteristically has fallen
into one of three schools of thought:

(1) Some scholars say, in effect, that the Communist Revolution
in China is but the latest phase of the great permanent revolution
that has been going on in China for 25 centuries. It is but a
ripple on the sea of history. Some have said that although the
Chinese may call themselves Communists, they are more agrarian
reformers than proletarians, more Chinese than Communist.

(2) Members of the Soviet conspiracy school, on the other hand,
see in the Communist takeover of China the familiar pattern of
Soviet infiltration, aid, training, influence, organization and subversion. Communism is Communism wherever it rears its ugly
head, this group asserts, and China is no exception.

(3) Advocates of the United States subversive interpretation (and
they are the smallest in number but often the most vocal) see
"the loss of China" as an American blunder brought about largely
by subversives and other dupes within the United States Government. Had we been more alert and forthright, this group insists,
we might have "saved" China.

Fortunately or unfortunately, politics, history, and international relations are not this simple. No single, simple explanation may be applied to a complicated, confused historical
situation.

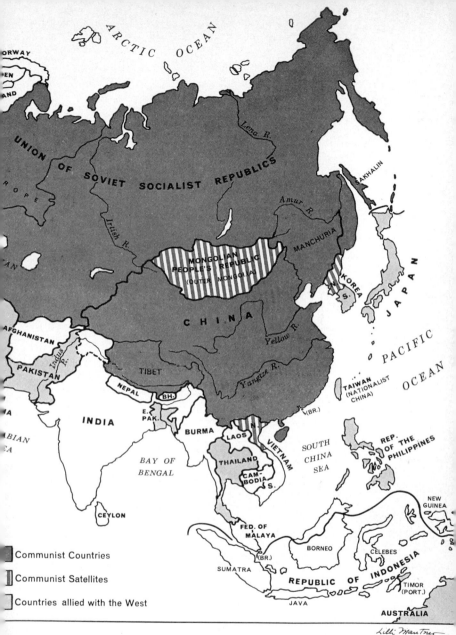

Communist Countries

Communist Satellites

Countries allied with the West

# COMMUNIST WORLD: EAST

Chinese Communist imperialism has pushed into border lands such as Laos, South Vietnam and the northern frontier regions of India and Pakistan.

1

This picture of Mao, taken in 1954, shows him announcing appointments to the state administration and national defense council.

The people assembled in front of Lhasa's Potala Palace are listening to an explanation by a member of the Military Control Committee of a State Council Order bearing on the restoration of order in Tibet.

The small farm boy working in the field is one of the 68,400 people included in this People's Commune.

This 1961 picture of Chinese women working in a Shanghai factory shows them in a rôle unknown to their sex in old China.

The first secretary of the Party's branch committee in a Commune is leading the discussion of Mao's works. The others present are members of a production brigade.

L

Machinery is used to harvest wheat on the vast lands of this Chinese People's Commune.

Recent research and analysis, and the opinions of most experts, now suggest that a combination of circumstances resulted in the Chinese Communist victory in China. Certainly, the Chinese Communists are Chinese who operate in China; they are not Russians. At the same time they definitely are Communists. The revolution is more than an agrarian reform. Clearly, the Soviet Government trained and aided the Communists in China. Soviet aid was probably not decisive, however, because the Chinese Communists were largely out of contact with the Soviets during the war. To be sure, Communist agents did work their way into the United States Government, but their influence does not appear to have been anything large enough to explain the world-shaking developments in Asia.

What were the critical factors then? How can one explain the disintegration of the Nationalist Government of China, and the progressive take-over of all of China by Communist forces despite United States aid to the legal government of China?

Briefly, these critical factors help explain the victory of the Communists in China:

**1. Ten years of war and economic disintegration.** World War II started for the Chinese in 1937 when Japan invaded China. By 1940, Japanese forces controlled all of the important industrial areas and most of the large cities of China. China's economy began to deteriorate. Food became scarce. Families fled their homes. Schooling had to be postponed. People looked for a formula, some quick means to improve their lot. Communist promises seemed worth testing. What was there to lose?

**2. Corruption of the Kuomintang — the Nationalist Government.** In the face of war, economic chaos, and subversion, the Nationalist Government of China, which in 1936 had been effective and popular, by 1945 was neither. Corruption within the government became widespread. Many Chinese, particularly the impatient student class, attributed all of China's woes to the *Kuomintang*. There were plenty of woes and consequently plenty of criticism.

**3. Superior Communist zeal and organization.** Sensing victory, the Communists were able to stimulate enthusiasm and demand devotion from their followers — qualities not easily roused in the older, tired, disillusioned members of the Nationalist Government. Also, the Communists excelled in organization.

The Chinese Communists had studied Lenin well. The Chinese
Communist Party was well organized and highly disciplined

**4. Soviet assistance.** Direct Soviet economic and military aid
to the Chinese Communists between 1937 and 1945 was meager
Indirect assistance immediately following the war was significant
The Soviets substantially improved the military position of the
Chinese Communists by giving them Japanese weapons and by
keeping Nationalist troops out of Manchuria.

**5. United States policy.** The debate over United States pol
icies during these critical years still goes on. In retrospect i
would appear that this country did not understand the true
nature of the problem until too late. Perhaps there was nothing
we could have done. In any case, what we did proved insufficien
to stem the Communist tide. By the fall of 1949 the Kuomintang
forces had retreated to Formosa, and the Communists were in
virtual control of mainland China.

## 62. *What is the record of the first decade of Communist control of China?*

During its first decade in power, the Communist regime in
China has made vast efforts to transform a backward country
into a modern industrial power. Existing industries were greatly
expanded. New enterprises, particularly in heavy industry, were
established throughout China, some with Soviet aid, other
through Chinese efforts alone. Industrial cities have grown up
in parts of China which hitherto had known no industrial devel
opment. Education, particularly scientific and technological
training, has been expanded. Elementary sanitation practice
have been widely introduced. In agriculture, after a blood
so-called "land reform," the regime initially tended to regard
the peasant solely as a source of capital accumulation. In th
late 1950's the building of dams and irrigation systems wa
greatly stressed. When the communes were created in 1958, th
Chinese Communists felt that they had discovered a way t
increase agricultural production by leaps and bounds.

As in the Soviet Union, the all-out drive to bring about indus
trialization and modernization was accompanied by a tota
regimentation of the population. Not only political freedom

but even the "small freedoms" of private life were sacrificed. Through the Communist Party and its handmaiden, the Communist Youth League, a population of 700,000,000 was organized to attack and attack again on the production front. People were told that three years of toil would bring a thousand years of happiness.

What have been the results of this great drive? After back-breaking efforts that have exhausted a population used to hard work, there is neither victory nor defeat. China today is in a state of vast confusion and economic dislocation.

The expected agricultural "break-through" has not materialized. Great natural disasters (floods, droughts, pests), combined with peasant resistance to regimentation, have resulted in severe food shortages. The regime has made concessions of "small freedoms" to the overworked peasants to try to win their cooperation. The fanatic Party cadres (group leaders), once the driving hammer of the Revolution, have been curbed. In the cities, students, workers, and residents seek slowly to restore the personal lives of which they were deprived by the Party. But now they must struggle against hunger, shortages, and apathy.

One must ask whether we are witnessing the beginning of breakdown, or a period of adjustment, at the conclusion of which the economic revolution will once again go into high gear. Not even the Communist leaders in Peking can answer that question today. The impressive achievements in basic industrialization and capital construction have not been wiped out by the troubles of the past few years. Modern industries remain, though seriously handicapped by shortages of materials. The irrigation networks and water control systems may yet "pay off." But the chaos resulting from the attempt to revolutionize the backward economy of China in a few short years may call for a profound alteration of the system. The Soviet Union went through a similar period of forced development and massive misery during the 1930's, and pulled through the crisis. We must envisage the probability that China too will emerge from its crisis.

There is little that the outside world can do to influence the course of development. The might of the Peking regime extends over every corner of China, preventing all but a trickle of information from the outside. Even the Soviet Union has ceased to wield significant power over the men of Peking. The crucial question is whether the Communist leaders can use their power effectively enough to get the economic revolution started once again, and attain the grandiose goal on which the regime has staked its very existence.

## The Chinese Communist System

### 63. How does the Communist system in China differ from the Soviet system in Russia?

Both Russia and China are "Communist." Both Moscow and Peking regard the United States as their principal enemy. At the same time, we would do well to remind ourselves that Russia is Russia and China is China. There are at least three important areas of difference: cultural tradition, political organization, and stage of economic development.

**Cultural tradition.** The Chinese cultural tradition is primarily Asian in its roots. The Soviet system is primarily European. Marxian concepts in the Chinese language may have a somewhat different meaning from the same concepts expressed in Russian. Further, despite Communist efforts to stamp out Confucianism and China's traditional ways (pp. 146–147), even Party members remain surprisingly Chinese.

The Chinese Communists have consistently attempted to adjust their approaches to the Chinese environment and traditions.

**Political organization.** The Chinese People's Republic and the Union of Soviet Socialist Republics — the very titles suggest basic differences in terms of the organization of the State. There are, for example, Autonomous Regions in Communist China but no separate Republics — even for largely non-Chinese areas such as Sinkiang and Tibet.

Chinese Communist Party leadership has been welded together, steeled, and forged into a well-coordinated *team*. Despite Mao Tse-tung's very real importance as *the* great leader, it would appear that there is a bit more of the true *committee* rule in the Chinese than in the Soviet system.

Certainly, the decision-making process in Communist China, as in the Soviet Union, takes place strictly at the top. But the Chinese Communists have consistently made a greater effort to convey the *image* of "popular participation in government" than has the Soviet Union.

**Stage of economic development.** China is a "have not" nation. The USSR is (relatively) a "have" nation. (See comparative statistics on industrial development, pp. 139–140.) If there is still imbalance between Soviet industry and agriculture, there is far less than in China — and the imbalance is somewhat corrected by the extensive foreign trade of the USSR. The imbalance between a huge, growing population and China's relatively decreasing amount of arable land is becoming a very serious problem.

These "stage of development" differences (and growing difficulties) led the Chinese Communists to introduce the communes in 1958 (see page 144). Accordingly, Communist China has developed economic (agricultural and industrial) and political (administrative, military, and Party) organizations and practices which are very different from those performing the same functions in the Soviet Union.

What may we conclude? Certainly not that Communist China is any less of a threat to the Free World, or any less "Communist," than the Soviet Union. The point is quite another one. The Peking leaders are both Communist *and* Chinese, and it is this explosive blend of traditional pride, sensitivity, antiforeignism, dialectical materialism, urgency, Leninism, and zeal that is cause for concern.

## 4. *How strong is the Chinese Communist economy?*

If we look at the economy of Communist China in terms of the three approaches employed in analyzing the Soviet economic picture, what do we find?

**Present levels of economic development.** In terms of comparative present levels of economic development, Communist China is today a very long way behind the USSR, not to say the U.S.A. Moreover, it is important to remember, when considering these figures and making general comparisons, that the population of China is not 185,000,000 as in the United States, or 210,000,000 as in the USSR, but more than three times these figures — 700,000,000! Here are some official Chinese Communist figures on economic development.[1] They are regarded by Western specialists as exaggerated, and may be as much as 20 per cent too high.

|  | Communist China's Production in 1959 | | Approximate Percentage of Production | |
|---|---|---|---|---|
| Industry |  |  | U.S.S.R. | U.S. |
| Steel | 13,350,000 | tons | 22 | 16 |
| Coal | 347,800,000 | tons | 69 | 89 |
| Electricity | 41,500,000,000 | kwh | 16 | 5 |
| Crude Oil | 7,000,000 | barrels | 3 | 1 |
| Agriculture |  |  |  |  |
| Grain | 270,050,000 | tons | 215 | 139 |
| Pigs | 180,000,000 | heads | 337 | 308 |
| Cattle | 65,430,000 | heads | 88 | 64 |
| Horses | 7,600,000 | heads | 69 | 246 |
| Sheep | 112,530,000 | heads | 83 | 335 |

**System.** Perhaps on an even stricter basis than in the USSR the people of China are asked (told!) to forgo consumer items in the interest of industrial development and economic progress. This means, again, that one ton of steel has a relatively higher strategic value in Communist China than it does in the United States. However, as will have been noted, the difference in levels of development between the Chinese and the United States economies is so huge that even strict allocation of resources can make little difference at the present time.

**Rate of growth.** Communist statistics are not always reliable. This makes it difficult to say with any certainty what the present annual rate of economic growth in China may be. According to official Chinese Communist figures the estimated national income increased from 26,600,000,000 U.S. dollars in 1952 (the year before the initiation of the First Five year Plan) to 67,725,000,00

[1] Data on charts from "The Communique on the Progress of China's National Economy in 1959," *Peking Review*, January 26, 1960, pp. 9–13

U.S. dollars in 1959. Between 1950 and 1958, the *annual* rate of increase of the value of industrial and agricultural output was, respectively, 28.1 per cent and 9.8 per cent. The number of workers and employees is reported as having gone up from 10.12 million in 1952 to 45 million in 1958.[2]

## 65. *Is the Peking regime popular with the people?*

It is always difficult to determine the feelings of a people toward their masters in a totalitarian state. Virtually every avenue of public expression is closed to those who would voice open opposition. This is especially true in the case of Communist China with its great mass of illiterate peasants. It can also be dangerous to complain or oppose. Since the establishment of the Red regime, however, gaps in the Bamboo Curtain have given the outside world some insight into the attitude of the Chinese toward their rulers. It is evident that dissatisfaction exists. Tensions at times have exploded in open revolt.

Before indicating an example or two of this unrest within Red China, a note of caution must be struck. While the Communists have encountered opposition, it does not necessarily follow that they are threatened with widespread revolt in the near future. A number of factors must be taken into consideration.

The Chinese are a proud people strongly attached to their country. Today, after decades of seeing their ancient land endure the status of a second-, even third-class nation among the great powers, the people are aware that China has emerged as a world power. They are proud of this fact. It is constantly drummed into their minds by every propaganda tool at the disposal of the Party. China's industrial power is growing. New lands are being opened through vast irrigation projects. The Chinese Communist army has proven itself in battle. The world listens when China's leaders speak. These facts cannot but impress the Chinese people. They endure hardships, as they always have, but they are bombarded by new, clever slogans meant to justify this suffering: "let's tighten our belts, the future is bright and beautiful;" "let's sacrifice ourselves for the happiness of the

[2] Data from Chao Kuo-chun, "The Structural Aspects of Planning in China," *International Studies* (Asia Publishing House), January, 1961.

next generation." All that has been gained, they are told, will be lost if the Communist leadership is destroyed. If China is to prosper, they must submit to the will of the Party.

The leaders of Communist China have shown that they are aware of the grave danger that exists in a dissatisfied people. They have also demonstrated a willingness to bend slightly when the winds of popular discontent become too great. This flexibility has been recently seen in the slowing down of the "great leap forward" drive and the changes which have taken place in the management of China's communes. The regime can afford a failure here and there. It cannot afford total, evident failure of its program.

Finally, it must not be forgotten that the Communist leaders are able to maintain a close surveillance over public opinion. Controlling the armed forces of China and a vast secret police network, the Party possesses the power to crush unorganized regional uprisings. The revolt of 20,000 Moslems in the western reaches of a land as vast as China can easily be put down with little more than a rumor of it going beyond the borders of the province.

In short, in China as in the Soviet Union, there are no genuine elections, no public opinion polls, and no independent newspapers. For all of these reasons there is no way of knowing precisely how popular or unpopular the Communist regime may be with the people of China. Available evidence suggests that the Communist regime in China has become increasingly *un-popular* during the past several years. Unless the Peking regime can pull out of the present economic difficulties, this unpopularity is likely to continue or even to increase.

## Daily Life in Communist China

**66.** *How does daily life in China today compare with life in China about twenty-five years ago?*

What was the situation in China twenty-five years ago? That would have been about 1937. In July of that year, Japanese forces in Manchuria launched their attack on North China. The war in China was on. The Communists, by this time, occupied a small area around the city of Yenan in Northwest China.

Throughout the mid-thirties the Chinese people were never well off by Western standards. They were, for the most part, poor. Almost everyone, however, looked forward to a few special festivals a year when a real feast was the order of the day. The Chinese New Year was one of these.

Chiang Kai-shek was a popular hero. China showed prospects of healthy growth both politically and economically. On both scores the problems were huge, and on the whole the government made little progress in overcoming basic social problems. In times of famines and floods there was much suffering. But the Chinese were not living under a totalitarian regime. One could speak freely, travel freely within China, and leave the country freely — three rights which do not exist in China today.

In the 1930's most well-educated Chinese had studied both their Confucian tradition and Western science, possibly even at one of the Christian missionary colleges which had grown up in many parts of China. Today Confucianism, along with Christianity and much of the rest of significant Western learning and culture, is frowned upon by the Chinese Communist regime.

Gone, too, is most of farm and family life as China had known it for centuries. To be sure, the peasants' lot in rural China was not always a happy one. So one might be tempted to say "objectively" perhaps it's just as well — except that conditions in Communist China today, in terms of both freedom and food, are probably as bad as they have ever been in China's long history (see pp. 144–145 on the communes).

With respect to life in the cities — Chinese and Europeans who have recently come from Red China agree that Communist lack of technical know-how, mismanagement, and terror have reduced the once prosperous business centers to a cross between ghost towns and slave camps. Morale is low. People are tired, and they do not care.

In foreign policy, not since the T'ang Dynasty have the Chinese people been saddled with a regime dedicated to the expansion of Chinese influence and control over all their neighbors. North Korea, North Viet Nam, and Tibet are already part of this new Chinese empire.

## 67. *What is life like in a Chinese commune?*

Since 1958 the People's Commune system has been the pattern of economic and social organization of millions of Chinese. The Communists have assigned each of the communes a name like "Prosperity and Peace," "Everlasting Happiness," or "Sputnik." But, as Shakespeare said, "What's in a name?" The Chinese communes are, in fact, huge work camps — human ant hills — where there is little prosperity, happiness, or peace. How do we know? We have the inside story from hundreds of former inmates who have fled through the Bamboo Curtain to the sanctuary of Hong Kong, Macao, and the Portuguese islands off the mainland of China. Before we sample the first-hand, eye-witness facts, we might take note briefly of the origin of the communes.

**Origin of the communes.** Mao Tse-tung announced in 1958 that all of China was to be reorganized into huge co-operatives of an advanced type which would contain within them "the shoots of pure Communism." Khrushchev promptly said: "We tried communes in Russia, but they didn't work." But the Chinese Communists went right ahead. The economic situation was unfavorable and worsening. The Communists decided to mobilize their greatest resource — people. Farm households and collectives were combined, merged, and recombined. By the fall of 1958 the original three quarters of a million collectives and smaller communes had been merged into some 26,000 large communes each averaging nearly 5,000 farm households and 10,000 workers.

Here is a description of life in one Chinese commune as gathered from accounts by some of the more fortunate Chinese who managed to escape to Macao:

**Eye-witness account.** "In the Three Joss Sticks commune, the work whistles started sounding at 4:30 a.m. Breakfast was at 5 a.m. Twenty minutes later, men and women marched to the fields. At 11:30 a.m. two sweet potatoes were distributed to each worker. A double-time march to the dining room got the work brigades back just in time for a 6 p.m. meal of rice and vegetables. After that, there was work in the fields under flood lights, or political sessions in camp. The whistles signaled everybody to bed at midnight."[3]

**Summary description.** *Life* Magazine summed up the situation in this way:

> All over China the family-centered, individualistic Chinese are being reduced to 653 million indistinguishable and interchangeable parts in a vast, inhuman machine. This machine is the commune, the most frightful form of regimentation in history.
>
> In a People's Commune the members eat, sleep, produce, act, think, even procreate, not as individuals, but as an integrated social unit. They need a pass to leave the area they live in. When they start out for work in the morning — after reveille, gymnastics and a mess-hall breakfast — they march off in formation, under flags. India's Prime Minister Nehru recently described China as one big army camp, explaining, "They go to work at a certain time, they come back for lunch at a certain time, all together, the whole village, the whole commune." And not only the men. Women, children and the aged live in barracks, too. In the cities, workers live in barracks next to their factories. There is military training for all.[4]

**Conclusion — How has the system worked?** How has the experiment worked? Has it solved China's age-old problem — that of too many people and too little food? The answer would appear to be not only that the experiment has not worked well, but that it has been a real failure. Evidence for this tentative conclusion is of two kinds: First, the fact that in the past three years China's agricultural production has declined by leaps and bounds — with the result that today Chinese face widespread famine (see page 137). Secondly, there is increasing evidence that the Chinese Communists have been backing away from the commune idea in its original form. The Chinese Communist press even hints that some modification and relaxation has been the pattern of the last year. While outward admission that the whole experiment has been a dismal failure would perhaps represent too great a loss of face for Mao Tse-tung, this appears to be, in fact, a rather accurate description of the People's Communes after the first five years.

---

[3] From a copyrighted article in *U.S. News & World Report*, Vol. XLVI, No. 4 (April 6, 1959), pp. 96–97.

[4] James Bell, "Misery, Oppression, Fear Inside China's Communes," *Life*, Vol. 46, No. 1 (January 5, 1959), pp. 64–65.

**68.** *What is the Communist attitude toward the great Chinese tradition, Confucianism, Taoism?*

In an article entitled "Communists and Confucius," the Chinese scholar Lin Yutang[5] describes the attitude of the Communist regime toward the Chinese cultural tradition:

> . . . Both Confucian and Taoist ideas are officially regarded as 'poison' just as Christianity is regarded as dope for the poor. Confucian books are not so much *verboten* [forbidden] as ignored. All ancient books are supposed to contain "poison." History books for students are systematically rewritten. Communist workers are replacing village elders. Elders and anyone else respected by the village community, or anyone acquainted with organizational technique, is a potential leader of the opposition, and as such is liquidated, no matter how innocent the partisans know the person to be. It is an ideological necessity. . . .
>
> Madame Sun Yat-sen expressed the Communist orthodox viewpoint best when she said, "Confucian teachings are feudalistic and autocratic from beginning to end. We must realize how deeply Confucian influences have been imbedded in our art, literature, social sciences and morals. We must make great efforts to uproot Confucian ideas from every nook and corner of our life and thoughts.". . .
>
> In every country, society lives by a set of moral values. In Christian countries, these virtues — such as honesty, kindness, justice and the value of the individual — are represented by the Christian code. In China, they happen to be represented by Confucianism. Thus Communism finds it necessary to strike at the core of Confucian teachings by breaking up family loyalty. The denunciation of their parents by boys and girls of 13 and 14 is encouraged. . . .

But Lin Yutang ends on a hopeful note. He is not convinced that tyranny can long prevail on earth.

> Generally, morals teachers outlast politicians. Gandhi will outlast Nehru, and Confucius and Lao Tzu [the father of Taoism] will outlast Mao Tse-tung. The Confucian golden rule must survive. As for the witticisms of Lao Tzu, his depth, his brilliance and his profound iconoclasm will always recommend themselves to the searching human mind. His teachings on gentleness and humility will always stand . . . irrespective of political persecutions.

[5] In "Religion in the Land of Confucius," *Life*, Vol. 38, No. 14 (April 1955), pp. 82–85.

Can the Chinese people, apart from their ideological rulers, accept the Communist negation of their traditional ways and beliefs? The answer is they have to. Can they accept the more rigorous, severe totalitarian pattern of life geared to production for the state? The answer is again they have to.

But thoughts and ideas are somewhat like seeds. They have a way of lying dormant underground until a more favorable climate brings them again to life. As to when or how this will happen and the Chinese people return openly to Confucian ideals and the tolerance of Lao Tzu, that is a matter of international politics. But, as a Chinese, I hope that it will be within my lifetime.

Some experts on China do not agree completely with Lin Yutang's evaluation. They point out that the Chinese, like the Russians, are tending to speak in praise of parts of their heritage after reinterpreting it, of course, in terms of Communist doctrine. Confucianism as a system is attacked, but individual Confucian thinkers have been praised. Furthermore, one may maintain seriously that Communism and Confucianism are not directly opposed to each other on all points. It would be wrong to assume that the Chinese Communists are negative to the whole Chinese past.

## The Military Establishment and Science

### 59. *How strong is China, militarily?*

**The role of military power.** Military power has played a key role in the rise of the Chinese Communists to power. Mao Tse-ung put it this way: "Political power grows out of the barrel of a gun." But for many years the Communist Party in China was a minority group and vastly inferior in military strength to the Kuomintang. Mao's skill as a strategist lies in his formulation of the theory of "protracted war." This took into account the military weakness of the Chinese Communist Party, and sought over a long period of time to wear down the morale and military efficiency of the enemy while gradually developing Communist strength. (See pp. 131-134 on the history of Communism in

China.) The strategy and tactics of a "protracted war" called for the avoidance of quick decisions on the strategic level, but insisted on quick decisions in a particular battle or campaign. It emphasized the use of mobile warfare and guerrilla forces, and sought to avoid positional warfare.

Mao's strategy and tactics were effective in the wars against the Japanese and the Kuomintang, but failed to prove decisive in the course of the Korean War when the Chinese were confronted with UN ground forces possessing superior firepower and supported by superior airpower. While Mao's military doctrine remains applicable to local wars involving the use of guerrilla forces and small mobile units (for example, in Southeast Asia) its usefulness in the event that China found herself in conflict with an enemy armed with nuclear weapons and missiles appears limited.

**A decade of modernization — present strength.** During the past decade, Communist China has been in the process of modernizing its armed forces. Today Communist China is the only power of major military importance among Asian states. The People's Liberation Army has a total of over two and one half million men in active service in ground, naval, and air forces. Communist China's ground forces are second in size only to those in the Soviet Union. In addition, the Communist Chinese have more than a half million troops in public security units plus a huge militia organization.

The ground forces of the People's Liberation Army, as the Chinese Communists call their armed forces, are equipped with such modern conventional weapons as 57-mm recoil-less guns, heavy mortars, 70-mm howitzers, and Soviet tanks. The air force is believed to include some 300 jet light bombers and 1500 jet fighters, approximately 400 of which are Mig-17's. There have been reports that a few of the newer Mig-19's have been added to the Chinese Communist air force and that the Chinese Communists are beginning production of their own Mig-15's and Mig 17's. Though Communist China's navy consists of some 637 ships, including four destroyers and approximately 12 large, long range submarines, the general effectiveness of this force is considered inferior to that of Japan's navy. In general, both air and naval forces appear to suffer from inadequate training.

**Formidable conventional forces.** Whatever the immediate shortcoming, in terms of conventional forces, Communist China must be ranked as a formidable military power. However, insofar as it possesses neither nuclear weapons nor advanced delivery systems (that is, missiles), its military power is vastly inferior to that of the United States and the Soviet Union. Because of its relative military weakness when compared with the United States, Communist China remains militarily dependent on the Soviet Union. Without Soviet support, which the Soviet Union has shown reluctance to provide, Communist China must pursue any military objectives that might involve a direct confrontation with the United States with extreme caution. This does not prevent Peking from engaging in such activities as border incursions, indirect aggression, or subversion, which are not likely to prompt an all-out military response on the part of the United States.

**Nuclear poverty.** Recognizing its military weakness in relation to the nuclear powers, Communist China has announced its intention to make its own nuclear weapons and missiles. In May of 1958 the Commander of the Chinese Communist Air Force declared that China would certainly be able to make atomic bombs "in the not-distant future." He also indicated that the Chinese were prepared to make their own "rockets." The Chinese no doubt hope that the detonation of a nuclear device, the progressive acquisition of a nuclear capability, and the development in time of an advanced delivery system in the form of missiles will enable them to press more vigorously for the achievement of their political and military objectives in the Far East.

## 70. *What is the status of science in Communist China?*

Writing in *Sciences in Communist China,* published by the American Association for the Advancement of Science[6], Dr. Theodore Hsi-en Chen of the University of Southern California summarizes the status of science and scientists in Communist China in the following ten points:

**Big Leap Forward.** The Big Leap in material construction has its counterpart in science. The call for a "grand march on sci-

[6] Sydney H. Gould, Editor (Washington, 1961).

ence," together with the use of "shock" methods, intensive drives, and emulation campaigns, has produced new interest and new activities in science and technology. Technical institutes on secondary and higher levels are turning out a vast army of engineers, technicians, and technologists.

**Better facilities.** Scientific study has been provided for since the the scientists aired their criticisms in 1956–1957. Living conditions for scientists have been improved; their salaries are in the highest brackets of the national scale. Library and laboratory facilities have been expanded beyond the narrow limits of Soviet publications and equipment of earlier years. Within the area of technical study, the scientists enjoy a broader scope than was permitted before 1956.

**Emphasis: applied science.** Emphasis is put on technology. Science is closely linked with production and industrialization. Violent opposition to "science for its own sake" tends to push theoretical science into an inconspicuous corner. Some lip service is paid to theoretical science, but scientists are subject to constant pressure to make practical application and avoid being called impractical theorists. The engineer, the inventor of new tools, or the person who introduces innovations in production methods wins immediate acclaim while the theoretical scientist may be criticized for his bourgeois scholasticism.

**Political restrictions.** Scientists are so hemmed in and so burdened with political requirements that there is little room for initiative and creativity in their work. The Communists urge that scientists should learn the "Communist way of bold thinking and bold action." What they mean by boldness refers to bold departure from old methods in order to devise new methods, new tools, new machines, etc. — in other words, bold technological innovations and applications. Any departure from the prescribed plans, however, might be attacked as "disobedience to leadership."

**Technical revolution.** This technical revolution is not empty talk. There is a mushroom growth of new ideas in technical innovations and improvements. Numerous new tools and machines have been invented. In the machine building industry alone, 180,000 manual operations are said to have been replaced by mechanical and semimechanical devices. "A colossal mass movement for technical innovations and technical revolution is sweeping China with hurricane force," declared one writer. No such claim, however, could be made for the study of basic science or theoretical research.

**Let-downs and dislocations.** Intensive drives and "shock" campaigns do produce spectacular results, but are often accompanied by letdowns and dislocations in other areas. The steel drive of

1958, for example, did raise the production of steel to amazingly high figures, but concentration on steel caused neglect of agriculture and the breakdown of the transportation system, and even the steel that was produced was found to be unusable in many instances. Likewise, the Big Leap Forward in science is producing spectacular results in technical innovations, but from the standpoint of a long-range and balanced program of scientific development, much is lacking.

**"Down with personal gain and profit."** Communist scholars doing research and writing have been censured for spending time in writing at the expense of political activities. The primary duty of scientists is considered to be the training of a host of cadres to take up the technical tasks of the industrial revolution and research on projects of definite benefit to socialist construction.

**A non-political job.** If scientists accept the Communist ideology and the centralized planning of the state, if they are content to work in prescribed areas, if they submit to thought reform and pledge allegiance in approved manner, they can manage to get along quite well. They can enjoy material living conditions considerably better than those available to the rest of the population. If their work is judged to be of value to the state, they may be provided with fairly liberal library and laboratory facilities and research funds.

**Handmaid of politics.** As long as science in Communist China serves politics, it is well supported and scientists may be strongly motivated by the clear and specific goals presented to them by powerful propaganda. But the scope of science is definitely restricted. Within the prescribed limits, the scientists may enjoy some degree of freedom in the pursuit of their activities, but few dare venture beyond the limits. To what extent this strict political control inhibits the creativity of scientists and shackles the development of science, the future will tell.

**Self-criticism.** Having no alternative, China's scientists have made abject public confessions pleading guilty of individualism, selfishness, disregard of public welfare, neglect of politics and the class strugggle, pro-Americanism, and many other "bourgeois sins." They have vowed to make a clean break with the past and to start anew under the close guidance and direction of the Communist Party. They pledge to study Marxism-Leninism, to work for the proletarian-socialist revolution, and to "surrender their hearts" to the Communist Party. Have they really surrendered? The incisive criticisms they made of the Communist regime during the brief "Hundred Flowers" season of 1957 and the complaints they voiced against political control of science at that time give us reason to believe that underneath the outward conformity there still exists in the hearts and minds of the scientists a good deal of resistance to Communist pressure. The events of that short season provided ample evidence that China's intellectuals still had plenty of fighting spirit and unconquered integrity despite the years of political indoctrination and "thought reform." China's intellectuals have bowed low but their backs are not broken, and the day may yet come when they will stand erect and make their contributions as free men in an atmosphere of intellectual freedom.

## 71. *How soon will Peking have atomic or hydrogen weapons?*

Very little is known in the West about Communist China's program for the development of nuclear weapons. Scientific work in such fields as nuclear technology is usually described as designed to further research in the peaceful uses of atomic energy. China is believed to have the uranium resources necessary for the production of plutonium, the explosive element used in the basic atomic and hydrogen weapons. A number of Chinese scientists have been trained in nuclear technology at the Joint Institute of Nuclear Research established in the Soviet Union in 1956. A research reactor, provided by the Soviet Union, was put into operation in Peking in June of 1958. In late 1960, the Chairman of the Chinese People's Republic, Liu Shao-chi, indicated that China had four nuclear reactors that could be converted to military uses.

Nor do we know the extent to which the Russians, aside from enabling Chinese scientists to study in the Soviet Union and providing the Chinese with a nuclear reactor, have actually assisted the Chinese in a program leading to the production of nuclear weapons.

While rumors have circulated regarding the date when Communist China might be expected to detonate a nuclear device, the most authoritative statement on the subject would appear to be that made by Arthur H. Dean, the head of the United States delegation to the Conference on the Discontinuance of Nuclear Weapons Tests, in August, 1961. At that time, Dean said that Communist China may produce a bomb in 1962 or 1963.

Whatever the specific date the Chinese detonate their first nuclear device, they can be expected to have a modest nuclear stockpile within the next few years. Even then, without an effective means of delivery, Chinese Communist strategic capability will remain limited.

## Popular Attitudes

## 72. *Is the average Chinese anti-American?*

Politically, there are two Chinas: One is represented by the Republic of China on Taiwan, or Formosa; the other by the Chinese Communist regime on the mainland. The United States still recognizes the Nationalist Government as the only legal government of China. The Soviet bloc (and a number of non-Communist nations) have recognized the Communist Government in Peking.

This does not mean all Chinese on the mainland are pro-Russian and anti-American. Neither are all Chinese on Formosa pro-American. The situation is more complicated.

Most educated Chinese have mixed feelings about the West. They remember — firsthand, from stories related by their parents, or from history books — the tragic past record of Western imperialism, intolerance, and exploitation in Asia. They recall, for example, a sign in the park in the Shanghai "white" international settlement which read: "No dogs or Chinese allowed!" The United States came on the scene too late to be accused of some of the acts committed by the British, French, and Dutch colonialists. In fact, United States policy and practice in bringing the Philippines to independence is generally regarded as something of a model of good colonialism, to the extent that it is possible for colonialism to be good.

But Chinese do not always make a fine distinction between the various Western nations. As Americans, we are in this sense guilty by association. Moreover, the Chinese have always been, understandably, sensitive to discrimination against Orientals in the

United States, in fact to any kind of discrimination against the colored races.

At the same time, many Chinese remember the long tradition of warm friendship with America. Tens of thousands of Chinese have studied in Western Europe and America. United States soldiers fought side by side with Chinese soldiers in World War II. Over the years, relations between China and the United States have generally been cordial. Most Americans respect the Chinese for their proud tradition and great culture. What American is not fond of Chinese food? Most Chinese admire Americans for their high standard of living (even for the "common man") and for their generosity and willingness to help people in trouble throughout the world.

Now we come to the unfortunate chapter in the story: the past decade. The Communist regime in China has mounted and sustained for more than ten years a vicious anti-American campaign. It has included a program designed to show (falsely) that the United States used germ warfare during the Korean War in an effort "to exterminate the Chinese people." The United States is pictured as a ruthless, capitalist, imperialist nation run by big business and populated by millions of disgruntled, starving farmers, and destitute workers. In short, through lies, distortion, and exaggeration, the regime in Peking seeks to exploit the ignorance and hopes of the unfortunate millions of Chinese and to turn them all into militant anti-Americans.

How successful have the Communists been? Are most Chinese today anti-American? Probably not. We don't know. We can only hope that the average Chinese still maintains that combination of wisdom, practicality, and quiet resistance to tyranny that has sustained the Chinese nation for more than 3,000 years.

## 73. What do the Chinese think of the Russians?

Officially, the Union of Soviet Socialist Republics and the People's Republic of China are allies "in the struggle for peace against capitalism and imperialism." The Russian people and the Chinese people, we are told, are bound together by "time-tested ties of comradely friendship." "Proletarian internationalism" (Communists, stick together!) is the slogan; Moscow-Peking solidarity is the watchword.

Unofficially, the Russians tend to look down on the Chinese, while the Chinese resent Russian high-handedness. Relations between the two peoples — official and unofficial — seem to have grown increasingly distant and difficult during the last few years.

A former Chinese Communist official who recently fled to Hong Kong puts it this way: "Who were these 'foreign advisers?' Soviet experts, of course, who looked down on us condescendingly from the height of their own arrogance and experience."

Among the items that have contributed to increasingly bad feelings between the Russians and the Chinese are the following: (1) The ultra-sensitive national pride of most Chinese (even those who may consider themselves Communists). (2) The widespread suspicion among Chinese that the Soviets may not be enthusiastic about helping China. (Why in the matter of economic aid give preference to India over China?) (3) Certain specific disputes over who should "control" Korea, and Japan. (4) Disagreement over strategy and tactics, particularly such matters as the "road to socialism" and the question of "coexistence." The Soviets are *opposed* to communes and *for* temporary coexistence; the Chinese Communists have taken the opposite position. (5) The clash of peoples and culture in Central Asia as Chinese population pressures push into the buffer zones which have traditionally separated Russian and Chinese interests.

The Chinese Communist attitude towards the Russians may be summed up by this story: Chinese Communist foreign minister Chou En-lai went to Moscow. During an important meeting there a Soviet official suddenly said to Chou, "Why do you insist on speaking English? You know Russian well; why don't you speak Russian?" Chou is supposed to have replied: "Why don't you Russians speak Chinese?"

But the following joke circulating in Moscow and Warsaw puts the problem in a nutshell: One Russian says to another, "What's the difference between an optimist and a pessimist?" His friend replies, "I don't know, what is the difference between an optimist and a pessimist?" The first Russian answers, "An optimist studies Russian. A pessimist studies Chinese!"

Does this mean that Moscow and Peking are likely to fall out with one another? Probably not, at least not in the foreseeable future. The international political advantages of joint effort against the West are probably sufficient to keep whatever bad feelings may exist in check. (See Moscow-Peking Axis relations, page 183.)

# 7 Russia and China in World Affairs

## Fundamentals of Foreign Policy

**74.** *How does the Soviet approach to foreign relations differ from the traditional American approach?*

First, let us clarify the question: What is foreign policy? Foreign policy is the sum total of a nation's official attitude and actions toward other nations and other areas of the globe. It is a government's aims and needs as applied and reflected in its external relations. What is our attitude toward each of the different countries of Latin America? Would we sign a trade agreement with Turkey? What should we do if the Soviets attempt to take over West Berlin? Is a mutual defense pact with Japan in our best interests? Is NATO a useful instrument? Should we support the United Nations? These and a thousand other urgent questions must be answered by those responsible for foreign policy. The precise nature of a given country's foreign policy may be judged by the speeches of its leaders, by treaties and agreements, and, most of all, by that nation's behavior pattern over the years.

The famous German student of power politics, von Clausewitz, described *war* as "diplomacy by other means." The Soviets have turned this notion around. To the Communists, — in Moscow or in Peking, — diplomacy is *"war* by other means!" The issue is clear. To the Communists their enemies include all nations of the Free World, particularly the two power centers: the United States and Western Europe. The means employed by Communists include anything short of total war — propaganda, atomic blackmail, subversion, espionage, economic entanglement, conference diplomacy, pressure, intimidation, limited war.

With respect to underlying assumptions and the approach used, Soviet or Communist foreign policy differs in two important ways from that of the United States or other Free World Nations.

First, the Communists believe in the non-permanence of the non-Communist world: that is, they believe that the governments of all the nations outside the Moscow-Peking orbit will, eventually and inevitably, collapse or be overthrown. When this happens, the Communists assert, these bourgeois regimes will be replaced by Communist governments. Therefore, coexistence with such capitalist governments is thought of as strictly temporary.

Secondly, the Communists pursue a policy which they term "people's diplomacy." This means that rather than deal strictly on a legal, government-to-government basis in the tradition of Western diplomacy, the Communists appeal directly to the people of another country. To influence or subvert the foreign nation, the Communists use every means and every weapon available. Such a policy is designed to sell Communism, to discredit the United States, and to promote Soviet aims among the peoples of the world.

This is an entirely new kind of foreign policy based on the ideology of Marxism-Leninism, but utilizing all the methods, power, and resources of the modern totalitarian state.

The differences between the American and Soviet approaches to foreign relations can be summed up in three phrases: (1) self-determination, (2) limited goals, and (3) means.

**1. Self-determination**—The fundamental attitude of the United States toward other peoples is that they should have the right to determine their fate themselves, without any other nation's telling them what they can or cannot do. An important aspect of this principle is the closely related one of democracy, especially the right of the peoples themselves to determine their policies through democratically elected representatives. In other words, our policy generally has been "hands off" — unless other nations have threatened us, or unless they have asked us to intervene in some way.

The Soviet policy has been the opposite. While paying lip service to the principle of self-determination, the Russians have repeatedly, and as a matter of policy, interfered with the affairs of other states whenever they thought it to their advantage, and whenever they thought they could get away with it. They have imposed oppressive governments on other peoples against their will, and have denied them the right of choosing their representatives democratically.

**2. Limited goals** — You might argue that there really is no difference between Soviet and American foreign policies — that the Russians want all the world to be Communist, while we want all of it to be democratic. But there *is* a difference. While it is true that we would like the whole world to be democratic, we have not adopted a policy of wholesale intervention in all countries of the world for the purpose of imposing American-style regimes on people everywhere. Our goals are limited. We are content to live peacefully with dictatorships and monarchies, as well as with democracies, so long as they do not threaten us.

Soviet goals, by contrast, are unlimited. Communist leaders have stated openly and repeatedly that their goal is World Communism, and that they will not be satisfied until *every* country in the world has a Communist regime, modeled after that of the Soviet Union. Since World War II they have helped to impose such regimes on 16 countries, and they are actively working every day to achieve their unlimited goal.

**3. Means** — The Soviet objective to enhance Soviet power and prestige and to establish Communism throughout the world would not be such a threat to us if it were not for the fact that they are willing to use *any* means for achieving this goal. Lenin preached, and Stalin and his successors followed, the idea that any means, including lies, deceit, theft, subversion, sabotage, and murder are acceptable for furthering the cause of World Communism.

The United States finds it difficult to combat such a ruthless foe by traditional, peaceful means. The Communists have no reluctance about using force. This country does not use force to impose upon other people a type of government which they do not want. At times, however, we have found it necessary to engage in what some might consider "dirty work." For example, the United States, like all great powers, engages in espionage. Although interference in the affairs of other nations is not a part of our foreign policy, we sometimes have found interference necessary. We try to use honorable means wherever possible. If the Soviet threat were removed, we could, no doubt, move more quickly to abolish such unbecoming means altogether.

## 75. Does the Soviet Union live up to its treaties and agreements?

A careful study of performance with respect to the treaties and agreements made by the Soviet Union during more than four decades reveals one indisputable fact: The Soviet Government has consistently violated, broken, or torn up virtually every treaty and agreement it has ever made. No nation in history rivals the Soviet record of hypocrisy and insincerity.

A United States Senate staff study entitled *Soviet Political Agreements and Results*[1], published in 1956, puts it this way:

> The staff studied nearly a thousand treaties and agreements . . . both bilateral and multilateral, which the Soviets have entered into not only with the United States, but with countries all over the world. The staff found that in the 38 short years [up to 1955] since the Soviet Union came into existence, its Government had broken its word to virtually every country to which it ever gave a signed promise. It signed treaties of nonaggression with neighboring states and then absorbed those states. It signed promises to refrain from revolutionary activity inside the countries with which it sought "friendship," and then cynically broke those promises. It was violating the first agreement it ever signed with the United States at the very moment the Soviet envoy, Litvinov, was putting his signature to that agreement, and it is still violating the same agreement in 1955. . . . It broke the promises it made to the western nations during previous meetings "at the summit" in Teheran and Yalta. It broke lend-lease agreements offered to it by the United States in

[1] 84th Congress; Senate Document No. 125 (extract from the foreword by Senator James O. Eastland).

order to keep Stalin from surrendering to the Nazis. It violated the charter of the United Nations. It keeps no international promises at all unless doing so is clearly advantageous to the Soviet Union.

I seriously doubt whether during the whole history of civilization any great nation has ever made as perfidious a record as this in so short a time.

This aspect of the Soviet approach to foreign relations must be kept in mind *at all times.*

# 76. *What good are Summit meetings?*

If the Kremlin doesn't live up to its agreements anyway, then what good are Summit meetings? Why bother meeting with the Soviet leaders? Isn't it a waste of time? Not necessarily!

Even though a specific agreement may not be reached, and even though we must assume the Soviets will break any agreement the moment they can get away with it and as soon as it suits their purpose, still there are reasons why, under certain conditions, high level meetings with the Soviet leaders are important. Here are three reasons:

**Propaganda effect.** Imagine for a moment that Khrushchev, with the fanfare for which he is famous, has invited President Kennedy to come to Vienna to "talk of peace." At the UN, the Soviet representatives play up the important pending meeting. The huge Communist presses throughout the world begin to roll. "We are on the threshold of a new era of peace and friendship" says *"Red Flag"* in Japan, *l'Humanité* in France, Communist dailies everywhere. Moscow Radio echoes the growing chance of "peace in our time." But President Kennedy says, "No, the United States does not wish to meet with the Soviet Union until the latter demonstrates its real desire for peace." We therefore refuse to meet with Khrushchev. President Kennedy's point may be a good one — but it is not likely to impress the vast uninformed, hungry, and hopeful masses of the world. It can only serve to further convince the misinformed that the United States is against peace! And the Kremlin will have won another round in the propaganda fight. The United States can ill afford to let the Kremlin become, in the eyes of the world, the champion of peace!

**Face to face evaluation of Khrushchev.** There is an advantage in being able to hear first-hand from the top leader his policies and problems — insofar as he reveals them. The opportunity for the President and his advisors to size up Khrushchev and company, to talk directly, to sense his mood, must not be dismissed. At the same time, we must remember Khrushchev is an actor, a poker player. He can at times "turn on" emotions for effect. He is not likely to reveal his ace in the hole. Thus, this aspect should not be overrated.

**Making our position clear.** One of the great dangers of our time is that the Soviet leaders may misjudge our motives or underestimate our determination. A frank, forceful presentation by our President can be helpful in reinforcing policy and actions. Khrushchev fancies himself as something of a people's psychologist. He is not likely to miss the mood of genuine determination in which the President presents this nation's decision to stand firm and to resist further Communist aggression in any place, at any time. This concept of personal diplomacy is simply one more part of the picture of total diplomacy. It could mean the difference between war and peace.

Thus, our leaders go to the "Summit" and talk, and the results are about as expected. Those who are disappointed were simply expecting too much!

## 77. *Do the Russians really believe in disarmament or the United Nations?*

We must record a qualified "NO" on both scores. Qualified, because the disappointing record of Soviet words and deeds adds up to the unpleasant fact that the Kremlin honors its agreements only when it serves Soviet interests. This means that we can never trust the Communists. But this also means that we should not discount entirely all Soviet statements on disarmament or the UN. If approached realistically, it is entirely possible that we may find in the future, as we have in the past, certain limited areas of mutual agreement and advantage between this country and the USSR.

All of this does not, of course, change the basic facts of life —

namely, that the Kremlin considers both the disarmament question and the UN issue relatively unimportant. The idea of a sincere agreement or compromise with "the capitalist world" — as has been suggested — is simply not part of Soviet thinking and planning.

**The Soviet Union and disarmament.** A 641-page study by the Brookings Institution (published in August, 1961) of the Soviet record in disarmament negotiations over the past 15 years is hardly reassuring. The conclusion of the study is that in the past decade and a half the Soviet Union "has not yet shown a desire to sacrifice" its system of Iron Curtain secrecy in order to obtain real disarmament. As we know, the Kremlin broke a tacit agreement for a nuclear test-ban, and despite the protests of the people of the world went ahead in the fall of 1961 with dangerous nuclear tests which have polluted the atmosphere with radioactive fallout.

**The Soviet Union and the United Nations.** It is obvious from the record that the Soviet Union does not really believe in the UN. The Russians have repeatedly thwarted the will of the majority of the Security Council by imposing their veto. They have consistently refused to let the UN have jurisdiction over matters which the Soviets considered vital to their interests. They look upon the UN primarily as a sounding board for their propaganda, rather than as a world organization for the preservation of peace.

It seems clear that the Soviets would have preferred that the UN had never come into existence, that they have never really taken it seriously. During the early negotiations for the creation of the UN, Stalin showed that he had paid the question little attention. He seems to have agreed to the creation of the UN reluctantly, and as a concession to Western pleading during the era of good feelings that existed toward the end of World War II. At one time, Stalin refused to send Molotov to the founding conference of the UN at San Francisco, and it was only after a personal plea from President Truman that he finally agreed to let his Foreign Minister attend. The Stalin record within the UN was correspondingly bad. The Khrushchev record is even worse. It includes the astonishing spectacle of the Soviet leader noisily pounding his shoe on the desk of the UN General Assembly before the distinguished representatives of the nations of the world. This rude act is symbolic of the disdain and distrust with which the Kremlin looks upon the UN.

## 78. What does the Kremlin mean by "peaceful coexistence"?

Stripped of its propaganda content, peaceful coexistence may be defined briefly and precisely: By peaceful coexistence the Soviets mean simply the absence of nuclear war. Thus seen in the cold light of reality, Communist pronouncements on the desire for peaceful coexistence are at the same time true and meaningless or misleading.

They are true in the sense that Khrushchev is certainly for coexistence. Given the United States' nuclear retaliatory striking power, the alternative to coexistence, i.e. nuclear war, is *nonexistence* — national suicide.

Such statements are meaningless and misleading because they are too often equated or confused with the concepts of cooperation, agreement on principles, mutual trust, conciliation, or friendship.

To the Kremlin, peaceful coexistence is no more than a necessary strategy and a clever slogan dictated by the relative power positions of the two great super-states. But it is used to convince the naive and the uninformed that the Soviet Union stands for peace.

If we keep this definition in mind and remember the astounding record of Soviet aggression, hypocrisy, and intimidation, Kremlin talk of coexistence may be evaluated for what it is, pure propaganda! Here is a typical statement on peaceful coexistence by Khrushchev:

What, then, is the policy of peaceful coexistence? In its simplest expression it signifies the repudiation of war as a means of solving controversial issues. However, this does not cover the entire concept of peaceful coexistence. Apart from the commitment to nonaggression, it also presupposes an obligation on the part of all states to desist from violating each other's territorial integrity and sovereignty in any form and under any pretext whatsoever. The principle of peaceful coexistence signifies a renunciation of interference in the internal affairs of other countries with the object of altering their system of government or mode of life or for any other motives. The doctrine of peaceful coexistence also presupposes that political and economic relations between countries are to be based upon complete equality of the parties concerned, and on mutual benefit.

## The Role of Diplomacy and Force in Soviet Foreign Policy

## 79. *What is the Communist concept of diplomacy?*

Diplomacy is a nineteenth century term. "Total diplomacy" may be a somewhat better way to characterize international relations and negotiations at nuclear mid-twentieth century, but even this phrase is misleading. In the complex technological world of today no one man knows enough to make a personal, on-the-spot decision on a vital question affecting the future, perhaps the very existence, of his country. In short, the range of decision-making power, the initiative allowed the typical Western diplomat, is considerably smaller today than it was fifty or even twenty-five years ago. Yet the Western diplomat, compared to his Soviet counterpart, has a wide latitude in negotiation where his judgment and imagination play an important role.

The Soviet diplomat is quite different. He has never had real decision-making power. All Soviet decisions, big and small, are strictly made-in-Moscow. The Soviet diplomat doesn't really negotiate at all. Instead, he *represents* — reflecting the official Kremlin line or position of the moment on a particular issue. This is a different kind of diplomacy. Unless we understand this difference — and the concept behind it — we may not appreciate the difficulties faced by our representatives whenever and wherever they must negotiate with their Soviet opposite numbers.

Dr. Philip E. Mosely, formerly Director of the Russian Institute at Columbia University and presently Director of Studies of the Council on Foreign Relations, New York, has had wide personal experience in negotiating with the Russians. He sums up the problem this way:

. . . The Soviet negotiator is tight as a spring, deeply suspicious, always trying to exert the Soviet will-power outward and to avoid reflecting non-Soviet facts and aspirations inward, a rigid agent knowing only the segment of policy which he must carry out with mechanical precision. Does this mean that "negotiation" in any real sense of the term is impossible? Admitting that negotiation under these conditions is a very limited affair and very difficult and un-rewarding, it may still be both possible and essential. But it requires a special approach. Naturally, a knowledge of Russian in its Soviet nuances is important. It is equally important to understand the role of the Soviet negotiator in relation to his own government and to its ideology. The Department of State has carried on a far-sighted policy of equipping a substantial number of its representatives through language and area training and through service in missions in the Soviet-dominated areas to deal with Soviet problems, and as these young men mature in experience they will fill an important need. The Army and Air Force have also done a good deal along this line. . . .

Protected by two oceans and remote from the direct origins of previous world wars, Americans have been accustomed to ignore the rising storm and then, once it had burst upon them, to work solely for victory over the immediate menace. Thus, they tend to feel a sharp dichotomy between "war" and "peace" [between force and diplomacy]. When at peace they are reluctant to think of the possibility of war. When at war they concentrate solely on winning the war, as if it were a grim football match, and refuse to worry about the peace which is the goal of war. Through Lenin and Stalin Soviet thinking has fully absorbed the Clausewitz maxims that national strength and strong alliances determine the effectiveness of national policy in peace, and that in war one must never lose sight of the aims of policy for which it is waged. . . .[1]

## 80. *How does one explain the Communist use of force in Korea and Hungary?*

The Communists use force whenever and wherever it seems the most effective instrument to achieve their objectives. The Korean

[1] Philip E. Mosely, "Some Soviet Techniques of Negotiation" in Raymond Dennett and Joseph E. Johnson (Editors) *Negotiating with the Russians* (World Peace Foundation, Boston, 1951), pages 297 and 302.

War (1950–53) and the Hungarian Revolution (1956) are two classic examples of the Communist use of "naked force." In Korea, the Communists sought to impose their way of life upon South as well as North Korea — to "unify" Korea with tanks. In Hungary, the Soviet Union ruthlessly crushed the freedom revolution with massive Soviet tank, artillery, and infantry units and with elements of the Soviet secret police. In this way they prevented Hungary from swinging out of the Soviet orbit.

**The Korean War.** The Korean war is a case study in what the then President Harry Truman termed "naked Communist aggression." As a result of the Japanese defeat in World War II, Korea, which Japan had annexed in 1910, found itself divided between the Soviet backed North Korean Communist regime and the UN sponsored South Korean government.

During the Soviet military occupation of Korea north of the 38th parallel (1945–1949), the Soviets had trained a powerful North Korean Communist army and had turned the area into a Communist satellite. During the same period, United States occupation forces south of the 38th parallel had disarmed and repatriated the Japanese, had helped South Korea restore its shattered economy and disrupted life, and had helped the new government develop a security force of about 65,000 men.

The result might have been anticipated: North Korean Communist forces launched a massive invasion across the 38th parallel on June 25, 1950. They were supported by Soviet and Chinese Communist advisors. The aim: a cheap Communist victory, since neither South Korean forces in being nor Western determination seemed strong enough to present any real obstacle.

When United States military and diplomatic observers in the area reported to Washington what was happening, President Truman acted immediately. First, he ordered our air and naval units to assist in repelling the aggressors, and, a few day later, also committed this country's ground forces. Secondly, he called for an emergency session of the Security Council of the UN.

A United Nations mission happened to be in South Korea at that time. Based on an impartial report on the situation from this mission, the UN Security Council branded the North Koreans the aggressors and ordered the immediate withdrawal of North Korean units to their own territory. When the North Korean

Communists ignored the request, the Security Council called for UN members to supply military units for a United Nations force to repel the aggression. Forces from the Free World were placed under the direction of General Douglas MacArthur. Soon troops from Turkey, Australia, and Pakistan were fighting alongside American troops. India sent a hospital unit.

When the UN Forces had pushed northward to the Yalu River on the border of Manchuria, over a million Chinese "volunteers," in November of 1950, entered the war. This force actually was made up of well-trained units of the Communist Chinese regular army. This intervention increased the size and intensity of the war. Only after two years of see-saw battles with staggering losses on both sides did the UN Forces finally manage to push the Communists back again behind the 38th parallel. By this time it was clear that a cheap Communist victory was hardly at hand. In fact the UN was clearly on the offensive and winning. Both politically and militarily the war had become a Communist liability. Accordingly, just at this time Soviet UN representative Jacob Malik rose before the world body to suggest that the Soviet Union, "which the world knows has no soldiers in Korea and is neutral," sees no reason why that terrible war cannot be settled peacefully "if all parties are sincere." Suddenly, the North Korean and Chinese Communist forces for the first time were willing to negotiate. Very soon the war was over and an armistice was finally signed. Korea remains divided.

What are the lessons of the Korean war? They are many and they were mostly learned the hard way. These two are especially worth noting.

*Lesson No. 1* — The Communists will not hesitate to use military force to take over a country the moment they sense a combination of military weakness and lack of determination on the part of the free community of nations.

*Lesson No. 2* — Seventy-five per cent of the Communist prisoners taken during the Korean War refused to go back to North Korea or China. This situation is unique in the history of warfare. Like the wall the Communists have built in Berlin, or the constant stream of refugees from East to West, it is eloquent testimony on the nature of conditions behind the Iron and Bamboo Curtains. If conditions are as good as the Communists claim, why do so many people want to get out?

**The Hungarian Revolution.** Suppression of the brave Hungarian freedom fighters in 1956 by Soviet tanks, artillery units, and the secret police is an example of the Communist use of brute force to control restless satellites. The history of the Hungarian revolt goes back to the early postwar period when the Soviets imposed a Communist regime on that helpless nation, as well as other countries of Eastern Europe. The facts on what happened have been established by an impartial United Nations Committee, the UN Special Committee on the Problem of Hungary. That five-man committee (composed of one representative each from Denmark, Australia, Ceylon, Tunisia, and Uruguay) heard testimony from 111 witnesses, many of them key leaders of the revolution, who had managed to escape when Soviet tanks overran Budapest. Their report produced a sense of shock and revulsion all around the world.

The cases of Communist brutality cited one after another in this impartial report of what actually happened are difficult for most Americans to believe. But, this is the way Communism works. Here are two brief excerpts, only two of the thousands which might be cited, the first on military suppression, the second on secret police brutality:

  **Military suppression:** The accounts and information collected by the Committee concur in the fact that for the purpose of crushing the Revolution, Soviet tanks moved along the streets of Hungarian towns shooting indiscriminately at armed groups of individuals and at every building from which they believed they were being attacked. In addition to operations of this kind, which could be described as military, there are numerous instances of mortar fire across the Danube from Pest to Buda on inhabited quarters, of artillery fire on buildings from which there was no return fire and of haphazard shooting at defenseless passers-by. By way of example, it was reported to the Committee that twenty to thirty tanks went up and down one Budapest street for about an hour, firing at the buildings until they were completely destroyed. Another incident as told to Committee was as follows: "On November 4, ten armored cars came towards our positions at Szena Square by way of the Margit Bridge over the Danube. Their guns were pointed at each side of the street in turn. For one and a half kilometers they fired at each house, destroying a large number and killing many people, including women and children. When they arrived at Szena Square they fired at everything within a radius of one kilometer for several hours, although their fire was not returned."

Many witnesses have reported cases where Soviet soldiers shot at queues (lines) of Hungarians waiting outside bakeries or other food shops. These incidents, in most of which the victims were women and children, contributed in a special way to arouse public indignation, as did the many cases of shooting at ambulances, Red Cross vehicles and the doctors and nurses in those vehicles.

It therefore appears to the Committee that, especially after 4 November, Soviet orders were to crush all resistance by every means that would prove effective.

**Secret police brutality:** Besides the examples of brutality and degrading forms of treatment causing unspeakable physical suffering, numerous psychological methods were used such as mock executions, threats to families, interminable waiting by prisoners in inhuman conditions aimed at crushing their spirit and drawing a confession from them. The following extracts of testimony given to the Committee will throw some light on this subject.

The chairman of one of the Workers' Councils gave the following testimony:

". . . They took me to a prison, chained my right hand to my left foot, and left me in a dark cell about three meters square. There was no heating, and this was in the middle of the winter of 1950. For clothing I had nothing but a shirt and undershirt, a pair of shorts and a pair of shoes, and I was left in chains in that hole. was there for twenty-four hours when I was given a little piece of bread, about twenty decagrams. It was so dark I did not know what the time was and I could not move because if I did so, my wrists and ankles bled. I had to freeze and starve . . ."

A mechanic reported as follows:

"When I was interrogated in the AVH (Hungarian Communist Secret Police loyal to the Kremlin) prison . . . I was subjected to two kinds of torture. One was physical and consisted of knocking out all my teeth. I was also starved. For six and a half months was in a concrete cell, where I had no opportunity to wash myself or keep myself clean."

A former university professor, an official and a member of the Communist Party declared:

"During the first three days I was left completely alone. Everything was taken away from me and I was put in a cellar. I could live; down below it was a crypt in which I was entombed; there was no life. It is very interesting; several years later I met other people who had gone through the same thing, and who said the same. The beatings were not too important, they did not bother us too much, in a way we could be amused, it was a diversion."[2]

So the UN Report documents case after case — the tragic, heartless story of Soviet suppression. It concludes:

1. What took place in Hungary in October and November, 1956, was a spontaneous national uprising due to long-standing grievances which had caused resentment among the people.

2. The thesis that the uprising was fomented by reactionary circles in Hungary and that it drew its strength from such circles and from Western imperialists failed to survive the Committee's examination. From start to finish, the uprising was led by students, workers, soldiers and intellectuals, many of whom were Communists or former Communists.

3. The uprising was not planned in advance. It was the universal testimony of witnesses examined by the Committee that events took participants by surprise. No single explanation can determine exactly why the outbreak occurred just when it did.

4. Since the second Soviet intervention on 4 November there *has been no evidence of popular support for Mr. Kadar's (Soviet puppet) government.* Mr. Kadar has proceeded step by step to destroy the power of the workers. Strong repressive measures have been introduced and general elections have been postponed for two years. He refuses in present circumstances to discuss withdrawal of the Soviet troops. Only a small fraction of the 190,000 Hungarians who fled the country have accepted the invitation to return.

5. Consideration of the Hungarian question by the United Nations was legally proper and paragraph 7 of Article 2 of the Charter does not justify objections to such consideration. *A massive armed intervention by one Power on the territory of another with the avowed intention of interfering in its internal affairs must, by the Soviet Union's own definition of aggression, be a matter of international concern.*

The Korean War — Communist aggression, attempted takeover of South Korea. The Hungarian Revolution — Soviet suppression and control of a captive people yearning for freedom. These are two case studies in the Soviet use of military force in the relentless pursuit of political objectives.

---

[2] United Nations Report of the Special Committee on the Problem of Hungary, General Assembly, New York, 1957, pp. 130–139.

## Propaganda, Intelligence, and Subversion

### 81. *What are the facts about Soviet foreign intelligence and espionage?*

In a Communist political tract called the *Soviet Political Dictionary,* intelligence-gathering or espionage is defined in the following terms:

> One of the basic means used by capitalist nations in their fight among themselves, and in particular in their fight against the USSR. Foreign Intelligence agencies began to send their spies into Soviet Russia immediately after its emergence. Foreign espionage in our country is closely tied up with diversionist and wrecking activities and is aimed at the undermining of Soviet military and industrial might.

This definition certainly offers no hint to the Russian people that perhaps their own government, the Soviet Government, may also be engaged in this sort of thing abroad. The facts are that the Kremlin, since the Communists have come to power in Russia, has spent (at a conservative estimate) something like ten times as much on intelligence, spying, and espionage as the United States.

There are three good reasons why foreign intelligence and espionage have played so large and important a role in the affairs of the Soviet Union.

**Reason number one** is the Communist heritage of conspiracy and intrigue. The Bolsheviks gained power in Russia through conspiracy and intrigue. It is their life, an essential ingredient of their system. To the Communists, spying comes naturally. Further, without it the Communists could not hope to maintain their rule at home or expand their control and influence abroad.

**Reason number two** is the Marxist-Leninist concept of permanent revolution and class war. One very important aspect of all Soviet foreign activity, even trade or culture, is intelligence, espionage, and subversion. This combination is regarded by the Kremlin as an important strategic weapon for the assault on capitalism. The strengths, weaknesses, and special vulnerabilities of every target country in the Free World must be discovered and analyzed. In this process, foreign intelligence and espionage play a major role.

**Reason number three** relates to military and economic considerations — the urgent Soviet desire to catch up with and overtake the United States. This has characteristically taken such forms as "If you can't invent it, steal it!" — or "What we can't figure out ourselves, our spies can find out from other more advanced nations." Here too, as we shall see, Soviet intelligence and espionage have played key roles in "building the Socialist economy," and in making the Soviet Union a world power.

Consider these startling facts. In the years up to 1945, Soviet intelligence had agents, many of them highly placed, in the following critical posts in foreign countries:

*The United States.* In the State Department, the Department of Justice, the Office of Strategic Services, the Office of Naval Intelligence, the Manhattan Project, and a number of other important government departments.

*Japan.* In the personal staff of Prime Minister Konoye, the Foreign Ministry, the headquarters of the South Manchurian Railroad, the House of Representatives, various military headquarters, and several other sensitive government departments.

*The United Kingdom.* In the American division of the Foreign Office, the code room of the Foreign Office in London, the British Embassy at Moscow, the Admiralty, Harwell center of atomic development, and a great many more key agencies and departments.

*France.* In the Foreign Affairs, War, and Air Ministries, and the secret code department of the French Admiralty.

*Germany.* In several critical ministries, both military and political.

*Canada.* As extensively as in Germany, plus: all branches of atomic research, the Bank of Canada, and the Canadian Wartime Information Board.

Between 1947 and 1953, a single Soviet spy stationed in Switzerland supplied the following information:

The location of RAF airports in Germany; a roster of all American officers stationed in Germany; the battle order of American troops in

Germany; a critique of the various maneuvers and exercises staged by Allied troops in Europe; the organization of the U.S. Air Force in the United Kingdom; Allied military installations and construction in Germany; the battle orders of the French Army in France and in Indochina.[1]

Soviet intelligence has thus been both extensive and effective. It provided the Kremlin, among other things, with the date of the planned German invasion of the Soviet Union (a month in advance) and with the information on how to construct an atomic bomb. Soviet intelligence is bigger and more active today than ever before. In late 1961 the FBI disclosed that the Soviet bloc now has 300,000 espionage agents — a number greater than the population of Miami.

In *Soviet Espionage*[2] David Dallin concludes:

> The Soviet espionage network abroad today is the largest on earth, probably larger than the intelligence systems of all other nations combined. Based on the one hand on forty-six embassies, legations and missions abroad, and on the other on fifty-three Communist Parties of the non-satellite world as well as a number of networks independent of Soviet embassies and Communist parties, [it] is one of the most remarkable phenomena of our times.

## 82. *How does the Kremlin use subversion as a foreign policy weapon?*

Subversion, the systematic undermining and ultimate take-over *from within* of free nations, is a standard and well-developed Communist technique. The cases of Czechoslovakia and Hungary are classic examples of the Soviet use of subversion as a foreign policy weapon.

Few men are more familiar with the details of this technique than Allen Dulles, Director of the United States Central Intelligence Agency from 1953 to 1961. Let us ask him for the facts on the Soviet take-over of Czechoslovakia and Hungary. He writes:

[1] Ladislas Farago, *War of Wits* (Funk and Wagnalls Company, New York, 1954), p. 172.
[2] *Soviet Espionage* (Yale University Press, New Haven, 1955), page 493.

**Czechoslovakia.** Beginning in 1945, Moscow exercised heavy pressure on the free Czech Government headed by President Benes. Hoping to be able to work with the Kremlin and anxious to insure the quick withdrawal of Russian troops, Beneš went to Moscow in March of that year. He sought agreement on the forming of a coalition government acceptable to the Soviets which would include some of the pro-Communist émigrés who had been collected in Moscow during the war and who flooded back to their home country to play roles preassigned to them by the Kremlin.

When the parliamentary government of President Beneš was actually reconstituted, the anti-Communist forces were badly divided among four or more parties. The Communist Party, as usual, presented a monolithic front. Under these conditions, the elections of 1946 gave the Communists 38 per cent of the votes. Thus they became the largest single party, their leader Gottwald was named Prime Minister, and the Communists were able to take over certain key ministries, including Interior, Information, and Finance, with a crypto-Communist in charge of Defense.

During all this period, Stalin had cultivated President Beneš and lulled him into a feeling of security as to Moscow's intentions. Meanwhile the Communists were building up their control of the Czech military forces, the trade unions, and the internal security policy. Finally, one of Moscow's principal "expediters", Valerian Zorin, now Soviet Ambassador to Bonn, was sent to Prague, and the minority Communist Party seized power in February, 1948, without firing a shot.

The principal Czech anti-Communist leaders either escaped abroad, committed suicide, or were eliminated by arrest. Non-Communist parties were liquidated by the armed seizure of their headquarters and newspapers. A purge commission dealt with all so-called unreliable political leaders. President Beneš was forced to resign in June, 1948, and the Communists took over and ever since have maintained supreme control.

There are many lessons to be learned from this historical precedent. When the Communists obtain an effective minority position in any parliamentary body, it is a sign of danger. If, in addition to that, they have important places in the government and in particular control the ministries of defense and interior, then the danger is greatly augmented and the country in question is ripe for a Communist take-over.

**Hungary.** The situation in Hungary as the war was coming to a close was dominated by the Soviet military occupation. Nonetheless, the Hungarian non-Communist political leaders bravely started out to form a free government and in the first postwar elections in November, 1945, the anti-Communist parties had over 300 seats to about 70 for the Communists.

Then the trouble started. The Soviet military authorities proceeded to arrest, to drive from the country, or terrify and blackmail the leaders of these non-Communist parties so that in the next elections in 1947, the Communists substantially increased their representation and became the largest single party, although the opposition groups still had a majority. The latter, however, were badly divided and facing the pressure tactics of the Communists supported by the Soviet military, they were reduced to impotence and the Communists took over. By 1948 most of the anti-Communist leaders were dead, jailed, or had fled.

Rakosi, one of the Hungarian *renegade* artisans of all this terror, still maintains a very precarious hold over the Hungarian Government as the stooge of Moscow. Today he is trembling in his boots since as you can well imagine he almost completely symbolizes the Stalinist line and the Stalinist techniques, and sooner or later the new anti-Stalinist look may mean his downfall. In February of 1952, however, he was in fine fettle and described with glee and in the utmost detail the entire history and techniques of the destruction of the free government of Hungary.

I recommend the study of his speech of February 29, 1952, by those who are interested in understanding what Khrushchev and Mikoyan mean today when they tell us that one of their main weapons is to undermine our democratic institutions. Rakosi points out how the presence in the country of the Soviet Army prevented any attempt to defend with force the security of the anti-Communist government and served to protect the Communists from "imperialist intervention."

Meanwhile the Soviet Union, he states, shielded the Communist plotters in Hungary from "diplomatic interference of the great Western Powers." Rakosi frankly admitted that Soviet interference in Hungary's internal affairs was both "quite frequent and of great help in the strengthening of 'the Communist Party.' " He then describes step by step the success of the Communist intrigue and points out that the Smallholders Party, the strongest anti-Communist party, was constantly compelled to expel or discard individuals discredited by Communist blackmail. This gradual day-by-day slicing off of hostile elements, i.e., non-Communist leaders, he described as "salami" techniques. In other words, he boasted that democracy in Hungary was cut away, piece by piece, just as we slice up a sausage.

These two illustrative examples, Czechoslovakia and Hungary, could be further emphasized by tracing the Communist take-over in Poland, Rumania, and Bulgaria. But two examples serve the purpose. It is useful to have the ballots but there are situations, and the Soviet Union is adept in bringing them about, where bullets prevail.

## 83. *Is Soviet propaganda better than ours?*

Why does Soviet and Communist propaganda sometimes appear to be more effective than similar programs carried on by the United States? This question is repeatedly asked by responsible Americans. Feeling that advertising and "selling" are natural for Americans, they wonder why we seem to have difficulty in gaining acceptance for democracy in many lands.

Before we become critical of our own professional people in the State Department, the United States Information Agency, the Voice of America, and other organizations charged with telling America's story abroad, we must take into account some of the difficulties they have to overcome.

**1. The memory of past "wrongs."** Clearly one of the most critical areas in terms of the future is that vast region we call the uncommitted or the underdeveloped areas — Asia, Africa, the Middle East, and Latin America. Of course, not all nations in these areas are uncommitted or even underdeveloped, but many of them are both. The point is that the memories of Western imperialism and colonialism are still fresh in the minds of many Indians, Indonesians, Africans, Egyptians, Algerians, and some Latin Americans. Because the United States is an ally of Western powers it tends to be linked with them in the popular mind. At the same time, the problems of these areas are as difficult and urgent as the populations are impatient and often unbelievably uninformed. Into this loaded situation come the Communist propagandists with promises of peace and prosperity, a basic change in the present situation — if only the people will reject Western leadership. And who is not for peace and prosperity? Who does not wish a change for the better?

**2. The Communist propaganda approach.** The Communists' approach to information and propaganda differs fundamentally from ours. Communists use the big and little lie — as a matter of policy. We try to tell the truth. Sometimes this hurts. Certainly it gives the Communists a temporary advantage. Would we do better to stop being so honest? Most authorities don't think so. Experience during World War II, when Hitler, Mussolini, and Tojo relied on the big lie, makes it clear that in the long run the truth wins. The short run is difficult, and often disappointing. But once the world becomes convinced that what we say is true and what the Communists say is not true — is in fact, deliberately distorted — we have won the game. We are making progress, but, of course, should and can do better.

**3. The scope of the Communist effort.** The Communists over the years have spent about ten or twenty times as much as the United States has spent on propaganda. Here is one of the keys to their success. Any football coach knows that a school with ten times as much to spend on its athletic program as other schools is almost a sure bet to have the best team.

What may we conclude? First, it may be suggested that instead of constant negative criticism, a positive approach to the problem might go a long way in meeting the challenge. Secondly, we must also remember that every American, each movie, any American businessman, student, teacher, or other traveler who goes abroad is helping create an image of Americans and the United States. If that image is good our Government can help keep it that way. If it is bad, it is not easy to change. In short, we are all propagandists for America — the question is only: Are we helping or hurting our cause?

## Trade and Aid as Foreign Policy Weapons

**84.** *How do the Soviets use trade and aid as foreign policy weapons?*

Khrushchev told a group of United States senators in 1954 "We value trade least for economic reasons and most for political purposes. . . ." Since that time the Soviet Union has pushed a huge economic trade and aid offensive. At the 20th Congress of the Communist Party of the Soviet Union in 1956, Khrushchev said: "In contrast to the 'let's arm' slogan of the North Atlantic bloc we put forward the slogan, 'Let's trade.'"

Soviet trade and aid, like propaganda, subversion, military action, and diplomacy, have one primary purpose: the ultimate destruction of capitalism and the Free World.

In the use of trade and aid as foreign policy weapons — economic warfare as it is called — it must be recognized that the Soviet Union has certain advantages over the democratically governed nations of the Free World. The Communist Government controls all of its foreign economic activity. Therefore, it can arbitrarily select one country as a target for Soviet attention and generosity. Whereas in this country the President must seek the approval of Congress, get the support of business groups, and worry about the budget, Khrushchev is free to act. The Communist Government, therefore, can move more quickly than a democratic government.

Even the most powerful business organizations and trading companies of the Free World — those called monopolies by the Communists — are dwarfed by the huge state-run trade agencies of the Soviet world. Apart from relative size, enterprises in the Free World are in business to make a profit for their shareholders. The United States Government has no right to tell American business where it must invest its money and do its business.

**1. The Soviet technique.** Russia, having selected the country to be won over, carries out foreign economic projects according to plan. The methods used reflect long-term goals and thinking. The underdeveloped or newly emanicipated area is helped through economic aid, grants, and cheap credit. Frequently there are bilateral deals. This means barter deals calling for a specific amount of goods to be exchanged. The price is always negotiated and often there is price discrimination. Usually the transactions take place at a time when the new country needs capital very badly for its development, or needs money for a huge project for the sake of prestige — the Aswan High Dam in Egypt is a case in point. When a country is short of cash, the Red Bloc may offer to take the goods at a price favorable to it, and the underdeveloped country is promised a certain quantity of badly needed goods in exchange. The delivery of these goods is set at a later date. At no time can the poor country collect Russian rubles (for no rubles are allowed outside the USSR) in order to obtain dollars or other currencies for the goods sold to Russia. They must wait until they receive the goods as part of the barter.

**2. Operation Egypt.** What happens after such a deal is made? An excellent example is provided by Egypt. A few years ago, when Nasser was shopping abroad for arms, the Russians were only too eager to sell him the badly needed arms in exchange for long-staple cotton which Egypt used to sell to Europe. Of course, the Russians could not make domestic use of the cotton, since their program called for the development of heavy industry rather than consumer goods. After the Egyptian cotton was delivered to Russia, Nasser discovered that it was dumped in Western Europe at much lower prices than the Egyptians previously had obtained, and in the very same markets with which Egypt had done business for years.

**3. Case study — Ghana.** On May 6, 1957, the Free World witnessed the birth of a new republic — Ghana. Its capital, Accra, was the scene of rejoicing for Africans, and representatives of the Red Bloc and the Free World were there to celebrate the event. There were gifts for the occasion from many countries. One Western country gave a plane to President Nkrumah, another a painting, and some gave ornamental objects. The Russian greetings were of a totally different and novel kind. They welcomed the birth of the new nation by sending three ships to Accra to load cargoes of cocoa beans, a basic export in the economic life of Ghana. President Nkrumah was delighted with Russia's gesture. It was only much later that the Free World learned how Russia made new friends and influenced the new nations of Africa.

The unusual part of this gesture was that the Soviet Union does not allow its people to use too much chocolate, nor do the Russians drink cocoa. The favorite Russian beverage is tea. Of course, President Nkrumah did not ask whether Russia needed or would use the cocoa. Nor did he ask himself whether the Soviet Union might sell the cocoa to those who do use it — at less than the price in the world market. He was glad to find a new customer for the cocoa — and Russia's gesture made an impression in Ghana. President Nkrumah went to Moscow in 1961 as one of the two representatives selected by the neutral countries that met at Belgrade to plead with Khrushchev for the preservation of peace. Prior to his departure for Moscow Nkrumah saw evil only in the West. After talking with Mr. Khrushchev, he still saw no evil in Russia. Who knows the extent to which his judgment was influenced by the memory of the three boatloads of cocoa sold on May 6, 1957?

**4. Target — Yemen.** Another example of the nature of Russia's economic aid involves Yemen, a little-known and underdeveloped country. Yemen is strategically located at the entrance to the Red Sea from the Gulf of Aden and therefore commands the entrance to the Suez Canal. The Imam of Yemen is one of the last autocratic rulers, and his country numbers some four million people. For years he has been at loggerheads with the British over territorial boundaries. In order to pursue his war against the British he needed more modern arms. These he was unable to buy from the Western powers because they were afraid of increasing tension in the Middle East. The Red Bloc was only too glad to help Yemen. Aid began to arrive quickly after an agreement was made, although no assessment of Yemen's needs had ever been made by foreign nationals. The country has been hermetically closed to all "infidels" for centuries.

In the space of some 20 months Russia and Czechoslovakia granted Yemen $80,000,000 in credits, and since 1958 an additional $20,000,000 have been granted. Over $30,000,000 worth of arms were delivered and 65 Russian technicians were landed to teach the Yemeni how to use them. The record does not show that Yemen ever before had invited foreigners in such numbers.

The foregoing are but three examples. Iran, Burma, Ceylon, Cuba — everywhere it is the same story. Soviet objectives in using trade and aid as foreign policy weapons may be summarized as follows:

1. To supply their economy, especially the industrial-military base, with imports that help the Red Bloc become more powerful and less dependent on the Free World.

2. To drive wedges between Free World nations at every opportunity.

3. To arm small nations — Yemen, Ghana, Egypt, Cuba — and to encourage them to threaten neighbors and to adopt policies hostile to the West.

4. To increase the reliance of Free World nations on the Red Bloc for markets and supplies, and thus to make the Free World more vulnerable to Red Bloc pressure.

5. To prevent by trade and credit manipulation any defections of neutral nations to the side of the West, e.g. Finland.

6. To convince the neutral nations that any nation, such as the Soviet Union, that in a relatively short time can achieve a position that enables it to grant large-scale aid to other countries has an economic system worth copying.

## 85. *How do Soviet foreign trade and aid compare with those of the United States?*

Trade and aid may be compared in three ways: in terms of purposes, in terms of scope, and in terms of focus or type.

**Purposes.** As already demonstrated, the Kremlin regards trade and aid first and foremost as strategic or political weapons. The basic design of the Communist foreign economic program relates to this one central purpose. The specific aims are to destroy the capitalist economy and to subvert the nations of Asia, Africa, the Middle East, and Latin America. No such sinister design dominates the trade and aid programs of the Free World, although one of the purposes of American trade and aid is clearly to counter Communist influences and penetration, especially within the newly emerging nations and in Latin America. President Eisenhower said: ". . . urgent as the outlay for our missile and other weapons may be, a strong program of military and economic aid is equally urgent." Governor Adlai Stevenson, when Eisenhower was President, said: "I think foreign aid is an essential tool for accomplishing America's peaceful purposes."

Two other important purposes of this country's trade and aid are (1) to strengthen the United States economy by stimulating business and industry and by providing essential strategic materials, and (2) to assist underdeveloped nations with basic economic development, health and educational programs.

**Scope.** In terms of scope over the years, United States trade and aid dwarfs the smaller and much more recent Soviet program. Foreign trade was important to this nation long before the twentieth century. Recent examples of our aid programs include famine relief to Russia in the 1920's and to China in the 1930's and 1940's, and the Marshall Plan after World War II.

By contrast, until very recently, Soviet foreign trade has ne

A member of the East German border guard leaps
over the barricade to freedom in West Berlin.
This photograph was taken at the Bernauer Street
sector of the border on August 15, 1961. In the
weeks that followed the barricade was made
higher!

M

Moscow garrison troops are parading in Red Square during the 1960 May Day celebration. Note that only Marx and Lenin are pictured on the banner.

The United States must keep pace with rapid Soviet development to maintain its nuclear advantage. In conventional warfare, U.S.S.R. ground forces, equipped with modernized weapons, would have the advantage. Most U.S. forces are still using weapons of World War II design.

| | Stockpile of Nuclear Weapons | Intercontinental Ballistic Missiles (ICBM's) | Polaris-type Missiles | Long-range Bombers | Medium Bombers | Attack Aircraft Carriers |
|---|---|---|---|---|---|---|
| U.S.A. | 35,000 to 40,000 | 24 to 48 | 80 | 785 | Over 2000 able to reach Russia | 15 (carrying 1500 planes) |
| U.S.S.R. | Perhaps half the U.S. Stockpile | 50 to 100 | NONE | 150 to 200 | 1500 perhaps 200 able to reach U.S. | NONE |

**THE NUCLEAR ARMS RACE**
Weapons and Delivery Systems
United States and Soviet Union

Nehru, Nkrumah, Nasser, Sukarno are pictured with Tito in this meeting of chiefs of state of the leading neutralist countries. The place: headquarters of the Yugoslav U.N. Mission in September 1960.

This model of the Aswan High Dam was used for purposes of hydraulic research prior to construction of the dam itself. The model was built in Moscow's Institute "Hydroproject." The Soviet Union is helping Nasser achieve his dream of building this huge dam.

O

Khrushchev is embracing Castro on the floor of the U.N. General Assembly, September 20, 1960.

In April 1961, when the small landing force at the Bay of Pigs had been rounded up, rallies were held outside the Cuban Embassy in Moscow and in Peking to demonstrate the solidarity of Soviet and Chinese support for Castro and his revolution.

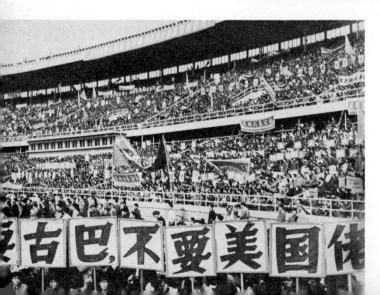

been large or significant. The Kremlin did not even enter the foreign aid field in any large way until 1954 or 1955. Since that time, Soviet aid to many nations has, however, been substantial and effective.

**Focus.** Soviet foreign trade has long been focused on strategic materials. The Soviets have concentrated on the acquisition of those items, particularly military, which the Soviet economy lacks or cannot produce in sufficient quantity or quality. That is why the West has been forced to construct a strategic embargo list which prohibits the sale to the Soviet Union of certain strategic and military items. Still, the Soviets have been able to buy jet engines from Britian, machine tools and equipment from us, and other essential items from Western Europe.

As already pointed out, Soviet aid is of recent vintage and smaller in scope than this country's. It is chiefly focused on projects with propaganda value and political implications — a hospital in Indonesia, a steel mill in India, paved streets for Kabul, the capital of Afghanistan.

Thus, we may summarize these differences by saying: (1) the United States aids more nations than the Soviet Union, and the aid is of a considerably larger magnitude, (2) our country provides a much wider variety of aid to meet a given nation's basic needs, and (3) our aid to underdeveloped areas has been concentrated on agriculture, education, health, and industry, probably in that order, while the Kremlin has sought to reap the political advantage that comes from more flashy, if less basic, projects.

## The Moscow-Peking Axis

### 86. *Is a split between Moscow and Peking likely?*

As has been suggested ("What do the Chinese think of the Russians?" p. 154), Red China's relations with the Soviet Union have rarely been ideal from the Communist point of view. The Chinese Communists obviously are dependent on the Soviet Union in the military and economic fields. It is equally apparent that the Soviet Union finds it convenient — if sometimes terrify-

ing — to have an Asian "ally" to harangue the United States and
to fight the Communist battles in the East. The Chinese Communists want atomic weapons. The Kremlin is reluctant to give
them to its unpredictable and "inscrutable" Oriental ally (see
p. 149). The Chinese Communists want to take Formosa. The
Kremlin has apparently counseled caution lest the Chinese Communists get themselves into a war with the United States which
might see the Soviets caught in the middle. Peking finds fault
with Khrushchev's policy of coexistence. Years ago Khrushchev
suggested that Mao's pet project, the commune system in China,
was not a good idea. Such symptoms as these raise questions as
to the permanence of the Sino-Soviet alliance.

At the 22nd Congress of the Communist Party of the Soviet
Union, held in Moscow in the fall of 1961, a serious rift developed between Khrushchev and Mao over policy towards the
Communist leadership in Albania. There have thus been many
points of friction between the two centers of Communism. Is a
split between Moscow and Peking imminent?

To answer this complicated question as specifically and as
authoritatively as possible, let us get the views of several experts
on the Soviet Union and Communist China.

Dr. Hugh Seton-Watson, professor of Russian history at the
University of London, has written several books on the Communist empire which are standard works in the field. What do you
think, Dr. Seton-Watson?

". . . If there is a showdown now, the Chinese will accept the
Russian demands. But they won't accept them in their hearts.
They'll be looking out for opportunities to create trouble later.

"One very obvious way they can and will try is by intriguing
inside the Soviet Union — in particular, inside the Soviet Communist Party leadership. If and when Khrushchev shows signs
of getting old and tired, and the struggle for succession grows
acute, the Chinese will put in their oar."[3]

Doak Barnett is a specialist on China. He was born in China
and is the author of *Communist China and Asia: Challenge to
American Policy*. He is presently lecturing at Columbia University. What is your view, Mr. Barnett?

"Even though China has had to pay its own way, Soviet as-

[3] "Will Russia and Red China Break?", Copyrighted interview in *U.S. News
and World Report*, Vol. XLIX, No. 17 (October 24, 1960), pages 72–77.

sistance has been absolutely essential up to this point, and I think the consequences would be extremely serious if there were a real rupture in economic relations between the Soviet Union and Communist China. [The Chinese] are still highly dependent on access to outside sources of capital goods. . . . Despite their difference, Peiping and Moscow are still bound together by many strong ties and common interests which are likely to hold them together for a long time."[4]

Dr. Robert C. North, associate professor of political science at Stanford University, is author of *Moscow and the Chinese Communists* and other important books on Russia and China. What is the nature of the conflict between Moscow and Peiping, Dr. North?

"It seems to me there are some fundamental dynamics behind this sort of conflict. One of the most important, I think, is Chinese nationalism.

"Now, by that I mean the whole drive on the part of the Chinese over a long period of time to reassert their national power and integrity. As a matter of fact, until the beginning of the nineteenth century, China saw itself as really the only great power on earth — the only really civilized nation, the only culture that really mattered in the whole of this world. And then in the course of the next 100 years after about 1839, the Chinese saw themselves degraded in the eyes of the world and in their own eyes. It seems to me that the resentments and frustrations of those 100 years have been in a sense stored up —"

Let us ask you one more question, Dr. North: "What about the military advantages of the alliance from the Soviet point of view?"

"It's an enormous advantage to the Soviet Union to have a frontier held by a Communist ally. Any kind of rupture which would in any sense damage the integrity of this long frontier would certainly work to the disadvantage of the Soviet Union and Khrushchev's leadership.

"Aside from this, of course, there are all kinds of prestige and psychological factors. If China and the Soviet Union split apart in a final fashion, I suppose the world Communist movement would be in a [perilous] state indeed."[5]

Dr. Philip E. Mosely is Director of Research of the Council on

4 *Ibid.*
5 *Ibid.*

Foreign Relations, New York City. He was formerly Director of the Russian Institute at Columbia University. Dr. Mosely, what about it? Is a split between Moscow and Peking imminent?

". . . Those who believe that the Moscow and Peking centers can be separated from each other must, it would seem, prove either that their goals are incompatible or that each of the two centers may judge itself better able, in separation or even in conflict with the other, to achieve its own goals. . . ."[6]

## 87. Does Peking's foreign policy differ from Moscow's foreign policy?

The Soviet Union has opposed the imperialism of other countries for reasons of political theory. Communist China is anti imperialist for these same reasons, but also perhaps equally in response to an anti-foreign sentiment which is more deep-rooted than in Russia. It derives in part from China's experience as a "semi-colonial" country, but there are deep cultural and racial elements also involved.

China has regarded itself proudly throughout history as the "middle kingdom" — that nation at the center of the universe. We should remember that twice before in history, Peking ha been the seat of an extensive empire encompassing most of Asia during the Han dynasty (202 B.C.–220 A.D.) and during the T'ang period (618–907 A.D.). One of the Chinese Communist goals i clearly to rebuild the glories and powers of the past. China therefore, has an imperialism of its own, at least in part a carry over from China's eminent past. While tsarist Russia's history too produced more than its share of imperialism and empire building, this tradition does not appear to be as important motivating force in the Soviet case.

Then, too, China's foreign policy under Communist rule ha tended to be less stable than Moscow's for the same period: 1949 53 — belligerency (the Korean war, take-over of Tibet); 1954–5 — "Panch Shila" (the five principles of peace, including peacefu coexistence); 1958–60 — "inevitability of war" and adventurism

[6] Philip E. Mosely, "The Moscow-Peking Axis in World Politics" in How ard Boorman et al., *Moscow-Peking Axis: Strengths and Strains* (Harpe and Brothers, New York, 1957), p. 201.

(including an invasion of the Indian border region); 1961 — back to declarations of concern for peaceful coexistence and economic co-operation. The Soviet Union, as we have seen, also employs a zig-zag Leninist line which, depending on the strategy of the period, has ranged from a tough warlike attitude to friendly coexistence. China's shifts, however, have been more pronounced, with a pervading spirit of instability and immaturity. This situation is thought to be of some concern to the Kremlin. What will the Chinese do next? (See also pp. 183–185 and 191–192.)

Doak Barnett sums up the challenge of Chinese Communist foreign policy when he writes:

> Since 1949 the clashes of Chinese Communist and American interests all along China's periphery have been bitter and violent. For almost half of the past decade, in fact, the United States and Communist China have been either engaged in military struggle or poised on the brink of conflict. The war in Korea from 1950 to 1953, and subsequent crises over Indo-China and the offshore islands, have intensified the deep hostility and suspicion with which the two nations view each other.[7]

Thus, in a sense, Peking's foreign policy is more "active" than Moscow's, equally difficult, and perhaps more dangerous. Our forces have already engaged the Chinese Communist enemy in Asia. Given Chinese Communist arrogance, fanatical zeal, and ruthlessness, the prospects for genuine co-operation and settlement of differences between the "New China" and the Free World do not appear bright.

## Critical Issues and Areas

### 88. *What is the background of the Berlin crisis?*

For the third time in 13 years, the Soviets in 1961 launched a major threat to the freedom of West Berlin. What is the background of the Berlin crisis? How did we get involved in the situation in the first place? What is our policy?

[7] A. Doak Barnett, *Communist China and Asia: A Challenge to American Policy,* (Harper, for the Council on Foreign Relations, 1960), pp. 5–6.

**The background.** The clearest presentation of the background
of the Berlin crisis is the Department of State publication, *Background: Berlin — 1961,* which says in part:

Berlin lies more than 100 miles behind the Iron Curtain within the
Soviet-occupied zone of Germany. It is not, however, part of that
zone. It is a separate political entity for which the four major allies
of the war against Nazi tyranny are jointly responsible. Its special
status stems from the fact that it was the capital not only of Hitler's
Third Reich but of the German nation formed in the latter half of
the 19th century. In essence, the four major allies agreed to hold
Berlin, as the traditional capital, in trust for a democratic and united
Germany.

The Federal Republic of Germany, comprising the former occupa
tion zones of the Western Allies, is a democratic state. Its 53 million
people enjoy self-determination at all levels. Through their freely
elected Federal Government, they have taken their place in the
community of free nations.

By contrast, the 16 million inhabitants of the eastern zone are
ruled by the Soviet Union through its Communist creature, the East
German regime which calls itself the "German Democratic Repub
lic." *That regime is neither democratic nor a republic.* It was not
chosen by the people it controls and has never been freely endorsed
by them. It was imposed by duress and is maintained by all the
oppressive apparatus of a police state backed by the military force
of the Soviet Union.

Berlin contains four sectors. The 2,250,000 inhabitants of its
three western sectors live under a municipal government which they
have freely chosen. The eastern sector has some 1,100,000 inhabit
ants. In 1948, in violation of their commitments, the Soviets sepa
rated it from the rest of the city. Subsequently, in further violation
of their commitments, they permitted their German agents to declare
it the capital of the East German regime. Thus the people of East
Berlin, like those of the eastern zone of Germany, are ruled by a
regime they did not chose.

*The government of West Berlin is the only freely elected govern
ment behind either the Iron or the Bamboo Curtains.* Repeatedly
the Soviets and their German agents have sought to blot out this
island of freedom. Their methods have ranged from the brazen to
the devious, but their purpose has always been clear.

Every President of the United States since the Second World War
has deemed the defense of Free Berlin critical to the security of the
United States and of the entire free world. The United Kingdom

France, and the United States stand pledged to defend West Berlin by whatever means may be necessary. All the members of the North Atlantic Treaty Organization stand pledged to support them in discharging that obligation.[9]

**The problem.** The problem may be summarized very simply: The Kremlin is determined to force the West out of the city Khrushchev has characterized as a "cancerous tumor," a "bone stuck in our throats." Khrushchev has publicly declared his resolve to "eradicate this splinter from the heart of Europe." Stalin initiated that policy. In the summer of 1948, the Communists severed all land and water routes between Berlin and the western zones of Germany to force the Western Allies out of Berlin and starve the people of the city into the Communist fold.

The Western Allies' response was a massive airlift. For the next year every pound of food and coal, and all else necessary to keep alive the people of West Berlin and supply the forces of the Western Allies in Berlin, was transported by air. In a total of 277,728 flights, American, British, and French airmen brought in 2,323,301 tons of food and supplies. At the peak of the airlift, planes were landing in West Berlin at the rate of one every 45 seconds.

Finally, the Communists conceded defeat and re-opened the overland routes. They have since used every means, legal, economic, and military to attempt to force the Western Allies out of Berlin. To seal off the Communist part of the city — to keep Eastern Europeans from escaping to the West through the Berlin "escape hatch," the Communists in the fall of 1961 began building their infamous wall. Khrushchev insists the West must go, that he will soon turn over authority for Berlin to the East German Communist regime. The Western Allies insist on our legal rights to stay.

**United States policy statements.** Three recent Presidents have clearly stated our Berlin policy. Here are their statements:

*President Harry S. Truman:* "I made the decision ten days ago to stay in Berlin. . . . I insist we will stay in Berlin — come what may."[10]

[9] Department of State Publication 7257, European and British Commonwealth Series #64, Released August, 1961, pages 1–2.
[10] From his diary, July 19, 1948.

*President Dwight D. Eisenhower:* "We have no intention of forgetting our rights or of deserting a free people. Soviet rulers should remember that free men have, before this, died for so-called 'scraps of paper' which represented duty and honor and freedom. . . . We cannot try to purchase peace by forsaking two million free people of Berlin. . . . We will not retreat one inch from our duty."[11]

*President John F. Kennedy:* "The world must know that we will fight for Berlin. We will never permit that city to fall under Communist influence. We are defending the freedom of Paris and New York when we stand up for freedom in Berlin."[12]

## 89. *Will Africa go Communist?*

Serious Russian interest in Africa goes back a hundred years to the days of the tsars. The first Russian contacts with Africa were in the mid-15th century, when the wanderings of a holy monk Varsonofii, took him to the city of Jerusalem and on to Egypt. A host of Russian "Orientalists" — geographers, botanists, engineers zoologists, and linguists — visited Africa during the eighteenth and nineteenth centuries.

The Soviets have made some effort to sustain this tradition, but more urgent problems and more attractive areas have tended to keep Soviet African studies (like African studies in America) the preoccupation of a few dedicated souls. It is, in fact, only within the past decade that the Kremlin has begun to concentrate it ideological, political, and economic sights on Africa.

Since Khrushchev came to power in 1955, the Soviets have stepped up their African campaign in two areas: trade and education. The economic penetration of Africa poses a serious threat to the Free World (see section on trade and aid as economic weapons, p. 178). The Soviets, well aware of the importance of education to newly emancipated peoples, have recently been bringing hundreds of Africans to Moscow for study. This effort, in many instances, has backfired. (See the section on racial discrimination in the USSR, p. 117.)

In 1960, the Soviets opened a new Institute on Africa with four

11 Radio-television report to the American people, March 16, 1959.
12 Statement for special issue of *Berliner Illustrirte*, 1961.

departments: (1) history, (2) art, literature, and culture, (3) linguistics, and (4) current events. This Institute is training a Soviet "Peace Corps" for Africa. Since that time, the Kremlin has intensified its drive to capture Africa.

Writing on the subject, "Will Africa Go Communist?", Stewart Alsop says: "The Communist bloc is now making a determined, carefully-planned play for power throughout Africa. The only question is whether we should let the Communists win the African cold war by default or whether we should try seriously to meet the Communist challenge in Africa."

Speaking first of the dangerous, recent Communist penetration of the Congo, Mr. Alsop concludes:

> Mind you, everything is not going to be jim-dandy in the Congo, or elsewhere in Africa — not in our lifetimes. All Soviet and Communist influence cannot possibly be excluded from the Congo. But we can prevent the establishment in the Congo of a totally disciplined, unitary, Communist satellite state, which could only come into being as a result of civil war and which would be like a cancer in Africa's belly.
>
> By the same token, Soviet-Communist influence is now paramount in . . . Ghana, Guinea and Mali. We cannot hope to prevent such Communist infections from developing from time to time — and indeed, . . . we must be prepared sometimes to let them develop, rather than to submit to blackmail. But we and our European allies do have the means — military, political, and economic — to prevent the Soviet bloc from becoming the dominant power throughout . . . Africa. That is what we can do, and that is what we must do.[13]

## 90. How serious is the Communist threat to Southeast Asia?

One of the constant crisis areas subject to intensive and increasing Communist pressure is Southeast Asia. Southeast Asia includes six divisions: Indochina (divided into Communist North and free South Viet Nam, Laos, and Cambodia), Thailand (or Siam), Burma, Malaya, Indonesia, and the Philippines.

For several reasons the region remains highly vulnerable to Communist penetration and subversion. First, it is an area of a

[13] *The Saturday Evening Post,* Vol. 234, No. 7 (February 18, 1961), pp. 13–15 ff. © 1961 by the Curtis Publishing Company.

great many different racial and ethnic groups, who often fight among themselves. These groups include sizable overseas-Chinese populations — potential fifth columns — in almost every nation of Southeast Asia (one-half of the population of Malaya, for example, is of Chinese racial background). Secondly, this is a region of extremes of poverty and of riches — with the vast majority of the people living under very unsatisfactory economic conditions. The atmosphere is one of desire for change. Thirdly, illiteracy is widespread. Few people know the facts on Communism or democracy. This makes the job of the Communist propagandist easier. Fourthly, the region suffers from chronic political instability. Very often a government has its hands full simply trying to maintain itself in power, especially since its enemies very often have their own private armies. Finally, Southeast Asia is a region where the memories of French, Dutch, and British colonialism are still fresh. For that reason the Communists have a huge propaganda advantage over the West.

As we know, the Communists are experts at fishing in troubled waters. Since the Communists came to power in Peking, the area of Southeast Asia has been right under their guns — political, economic, and military.

Through extensive propaganda and infiltration, and by using economic warfare and military invasion, the Chinese Communists have already brought North Viet Nam into the Communist camp. There have been several crises in Laos, one so serious that our President was forced to appear on television to explain the situation to the American people. Communist pressure is mounting against the South Viet Nam regime backed by this country. The Communist threat to Southeast Asia is serious; and it is likely to get worse before it gets better. The Chinese Communists seem determined to re-establish the powerful Chinese empire of the past. In this effort the Chinese are using the weapons of both traditional military force *and* Communist ideology.

## 91. *Are such "neutrals" as India and Indonesia really neutral?*

The so-called neutrals themselves are the first to say that they are *not* neutral. Both Premier Nehru, spokesman for India and often for the neutralist bloc, and Prime Minister Sukarno of Indonesia prefer to think of themselves as "uncommitted." The term "positive neutralism" has also been applied to their attitudes and policies, but this term confuses as much as it clarifies.

The main reason for neutralism — whether right or wrong — is a desire on the part of the "neutrals" not to be involved in the world struggle. The stand our government has taken on neutralism is that the United States is quite prepared to live in peace and amity with self-proclaimed neutrals. Quite probably this country is in a much better position to live with neutralism than is the Soviet Union.

How does neutralism relate to the problem of international relations in an era of cold and sometimes hot, little wars?

Two points are stressed by the neutralists: One is the climate of war theory, that military preparations and propaganda only contribute to the climate of war; the other is the importance of "non-alignment," of not being committed to either of the great power blocs. India and Indonesia have been insistent on both scores. Quite a different view of the problem is held by the NATO and SEATO countries. These nations stress the need for collective security.

This country believes that the problem is one of checking Soviet power and the Communist intention to destroy the West. The neutralists talk of tensions created by military blocs and defense pacts, which in the Western view are symptoms or consequences rather than the disease itself. So the neutralists, if the Western evaluation is correct, make the mistake of concentrating on the symptoms. But any doctor knows that symptoms are important only as a clue to the disease. We insist that the disease is aggressive World Communism backed by Soviet power and pushed by ruthless leaders.

Strict adherence to non-alignment, to the so-called positive neutralism, may be waning as the cold, unpleasant realities of Soviet power and Chinese Communist aggressiveness become unmistakably clear. Soviet suppression of the Hungarian freedom fighters, Chinese Communist take-over in Tibet, Chinese Communist invasion of Indian territory, the wall in Berlin, and the Kremlin's disregard of world opinion in going ahead with testing of giant nuclear weapons — are making it increasingly difficult for the neutrals to retain a neutral position.

## 92. *How strong is Communism in Latin America?*

The Communist offensive in Latin America is described in two publications of the Department of State. A brief excerpt from each will make clear the nature and scope of the Communist threat to Latin America.

Reporting in 1960 before the Subcommittee on Inter-American Affairs of the House Foreign Affairs Committee, R. R. Rubottom, then Assistant Secretary for Inter-American Affairs, defined the problem as follows:

. . . In Latin America it is estimated that there are 250,000 card-carrying Communists. Although it is sometimes said that this is a small portion of the population, we must bear in mind that this represents at least 20 times as many Communists as there are in the United States, which has a population approximately equal to that of Latin America. The leaders of these Communists have been fully trained behind the Iron Curtain and have demonstrated extraordinary skill in establishing Communist-front groups and in infiltrating into student, labor, and other groups. It has been estimated that it would take $100 million to finance a propaganda effort of the scope which the Communists are carrying out in Latin America today. This propaganda offensive includes not only the huge amounts of Communist propaganda which are being published and disseminated within Latin America but also large amounts of propaganda imported from the Communist bloc and distributed through bloc missions in the area. Communist-bloc radio broadcasts to Latin America extensively, and last year the Spanish-language broadcasts of Radio Peking were increased to the point that they are now second only to the worldwide English-language broadcasts.

All of these assets are now concentrated on supporting and spreading the Castro kind of revolution throughout Latin America. To this extent the Communists have moved away from the policy of collaborating with other non-Communist groups and are now emphasizing to a greater extent than hitherto the revolutionary approach which constitutes a direct threat to the other Latin American governments. Khrushchev has in speeches made it abundantly clear that he fully supports the Cuban revolution. He first made a reference to it in a speech before the Indian Parliament during his trip to that country earlier this year and has favorably referred to it on several occasions in addition to the endorsement which he gave a his Paris news conference. Communist theoretical publications in Peking, as well as Moscow, have also endorsed the Cuban revolution. It is noteworthy in this respect that the Cuban revolution is singled out while there no longer are favorable references to the other national movements of Asia and Africa which the Soviets formerly warmly endorsed. The Cuban revolution, in short, represents the pattern of revolution which the Communists would like to see spread throughout the underdeveloped world to replace national independence and strengthening of individual political and economic freedom.[14]

An even more recent statement on the Communist threat to Latin America is contained in the State Department's 1961 report on Cuba. In a section entitled, "The Assault on the Hemisphere," the report asserts:

. . . Under Castro, Cuba has already become a base and staging area for revolutionary activity throughout the continent. In prosecuting the war against the hemisphere, Cuban embassies in Latin American countries work in close collaboration with Iron Curtain diplomatic missions and with the Soviet intelligence services. In addition, Cuban expressions of fealty to the Communist world have provided the Soviet Government a long-sought pretext for threats of direct interventions of its own in the Western Hemisphere. "We shall do everything to support Cuba in her struggle," Prime Minister Khrushchev said on July 9, 1960, ". . . Speaking figuratively, in case of necessity, Soviet artillerymen can support with rocket fire the Cuban people if aggressive forces in the Pentagon dare to start intervention against Cuba."[15]

A few pages later the same report concludes:

Cuban interventionism has taken a variety of forms. During 1959 the Castro government aided or supported armed invasions of Panama, Nicaragua, the Dominican Republic, and Haiti. These projects all failed and all invited action by the Organization of American States. In consequence, after 1959 the Castro regime began increasingly to resort to indirect methods. The present strategy of *Fidelismo* is to provoke revolutionary situations in other republics through the indoctrination of selected individuals from other countries, through

[14] *Department of State Bulletin*, Vol. XLIII, No. 1098 (July 11, 1960), p. 63.
[15] Inter-American Series, No. 66 (released April, 1961), pp. 25–26.

assistance to revolutionary exiles, through incitement to mass agitation, and through the political and propaganda operations of Cuban embassies. Cuban diplomats have encouraged local opposition groups, harangued political rallies, distributed inflammatory propaganda, and indulged in a multitude of political assignments beyond the usual call of diplomatic duty. Papers seized in a raid on the Cuban Embassy in Lima in November 1960 display, for example the extent and variety of clandestine *Fidelista* activities within Peru Documents made public by the Government of El Salvador on March 12, 1961, appear to establish that large sums of money have been coming into El Salvador through the Cuban Embassy for the purpose of financing pro-Communist student groups plotting the overthrow of the government. The regime is now completing construction of a 100,000-watt radio transmitter to facilitate its propaganda assault on the hemisphere.

Most instances of serious civil disturbance in Latin America in recent months exhibit Cuban influence, if not direct intervention At the time of the November riots in Venezuela, the government announced the discovery of high-powered transmitting and receiving sets in the possession of Cubans in Caracas. In the following weeks about 50 Cubans were expelled from the country. Similar patterns appear to have existed in troubles in El Salvador, Nicaragua, Panama, Colombia, Bolivia, and Paraguay.

Other reports indicate increased Chinese Communist activity throughout Latin America. We may conclude that the Communist threat to Latin America is serious, and that it is likely to become worse before it gets better.

# 8 Communism in the United States

## Origin and Background

### 93. How did Communism get its start in the United States?

The major spur to the development of Communism in the United States, as in many other nations, was the success of the Communist Revolution in Russia in November, 1917. The ability of the Communist Party in Russia to seize the reins of government, and the belief that similar events might occur in other eastern and central European nations, appear to have convinced the most radical factions of existing socialist movements that the Communist philosophy was the surest and quickest way to power.

In the United States this communization of left-wing socialists came about in August of 1919 in Chicago, Illinois. Prominent among the founders were men such as Benjamin Gitlow, John Reed, Charles Ruthenberg, and Alfred Wagenknecht, whose names were to become legend in the history of the Party. At the outset, however, the Communist movement displayed the tendency toward division which is so typical of ideologically-oriented Marxist movements. In 1919 two separate parties proclaimed themselves the true representatives of the Communist idea, and waged a bitter oratorical struggle both publicly and privately. These were the Communist Labor Party and the Communist Party. Both were largely rather loose and undisciplined organizations of foreign-born radicals. Faced with the possibility of federal prosecution, both parties soon went underground, and continued their bitter factional struggles.

The Russian-controlled Comintern or Third Communist International, however, stepped quickly into the picture, strongly recommending that the two parties unify; and sent a Comintern representative to aid and advise a unity convention which was held in May of 1920. Although unity did not come immediately, by May of 1921 outward unity was achieved, and the Communist Party of the United States was admitted to membership in the Comintern.

Since membership in the Comintern meant adherence to the Twenty-one Conditions of iron discipline adopted by the organization's Second Congress in 1920, the Communist Party of the United States became increasingly dominated from Moscow (see pp. 33–34 on the Twenty-one Conditions). Not only were American Communist leaders trained in the noted Lenin School in Moscow, but increasing use was made of Comintern representatives to insure party discipline.

From these early days the goal of the Party has been the creation of a disciplined party, and has been characterized by complete subservience to the Russian Party.

## 94. What is the history of the Communist Party in the United States?

Once under the domination of the Comintern and Moscow-trained leaders, the Communist Party in the United States embarked on a history of subservience to the policies dictated by the Communist Party of the Soviet Union.

Under instructions from Moscow, the American Communists formed in 1921 an organization for open political action, while still maintaining their underground apparatus. This was called the Workers Party of America. The Party's first major objective was the penetration of the American trade unions, but in the early years of the Party's history, its propaganda was of such an openly violent and revolutionary nature that little success was encountered in subverting union leadership. The openly violent objectives of the Party, however, soon gave way to more subtle tactics, which enabled it to gain more substantial support. In the elections of 1928, for instance, the Workers Party of America was able to garner approximately 50,000 votes for its Presidential candidate, William Z. Foster.

It should not be concluded, however, that the Party was progressing during the 1920's without ideological splits and struggles. In 1923, for instance, there was a serious left-right struggle which shook the Party's unity. Even more serious was the 1928–29 Party purge ordered by Moscow to eliminate the element which might still adhere to the ideas of Leon Trotsky, as opposed to those of Stalin. This conflict lead to the formation of a splinter party preaching "Trotskyism" and called the Socialist Workers Party.

The clear indication of Moscow dominance exemplified by the Trotskyist purge in the late 1920's, however, does not stand alone. Throughout the 1930's the Communist Party of the United States indicated its subservience to the Soviet Union by strongly supporting the Loyalist cause in the Spanish Civil War, by following the Russian line to the letter when Stalin negotiated a Non-Aggression Pact with Hitler's Germany in 1939, by urging neutrality for the United States while that Pact was in force, and by then doing an abrupt about-face on the issue when the Soviet Union was attacked by Nazi Germany.

During the period of the Second World War, when the United States and the Soviet Union found themselves allies, the latter dissolved the Comintern as a gesture of friendship to the West. The Communist Party of the United States also was formally dissolved. At that time, under the leadership of Earl Browder, the Party called itself the Communist Political Association.

With the close of the war the need to cooperate with the West came to an end. There was no longer any compelling reason to maintain the fiction of "lovable Communism." The Party, once again under the leadership of William Z. Foster, changed its position and policies. "Browderism" (co-operation with capitalism) became a serious Communist crime, and the Party again became a disciplined and cohesive organization.

While the Party in the United States still attempts to maintain the fiction of independence, its policies and reactions (such as ignoring the Hungarian Revolution) strongly indicate that its true leadership is not American.

## Nature of the Communist Party in the United States and Its Front Organizations

**95.** *How does the Communist Party differ from the traditional American political party?*

The Communist Party (CPUSA) differs from, let us say, the Democratic Party or the Republican Party in the United States in at least five fundamental ways:

**1. Ideologically** — All Party members are *required* to subscribe to a specific ideology called Marxism-Leninism. Deviation, however slight, from the official Party line is not tolerated. Total dedication and absolute obedience are demanded of each and every member. While we may say that both the Republican and Democratic parties have philosophies of government, neither has an absolute ideology to which all members must subscribe without question.

**2. Organizationally** — The Communist Party is a tightly organized structure like a pyramid with every subordinate body directly responsible to the next higher echelon. In this sense, it resembles an army: the Party Secretary General is the commanding general; regional district chairmen are like major generals in charge of divisions; state chairmen are colonels commanding regiments; the Communist Party cells are the companies which fight the Party's battles in factories, schools, government offices, and in our armed forces. No such formal, strict organization is maintained by our traditional political parties.

**3. In terms of responsibilities of members** — To be a member of the Republican or the Democratic Party is one thing; to be a member of the Communist Party is quite another. Most Republicans and Democrats have never attended a meeting of their Party and most have not contributed a cent to the Party's campaign. Members of the CPUSA are *required* to attend Party meetings regularly, are *required* to pay monthly dues to support the Party, and are, like doctors, on duty twenty-four hours a day.

**4. With respect to goals and methods** — The Communist Party does not respect God, private property, liberty, or law. Nor does it respect our Constitution or any of the other great traditions of the United States. With the Communist Party, any strategy — legal or illegal, fair or foul — if it serves the ends of World Communism, is perfectly all right. In a very real sense, the Communist Party is un-American.

**5. On the matter of location of final authority** — No one man has absolute control over the traditional American political party. The authority rests with American political leaders and with the party's National Committee. Final authority and control in the case of the CPUSA comes from outside the United States. It is in the hands of individuals who are not even Americans — final authority rests with the Kremlin. This is why the United States Supreme Court ruled that members of the Communist Party of the United States must register with the Department of Justice as agents of a foreign power.

**96.** *Is it possible to be a good Communist and a loyal United States citizen at the same time?*

The Communist creed is incompatible with the fundamentals of our American heritage. The Communist Party cannot be regarded as a political party in the usually accepted sense of the term. Membership in the Party requires allegiance to an authority superior to one's own country. Absolute discipline and complete obedience to Party decisions and directives are required of all Communist Party members. Since the Communist Party of the United States regards itself as part of the World Communist movement, and because from the beginning it has been guided from Moscow, an American Communist is working for the Kremlin *against his own government*.

Communists stand for the overthrow of the United States Government and for the destruction of the American way of life. They call for the replacement of our constitutional, democratic system by a Communist regime and a planned society patterned after that in the Soviet Union.

As we have seen, Communists do not believe in God, the Constitution, duly elected government, individual rights and freedom, private ownership, or law. Purges, mass murder, and slave labor are sanctioned by the Communist Party *if they serve the ends of Communism.*

It is, therefore, quite obviously not possible to be, at the same time, a loyal citizen of this country and a Communist.

## 97. *What is a Communist front organization, and how can it be identified?*

The word "front" is well known to readers of detective stories or watchers of television. A store somewhere on Main Street, U.S.A. may appear to be a legitimate jewelry store. Actually, the display of goods for sale in the front part of the store is only a "front" for the gambling in the back room. A Communist front operates in much the same way.

A Communist front organization is an organization that conceals its real purpose and does not acknowledge its ties with the Communist Party. Its leaders may, in fact, be actually Party members or — as is more often the case — fellow-travelers. By posing as a legitimate, patriotic American organization, the Communist front organization can often gain support and accomplish Communist objectives which could not be attained if its Communist connections were generally known. The "front" fools the innocent public.

To help Americans distinguish between sincere civic or patriotic organizations dedicated to peace and democracy and phony Communist front organizations dedicated to destroying our country, the Justice Department publishes an official list of known subversive organizations.

*The Guide to Subversive Organizations and Publications* prepared by the Un-American Activities Committee of the United States House of Representatives lists thirteen points for the "guidance of the American people in detecting Communist front organizations." These points are:

1. Does the organization have Communist Party members or those trusted by the Communist Party, in its posts of real power — on its executive board, as secretary, organizer, educational director, editor, office staff?
2. Are meetings of the organization addressed by Communists or their trusted agents? Does its publication include articles by such persons?
3. Does the organization follow the Communist Party line?
4. Does the organization co-operate with campaigns, activities, publications, of the Communist Party or other front organizations?
5. Is the address of the organization in the same building with other front organizations or within the . . . vicinity?
6. Does the organization co-operate with Communist-controlled unions?
7. Does the organization's official publication reflect the line of the Communist Party, publish articles by pro-Communists, advertise Communist activities, or those of other front organizations or of Communist vacation resorts?
8. Are questions injected into meetings or in official publications, which have more to do with the current policy of the Communist Party, than with the professed purposes of the organization?
9. Are funds kicked back directly or indirectly to the Communist Party or to other front organizations?
10. Is printing done at a Communist printing house?
11. Does the organization use entertainers associated with pro-Communist organizations or entertainments?
12. Does the organization receive favorable publicity in the Communist press?
13. Is the organization uniformly loyal to the Soviet Union?[1]

## 98. *How do the Communists work?*

In numerous books, former Communists, FBI agents, and others have made clear the way Communists in the United States work to undermine our freedoms and to subvert our society. Perhaps the most meaningful, brief treatment of the subject is this passage by J. Edgar Hoover:[2]

---

[1] House Un-American Activities Committee, January 2, 1957, p. ix.
[2] From *Masters of Deceit* by J. Edgar Hoover (pp. 193–195). Copyright © 1958 by J. Edgar Hoover. Reprinted by permission of Holt, Rinehart and Winston, Inc.

Communists employ various tactics in devising methods to inject themselves into various phases of American life. Their obligation to defend the interests of the Soviet Union dictates their tactics in seeking to obstruct and undermine public confidence in our foreign policy. Thus, seizing upon the inherent desire of all Americans to reduce taxes, the *Daily Worker* editorializes that foreign aid should be curtailed and billions should not be taken "out of our pockets for a new phony 'emergency'. . . . The huge seventy-billion a year 'defense' budget is rushing America to inflation, and economic crisis." Actually, Communists would like to develop an economic crisis.

Then they urge the development of a peacetime economy by advocating trade between the United States and Russia because Russia would benefit. *Political Affairs* thus urges, "The only remaining untapped market for U.S. goods is the Soviet Union, China and the Peoples' Democracies, in which the threat of crises of overproduction has been removed forever . . ."

In seeking to curry favor with labor, Communists employ tactics of calling for immediate demands such as higher wages, a shorter work week, increased vacations. . . To that end a Communist labor tactician calls for putting ". . . ideological differences aside in order to work together in behalf of a *single immediate objective* or a *number of immediate objectives* . . . the unions must work together . . ."

The immediate demand tactics are also employed by the Communists to find favor with Negroes by urging the abolition of "Jim Crow Laws," "full representation," and "the fight for Negro rights." The controversy on integration has given the Communists a field day.

They also have a program ". . . to stimulate broad united-front actions in the rural communities in defense of the economic interests of the farming masses"; "to weld youth unity"; and to "work still harder" for mothers.

A primary tactic of the Communist Party is to preserve the legal status of the Party. Thus, any organization which has the duty to investigate or expose Communist activity is singled out for attack. For years the Party has campaigned against the House Committee on Un-American Activities, the Senate Internal Security Sub-Committee, and the Senate Investigating Committee. The Department of Justice and the FBI have not been spared, and we have come to judge our effectiveness by the intensity of Communist attacks.

The Red Fascists have long followed the practice of making full use of democratic liberties: elections, lawful agitation and propaganda, and free speech, press, and assembly. Their basic premise: Reap every advantage possible. However, if it will help, don't hesitate to use illegal methods, such as underground operations, terrorism, espionage, sabotage, lying, cheating. "We have never rejected terror on principle, nor can we do so. Terror is a form of military operation that may be usefully applied . . ." wrote Lenin. Morality is strictly a bourgeois device. To the Communists everything that promotes the revolution is moral, legal, and beautiful.

## Scope and Extent of Threat to the United States

**99.** *Is Communism a growing threat to our country?*

Two distinctions must be kept in mind at all times when we talk about the Communist threat to the United States. The first is the distinction between the internal and the external threat, though they are, of course, related. The second is the difference between numerical strength and real strength or capabilities.

The *external* threat to the United States and to the Free World, represented by World Communism — ideology and power — directed from Moscow and Peking, is serious, immediate, and growing.

Measured numerically, in terms of Party membership, the Communist threat *within* the United States is not great. According to the most recent information provided by an authoritative source, there are today only about 10,000 Communist Party members in the entire United States. Further, these members are now required by law to register as agents of a foreign government (see p. 209). Equally important, there is an increasing awareness on the part of the average American that Communism and Communists are dedicated to the destruction of our democratic way of life. This means that there is little danger that the Communists can take over our country — so long as we remain strong, alert, and dedicated to the principles of freedom within the law.

The threat to United States security from Communists in our own country is, nevertheless, serious in three respects.

**The threat of espionage.** An FBI report of May, 1960, *Exposé of Soviet Espionage*,[3] has this to say:

[3] 86th Congress; Senate Document No. 114, p. 1.

Recent Soviet propaganda has denounced the United States for aerial reconnaissance of the Soviet Union in terms designed to convince the world that the USSR would not stoop to espionage. In discussing this subject and the reception which President Eisenhower might expect on his visit to Russia, Premier Khrushchev was quoted in the newspapers on May 11, 1960, as wondering what would have been the reaction of the American people if the Russians had sent a plane over the United States on the eve of his visit to this country.

The facts are that at the very time Premier Khrushchev was advancing to the podium to speak before the United Nations General Assembly on September 18, 1959, two Soviet espionage agents were cautiously surveying a street corner in Springfield, Massachusetts, in preparation for a clandestine meeting with an American whom they were attempting to subvert. At the very time that Khrushchev was declaring that a means must be found to stop mankind from backsliding into an abyss of war, Vadim A. Kirilyuk, Soviet employee of the United Nations, was attempting to induce this American to furnish information regarding United States cryptographic machines and to secure employment in a vital United States Government agency where he could obtain classified information for the Russians. While this meeting was taking place Kirilyuk and the American were under observation by Leonid A. Kovalev, another Soviet employee of the United Nations who was conducting a counter-surveillance. Unknown to the Russians, however, this meeting was also being observed by Special Agents of the FBI who obtained photographs of the Russians.

Not only did these Russians stoop to spying, but they callously abused their status as guests of this country to spy in the most reprehensible manner — the subversion of an American on American soil.

**The threat of infiltration and influence.** The same FBI report cites specific cases of Communist infiltration of the United States Government. These involve Americans in the State Department, Justice Department, and other governmental agencies which help to shape American policy. Before discussing this infiltration of our Government, the FBI report states: "All these cases have withstood the exacting test of being tried under the democratic system of the American courts and the convictions obtained are ample proof of the charges made."[4]

[4] *Ibid.*, p. 13.

**The threat of propaganda and confusion.** The Communist Party of the U.S.A. supports a host of Communist and Communist front publications designed to bring Kremlin propaganda to the attention of every conceivable group. In this work, as in other efforts, the CPUSA is aided directly by the Soviet Union. As the FBI report says,

> Exploitation of our freedoms has also taken the form of propaganda. Not content with the distribution of over 20,000 copies of the illustrated monthly magazine, "USSR," which is in reciprocity for distribution of a similar American magazine in the Soviet Union, the Soviet Embassy has a carefully planned program of distributing press releases. As of February, 1960, the Press Department of the Soviet Embassy was distributing press releases to almost 7,000 individuals and institutions in the United States, including newspaper editors, business leaders, radio stations, public libraries, television stations, teachers, labor leaders, scientists, and leaders in trade and commerce.[5]

## 100. *What has our Government done to check Communism in the United States?*

The United States Government has sought to deal with the Communist threat *within* the United States in four ways: (1) investigation, (2) exposure and public enlightenment, (3) control legislation, and (4) prosecution.

**Investigation.** By far the most extensive and efficient agency of investigation is the Federal Bureau of Investigation. One of its several responsibilities is to discover and keep track of subversives, including Communists. Its record in the field is unexcelled. Its agents are trained professionals, responsible Americans who know their business. J. Edgar Hoover underlines the point when he says to Americans: "Don't try to do any investigating yourself. The innocent must be protected as well as the guilty identified. That is the job for the professional investigator. Hysteria, witch hunts, and vigilantes weaken our internal security."

**Exposure and public enlightenment.** The record of the House (of Representatives) Un-American Activities Committee has been

[5] *Ibid.*, p. 9.

attacked by a number of thoughtful, patriotic Americans who charge that, in its zeal to alert the American public to the very real Communist danger, the Committee sometimes has damaged the reputation of innocent Americans. At the same time, it should be stressed that certain of that Committee's staff studies on the Communist threat to the United States are very helpful in revealing the Communist's tactics of infiltration, deception, and subversion. Responsible investigation is essential, but it alone will not do the job. Responsible public education is also vitally needed. Don Whitehead[6] put the issue very well when he said:

> The top command of the FBI have no illusions that Communism can be destroyed in the United States by the investigation, prosecution, and conviction of Communist Party leaders who conspire to overthrow the government by force and violence. That is merely one phase of the job to be done in a world-wide struggle.
>
> The FBI knows that the bigger job lies with the Free World's intellectuals — the philosophers, the thinkers wherever they may be, the professors and scientists and scholars and students. These people who think, the intellectuals if you please, are the ones who can and must convince men that Communism is evil. The world's intellectuals themselves must see that Communism is the deadliest enemy that intellectualism and liberalism ever had. They must be as willing to dedicate themselves to this cause as the Communists have been to dedicate themselves to their cause.

**Control legislation.** Legislation on the books under which members of the Communist Party may be prosecuted includes the following:

*Smith Act of 1940:* The Smith Act appears to be aimed primarily at the individual (Communist). The act prohibits anyone from willfully advocating the overthrow of the government by force and violence, or from publishing any literature advocating such overthrow. The act also prohibits anyone from organizing a group which advocates the overthrow of the government by force and violence, or from being a member of such a group with knowledge of the group's intent.

*Internal Security Act of 1950:* This act appears to be aimed at the Communist organization, itself. The act establishes the Subversive Activities Control Board and empowers it to hold hearings

[6] *The FBI Story* (Random House, New York, 1956), page 327.

to determine whether an organization is a "Communist action" organization.

If a group is determined to be a "Communist action" organization (that is, an organization which has been determined to be under the control of the World Communist movement), it must register with the Attorney General within 30 days after it becomes or is declared such an organization. Under a 1961 Supreme Court decision, the Communist Party had until November 20, 1961 to register. If the organization failed to register, it became the duty of its executive officers to register for it within 10 days after failure of the Party to register.

If neither the Party nor its officers registered, then each individual member of the Party was required to register by December 20, 1961. Failure of the Party to register subjects it to a fine of $10,000 per day for each day of failure to register. Failure of the officers or members to register subjects them to a fine of $10,000 and/or 5 years in jail, per day of failure to register.

The Communist Party must also file with the Attorney General an annual report setting forth complete membership, financial records, and source of funds and expenditures. The Party must label all its publications and must acknowledge sponsorship of all radio and TV time.

The act also prohibits Party members from applying for or using passports or from working in a defense industry. It provides as well for the registration of Communist front groups with similar requirements. Further, it contains provisions for prosecution of individuals guilty of espionage, sabotage, or obstruction of justice. It also contains provisions by which the Immigration Service can exclude or deport certain aliens, such as those who advocate the overthrow of the government by force and violence.

*Communist Control Act of 1954:* This act is primarily a reaffirmation of the Internal Security Act of 1950. It states that the CPUSA is not entitled to any of the "rights, privileges, and immunities attendant upon legal parties . . . and whatever rights, privileges, and immunities which have heretofore been granted . . . are hereby terminated." (These rights, privileges, and immunities have not been defined.) This act also gives the National Labor Relations Board the right to deny representation to a Communist-infiltrated labor union.

**Prosecution.** In July of 1948, twelve top leaders of the Communist Party of the United States were indicted in New York for violation of the Smith Act. The trial began in January, 1949, and with the exception of the chairman of the organization, William Z. Foster, these Communist Party leaders were found guilty. The sentence of one was reduced in view of his World War II record. The others were each fined $5,000 and sentenced to five years in a Federal penitentiary. Their conviction was subsequently upheld by the United States Supreme Court. Four of the convicted men went into hiding. Two of these when caught were given additional sentences for contempt of court; two later surrendered and received additional contempt sentences.

In June of 1951, twenty-one "second-string" leaders of the CPUSA were indicted in New York, and seventeen were arrested. With the exception of four, all were subsequently convicted and given sentences of varying length.

This pattern was repeated at the state level. For example, in July, 1951, fifteen leaders of the Communist Party in California were arrested. Also in 1951, the Communist leaders in Baltimore, Pittsburgh, and Honolulu were indicted and arrested. In 1953 arrests took place in St. Louis, Detroit, and Seattle; and in 1954, in Colorado, Illinois, and Connecticut. The effect was, as intended, to weaken seriously the Communist conspiracy in the United States.

The Supreme Court decision of 1961, requiring the Party to register with the Attorney General by a specified date, places an additional weapon in the hands of our law enforcement agencies.

World Communism poses an internal threat to the United States and to other countries of the Free World. But the greater danger to this country and to the peace of the world stems from Communist plans to "bury" competing political and economic systems.

# 9 Combating Communism – Some Positive Suggestions

No book on the nature and challenge of the world of Communism in these critical days would be complete without some consideration of the question: What can we do about it? This is especially true at a time when so many public-spirited groups are coming forward, each with its own answer to the problem.

Perhaps there are no final answers. Clearly, there is no immediate single, simple solution. The problem is complex and confusing. As in any other specialized field, we must seek wise counsel, professional advice, and experienced judgment. This is no issue for amateurs, however dedicated! Above all, this is no time for despair.

Accordingly, our concluding chapter, "Combating Communism," seeks to accent the positive. To be anti-Communist is not enough. As J. Edgar Hoover said recently: "Both Hitler and Mussolini were against Communism. However, it was by what they stood *for*, not against, that history has judged them."

But to whom shall we turn for advice and inspiration? We live in a democracy where our heads of state are elected for a term of years and, after having served their nation well, retire from office. As ex-Presidents they are free to agree or disagree with the current administration. We live in a democracy where the views of management and labor, the thoughts of Catholics, Protestants, and Jews are given equal hearing — each has something to contribute. We live in a democracy in which differences in points of view constitute the strength of the society. We do not demand blind allegiance to the views of a leader or the tenets of a Party. Who has a monopoly on truth? We demand only freedom, tolerance, and truth as we may come to know it.

Included in this chapter are advice and suggestions from four living American Presidents, representatives of business and industry, and spokesmen for this country's three major religious groups. J. Edgar Hoover offers specific advice, and the author suggests steps that you as students may take. If we follow expert advice, we have nothing to fear from Communism, but only much to learn and much to do.

## Counsel from Four American Presidents

### President Herbert Hoover

Herbert Hoover, thirty-first President of the United States, 1929–1933. The quoted material is from a speech, "The Strengths of America, A Bird's Eye View,"[1] delivered at the Forty-Ninth Annual Meeting of the Grocery Manufacturers of America, New York City, November 11, 1957.

The minds of Americans are today greatly troubled. We have many domestic shortcomings. Many troubles beset us from abroad. They are indeed most serious, and it is urgent that we exert all our national strength to meet them.

But on this occasion it would be happier for me and possibly more comfort to some troubled minds if I were to review some of the great fundamental sources of strength of our country. If we have the will to use them, we can meet our dangers. And I would be glad if I could add reassurance to troubled minds which

[1] *Vital Speeches of the Day*, Vol. XXIV, No. 5 (December 15, 1957), pp. 154, 155.

President Eisenhower has so greatly inspired by his recent statements.

I have lived a long life and I have seen our country exert its strengths to overcome as great dangers as those which beset us today.

Despite the troubles of our past and despite the fact that we are only seven per cent of the peoples on earth, we have developed one of the most powerful nations in all history.

The signs of strength on the spiritual side may be found in the increasing attendance upon the worship of God. And in my lifetime I have seen our voluntary organizations and institutions engaged in charity and public welfare increase by tens of thousands in numbers and billions of dollars in service.

I have witnessed our people deny themselves to save the world, including our enemies, from the inevitable and gigantic famines which followed two of these wars. And among them we saved the lives of 15,000,000 Russians, then under the Communistic Government, from their terrible famine in 1922–23. And there is no less humanity in the American heart today.

Within my years I have seen our institutions of higher learning expand until today they turn out more trained men and women each year than all the rest of the world combined.

In my adult lifetime I have passed through several economic recessions and two great economic depressions which swept over our country. Each time we came out economically stronger than ever before.

With some training and understanding of science and technology, I have witnessed a vast growth of scientific discovery and its application to invention. They have given us the highest standard of living in the world. And with the advances of medical science our youth are taller than their fathers, and the span of life has been greatly extended.

I have watched our countrymen rise and fight two world wars to victory in defense of our country. The skill of our military leaders, the courage of our men, and the willingness of our people to make sacrifices are no less today than then.

We can well respect the accomplishments of Russian technicians. But we need not forget that they got the telegraph, the telephone, the electric lamp, the speaking sound track, the radio broadcast tube, the airplane, the atom and nuclear bombs from us. They secured the guided missile from the defeated Germans. They got their method of metal treatment and their radar from us and the British. They got their plastics, their antibiotics, their anti-viruses, their pain killers either from us or from the Germans, the British, and the French.

But with our own discoveries in science, our inventive genius, and our productive capacity, our country has risen to a position of effective retaliation to any irresponsible nation which might contemplate attacking us.

We possess many eminent scientists and engineers of great ability and ingenuity. We have more research laboratories in action than all the rest of the world put together. Our country has had a great warning. It is on the alert. I have no doubt of our ability to invent any other horrible weapon necessary to deter our enemy.

If you take a worm's eye view of the ills in American life and our foreign relations, you may worry that we are entering the decline and fall of the greatest nation in history.

If you take a bird's eye view you will see the increasing skills, growing productivity, and the expansion of education and understanding, with improving health and growing strength of our nation.

And from whence comes this strength? It lies in freedom of men's initiative and the rewards of their efforts. It comes from our devotion to liberty and religious faith. We will have no decline and fall of this nation, provided we stand guard against the evils which weaken these forces.

But we have need to exert all the strengths which God has given us.

## President Harry S. Truman

Harry S. Truman, thirty-third President of the United States, 1945–1953. The quoted material was included in a broadcast made by President Truman from the White House, April 11, 1951.[2]

[2] The Department of State Bulletin, Vol. XXIV, No. 615, p. 603.

I want to talk plainly to you tonight about what we are doing
1 Korea and about our policy in the Far East.

In the simplest terms, what we are doing in Korea is this: We
re trying to prevent a third world war. . . .

The Communists in the Kremlin are engaged in a monstrous
onspiracy to stamp out freedom all over the world. It must be
lear to everyone that the United States cannot — and will not —
it idly by and await foreign conquest. The only question is:
Vhen is the best time to meet the threat and how?

The best time to meet the threat is in the beginning. It is
asier to put out a fire in the beginning when it is small than
fter it has become a roaring blaze.

And the best way to meet the threat of aggression is for the
•eace-loving nations to act together. If they don't act together,
hey are likely to be picked off, one by one. . . .

If history has taught us anything it is that aggression anywhere
1 the world is a threat to peace everywhere in the world. When
hat aggression is supported by the cruel and selfish rulers of
 powerful nation who are bent on conquest, it becomes a clear
nd present danger to the security and independence of every
ree nation.

This is a lesson that most people in this country have learned
horoughly. This is the basic reason why we joined in creating
he United Nations. And since the end of World War II we have
•een putting that lesson into practice — we have been working
vith other free nations to check the aggressive designs of the
oviet Union before they can result in a third world war.

That is what we did in Greece, when that nation was threat-
ned by the aggression of international Communism. . . .

Another big Communist threat to peace was the Berlin block-
de. That too could have led to war. But again it was settled
•ecause free men would not back down in an emergency.

The aggression against Korea is the boldest and most dan-
;erous move the Communists have yet made.

The attack on Korea was part of a greater plan for conquering
ll of Asia. . . .

They want to control all Asia from the Kremlin.

This plan of conquest is in flat contradiction to what we be-
ieve. We believe that Korea belongs to the Koreans, that India

belongs to the Indians — that all the nations of Asia should b
free to work out their affairs — their own way. This is the basi
of peace in the Far East and everywhere else. . . .

The question we have had to face is whether the Communis
plan of conquest can be stopped without a general war. Ou
Government and other countries associated with us in the Unite
Nations believe that the best chance of stopping it is to meet th
attack in Korea and defeat it there. . . .

The course we have been following is the one best calculate
to avoid an all-out war. It is the course consistent with ou
obligation to do all we can to maintain international peace an
security. . . .

If the Communist authorities realize that they cannot defea
us in Korea, if they realize it would be foolhardy to widen th
hostilities beyond Korea, then they may recognize the folly o
continuing their aggression. A peaceful settlement may then b
possible. The door is always open.

Then we may achieve a settlement in Korea which will no
compromise the principles and purposes of the United Nations. . .

We are ready, at any time, to negotiate for a restoration o
peace in the area. But we will not engage in appeasement. W
are only interested in real peace.

Real peace can be achieved through a settlement based on th
following factors:

One: the fighting must stop.

Two: concrete steps must be taken to insure that the fightin
will not break out again.

Three: there must be an end to the aggression.

A settlement founded on these elements would open the wa
for the unification of Korea and the withdrawal of all foreig
forces.

In the meantime, I want to be clear about our military objec
tive. We are fighting to resist an outrageous aggression in Korea
We are trying to keep the Korean conflict from spreading to othe
areas. But at the same time we must conduct our military activi
ties so as to insure the security of our forces. This is essential i
they are to continue the fight until the enemy abandons its ruth
less attempt to destroy the Republic of Korea.

That is our military objective — to repel attack and to restor
peace.

In the hard fighting in Korea we are proving that collective action among nations is not only a high principle but a workable means of resisting aggression. Defeat of aggression in Korea may be the turning point in the world's search for a practical way of achieving peace and security.

The struggle of the United Nations in Korea is a struggle for peace. . . .

## President Dwight D. Eisenhower

Dwight D. Eisenhower, thirty-fourth President of the United States, 1953–1961. The quoted material is from The State of the Union Addresses given by President Eisenhower on January 7, 1960, and January 12, 1961, respectively.

[Part One[3]] Before us and our friends is the challenge of an ideology which, for more than four decades, has trumpeted abroad its purpose of gaining ultimate victory over all forms of government at variance with its own.

We realize that however much we repudiate the tenets of imperialistic Communism, it represents a gigantic enterprise. Its leaders compel its subjects to subordinate their freedom of action and spirit and personal desires for some hoped-for advantage in the future.

The Communists can present an array of material accomplishments over the past 15 years that lends a false persuasiveness to many of their glittering promises to the uncommitted peoples.

The competition they provide is formidable. We so recognize it.

But in our scale of values we place freedom first. Our whole national existence and development have been geared to that basic concept and [it] is responsible for the position of Free World leadership to which we have succeeded. [Freedom] is the highest prize that any nation can possess; it is one that Communism can never offer. And America's record of material accomplishment in freedom is written not only in the unparalleled prosperity of our own Nation, but in the many billions we have devoted to the reconstruction of Free World economies wrecked by World War II and in the effective help of many more billions

[3] 86th Congress; House Document No. 241, pp. 11–12.

we have given in saving the independence of many other
threatened by outside domination. Assuredly we have th
capacity for handling the problems in the new era of the world'
history we are now entering.

But we must use that capacity intelligently and tirelessly, re
gardless of personal sacrifice.

The fissure that divides our political planet is deep and wide.

We live, moreover, in a sea of semantic disorder in which ol
labels no longer faithfully describe.

Police states are called "people's democracies."

Armed conquest of free people is called "liberation."

Such slippery slogans make more difficult the problem of com
municating true faith, facts, and beliefs.

We must make clear our peaceful intentions, our aspiration
for a better world. So doing, we must use language to enlighte
the mind, not as the instrument of the studied innuendo an
distorter of truth.

And we must live by what we say.

On my recent visit to distant lands I found one statesman afte
another eager to tell me of the elements of their government tha
had been borrowed from our American Constitution and from th
indestructible ideals set forth in our Declaration of Independenc

As a nation we take pride that our own constitutional systen
and the ideals which sustain it, have been long viewed as
fountainhead of freedom. . . .

[Part Two[4]] On January 20, 1953, when I took office, th
United States was at war. Since the signing of the Korea
Armistice in 1953, Americans have lived in peace in highl
troubled times.

During the 1956 Suez crisis, the [United States] Governmer
strongly supported United Nations action — resulting in th
ending of the hostilities in Egypt.

Again in 1958, peace was preserved in the Middle East despit
new discord. Our Government responded to the request of th
friendly Lebanese Government for military help, and prompth
withdrew American forces as soon as the situation was stabilize

In 1958 our support of the Republic of China during the all-ou
bombardment of Quemoy restrained the Communist Chines
from attempting to invade the offshore islands.

[4] 87th Congress; *House Document No. 1*, pp. 2–4.

Although, unhappily, Communist penetration of Cuba is real nd poses a serious threat, Communist-dominated regimes have een deposed in Guatemala and Iran. The occupation of Austria as ended and the Trieste question has been settled.

Despite constant threats to its integrity, West Berlin has remained free.

Important advances have been made in building mutual security arrangements — which lie at the heart of our hopes for future eace and security in the world. The Southeast Asia Treaty Organization has been established; the NATO alliance has been military strengthened; the Organization of American States has een further developed as an instrument of inter-American cooperation; the Anzus treaty has strengthened ties with Australia nd New Zealand, and a mutual security treaty with Japan has een signed. In addition, the CENTO Pact has been concluded, nd while we are not officially a member of this alliance we have articipated closely in its deliberations.

The atoms-for-peace proposal of the United Nations led to he creation of the International Atomic Energy Agency. Our policy has been to push for enforceable programs of inspection gainst surprise attack, suspension of nuclear testing, arms reduction, and peaceful use of outer space.

The United Nations has been vigorously supported in all of its ctions, including the condemnations of the wholesale murder of he people of Tibet by the Chinese Communists and the brutal oviet repression of the people of Hungary, as well as the more ecent [United Nations] actions in the Congo.

The United States took the initiative in negotiating the significant treaty to guarantee the peaceful use of vast Antarctica.

The [United States] Information Agency has been transformed nto a greatly improved medium for explaining our policies and ctions to audiences overseas, answering the lies of Communist propaganda, and projecting a clearer image of American life and culture.

Cultural, technological, and educational exchanges with the oviet Union have been encouraged, and a comprehensive agreement was made which authorized, among other things, the distribution of our Russian-language magazine *Amerika* and the highly successful American Exhibition in Moscow.

This country has continued to withhold recognition of Commu-

nist China and to oppose vigorously the admission of this bel
ligerent and unrepentant nation into the United Nations. Re
China has yet to demonstrate that it deserves to be considered
peace-loving nation.

With Communist imperialism held in check, constructive ac
tions were undertaken to strengthen the economies of Free World
nations. The [United States] Government has given sturd
support to the economic and technical assistance activities o
the [United Nations]. This country stimulated a doubling of th
capital of the World Bank and a 50 per cent capital increase is
the International Monetary Fund. The Development Loan Fund
and the International Development Association were established
The United States also took the lead in creating the Inter
American Development Bank.

Vice President Nixon, Secretaries of State Dulles and Herter
and I traveled extensively through the world for the purpose o
strengthening the cause of peace, freedom, and international
understanding. So rewarding were these visits that their very
success became a significant factor in causing the Soviet Union
to wreck the planned summit conference of 1960.

These vital programs must go on. New tactics will have to be
developed, of course, to meet new situations, but the underlying
principles should be constant. Our great moral and material
commitments to collective security, deterrence of force, inter
national law, negotiations that lead to self-enforcing agreements
and the economic interdependence of free nations should remain
the cornerstone of a foreign policy that will ultimately bring
permanent peace with justice in freedom to all mankind.

The continuing need of all free nations today is for each to
recognize clearly the essentiality of an unbreakable bond among
themselves based upon a complete dedication to the principles o
collective security, effective co-operation, and peace with justice

## President John F. Kennedy

John F. Kennedy, thirty-fifth President of the United States
1961–    . The quoted material is from The State of the Union
Address[5] given by President Kennedy on January 30, 1961.

[5] 87th Congress; *House Document No. 73*, pp. 5–10.

. . Each day the crises multiply. Each day their solution grows more difficult. Each day we draw nearer the hour of maximum danger, as weapons spread and hostile forces grow stronger. I feel I must inform the Congress that our analyses over the last [ten] days make it clear that — in each of these principal areas of crisis — the tide of events has been running out and time has not been our friend.

In Asia, the relentless pressures of the Chinese Communists menace the security of the entire area — from the borders of India and South Viet Nam to the jungles of Laos, struggling to protect its newly won independence. We seek in Laos what we seek in all Asia, and indeed, in all the world — freedom for the people and independence for their government. This Nation shall persevere in our pursuit of these objectives.

In Africa, the Congo has been brutally torn by civil strife, political unrest, and public disorder. We shall continue to support the heroic efforts of the United Nations to restore peace and order — efforts which are now endangered by mounting tensions, unsolved problems, and decreasing support from many member states.

In Latin America, Communist agents seeking to exploit that region's peaceful revolution of hope have established a base on Cuba, only [ninety] miles from our shores. Our objection with Cuba is not over the people's drive for a better life. Our objection is to their domination by foreign and domestic tyrannies. Cuban social and economic reform should be encouraged. Questions of economics and trade policy can always be negotiated. But Communist domination in this hemisphere can never be negotiated.

We are pledged to work with our sister Republics to free the Americas of all such foreign domination and all tyranny, working toward the goal of a free hemisphere of free governments, extending from Cape Horn to the Arctic Circle.

In Europe our alliances are unfulfilled and in some disarray. The unity of NATO has been weakened by economic rivalry and partially eroded by national interest. It has not yet fully mobilized its resources nor fully achieved a common outlook. Yet, no Atlantic power can meet on its own the mutual problems now facing us in defense, foreign aid, monetary reserves, and a host of other areas; and our close ties with those whose hopes and

interests we share are among this Nation's most powerful as
sets.

Our greatest challenge is still the world that lies beyond the
cold war — but the first great obstacle is still our relations with
the Soviet Union and Communist China. We must never be
lulled into believing that either power has yielded its ambition
for world domination — ambitions which they forcefully restated
only a short time ago.

On the contrary, our task is to convince them that aggression
and subversion will not be profitable routes to pursue these ends
Open and peaceful competition — for prestige, for markets, for
scientific achievement, even for men's minds — is something else
again. For if freedom and Communism were to compete for
man's allegiance in a world at peace, I would look to the future
with ever-increasing confidence.

To meet this array of challenges — to fulfill the role we canno
avoid on the world scene — we must reexamine and revise ou
whole arsenal of tools.

One must not overshadow the other. On the Presidential coa
of arms, the American eagle holds in his right talon the olive
branch, while in his left he holds a bundle of arrows. We intend
to give equal attention to both.

**First, we must strengthen our military tools.** We are moving
into a period of uncertain risk and great commitment in which
both the military and diplomatic possibilities require a Free
World force so powerful as to make any aggression clearly futile
Yet in the past, lack of a consistent, coherent military strategy
the absence of basic assumptions about our national requirements
and the faulty estimate and duplication arising from interservice
rivalries have all made it difficult to assess accurately how
adequate — or inadequate — our defenses really are.

I have, therefore, instructed the Secretary of Defense to
reappraise our entire defense strategy — our ability to fulfill ou
commitments — the effectiveness, vulnerability, and dispersal of
our strategic bases, forces, and warning systems — the efficiency
and economy of our operation and organization — the elimina
tion of obsolete bases and installations — and the adequacy
modernization, and mobility of our present conventional and
nuclear forces and weapons systems in the light of present and

future dangers. I have asked for preliminary conclusions by the end of February — and I shall then recommend whatever legislative, budgetary, or executive action is needed in the light of those conclusions.

In the meantime, I have asked the Defense Secretary to initiate immediately three steps clearly needed now:

(a) I have directed prompt action to increase our airlift capacity. Obtaining additional air transport mobility — and obtaining it now — will better assure the ability of our conventional forces to respond, with discrimination and speed, to any problem at any spot on the globe at any moment's notice. In particular it will enable us to meet any deliberate effort to avoid or divert our forces by starting limited wars in widely scattered parts of the globe.

(b) I have directed prompt action to step up our Polaris submarine program. Using unobligated ship-building funds now (to let contracts originally scheduled for the next fiscal year) will build and place on station — at least [nine] months earlier than planned — substantially more units of a crucial deterrent — a fleet that will never attack first, but possess sufficient powers of retaliation, concealed beneath the seas, to discourage any aggressor from launching an attack upon our security.

(c) I have directed prompt action to accelerate our entire missile program. Until the Secretary of Defense's reappraisal is completed, the emphasis here will be largely on improved organization and decisionmaking — on cutting down the wasteful duplications and timelag that have handicapped our whole family of missiles.

If we are to keep the peace, we need an invulnerable missile force powerful enough to deter any aggressor from even threatening an attack that he would know could not destroy enough of our own force to prevent his own destruction. For as I said upon taking the oath of office: "Only when our arms are sufficient beyond doubt can we be certain beyond doubt that they will never be employed."

**Secondly, we must improve our economic tools.** Our role is essential and unavoidable in the construction of a sound and expanding economy for the entire non-Communist world, helping other nations build the strength to meet their own problems, to satisfy their own aspirations, to surmount their own dangers. The problems in achieving this goal are towering and unprecedented — the response must be towering and unprecedented as well, much as lend-lease and the Marshall plan were in earlier years, which brought such fruitful results.

(a) I intend to ask the Congress for authority to establish a new and more effective program for assisting the economic, educational, and social development of other countries and continents. That program must stimulate and take more effectively into account the contributions of our allies, and provide central policy direction [for] all our own programs that now so often overlap, conflict, or diffuse our energies and resources. Such a program, compared to past programs, will require:

more flexibility for short-run emergencies;

more commitment to long term development;

new attention to education at all levels;

greater emphasis on the recipient nations' role, their effort and their purpose, with greater social justice for their own people, with broader distribution and participation of their people, and more efficient public administration and more efficient tax systems of their own;

and orderly planning for national and regional development instead of a piecemeal approach.

(b) I hope the Senate will take early action approving the convention establishing the Organization for Economic Cooperation and Development. This will be an important instrument in sharing with our allies this development effort — working toward the time when each nation will contribute in proportion to its ability to pay. For, while we are prepared to assume our full share of these huge burdens, we cannot and must not be expected to bear them alone.

(c) To our sister Republics of the south, we have pledged a new alliance for progress — *alianza para progreso*. Our goal is a free and prosperous Latin America, realizing for all its states and all its citizens a degree of economic and social progress that matches their historic contributions of culture, intellect, and liberty. To start this Nation's role at this time in that alliance of neighbors, I am recommending the following:

That the Congress appropriate in full the $500 million fund

pledged by the act of Bogotá, to be used not as an instrument of the cold war, but as a first step in the sound development of the Americas.

That a new Inter-Departmental Task Force be established under the leadership of the Department of State, to coordinate at the highest level all policies and programs of concern to the Americas.

That our delegates to the [Organization of American States], working with those of other members, strengthen that body as an instrument to preserve the peace and to prevent foreign domination anywhere in the hemisphere.

That, in co-operation with other nations, we launch a new hemisphere attack on illiteracy and inadequate educational opportunities at all levels; and, finally,

That a food-for-peace mission be sent immediately to Latin America to explore ways in which our vast food abundance can be used to help end hunger and malnutrition in certain areas of suffering in our own hemisphere.

(d) This administration is expanding its new food-for-peace program in every possible way. The product of our abundance must be more effectively used to relieve hunger and help economic growth in all corners of the globe. I have asked the director of this program to recommend additional ways in which these surpluses can advance the interests of world peace — including the establishment of world food reserves.

(e) An even more valuable national asset is our reservoir of dedicated men and women — not only at our college campuses but in every age group — who have indicated their desire to contribute their skills, their efforts, and a part of their lives to the fight for world order. We can mobilize this talent through the formation of a National Peace Corps, enlisting the services of all those with the desire and capacity to help foreign lands meet their urgent needs for trained personnel.

(f) Finally, while our attention is centered on the development of the non-Communist world, we must never forget our hopes for the ultimate freedom and welfare of the eastern European peoples. In order to be prepared to help reestablish historic ties of friendship, I am asking the Congress for increased discretion to use economic tools in this area whenever this is found to be clearly in the national interest. This will require amendment of the Mutual Defense Assistance Control Act along the lines I proposed as a member of the Senate, and upon which the Senate voted last summer. Meanwhile, I hope to explore with the Polish Government the possibility of using our frozen Polish funds on projects of peace that will demonstrate our abiding friendship and interest in the people of Poland.

**Third, we must sharpen our political and diplomatic tools —** the means of co-operation and agreement on which an enforceable world order must ultimately rest.

(*a*) I have already taken steps to coordinate and expand our disarmament effort — to increase our programs of research and study — and to make arms control a central goal of our national policy under my personal direction. The deadly arms race, and the huge resources it absorbs, have too long overshadowed all else we must do. We must prevent that arms race from spreading to new nations, to new nuclear powers, and to the reaches of outer space. We must make certain that our negotiators are better informed and better prepared — to formulate workable proposals of our own and to make sound judgments about the proposals of others.

I have asked the other governments concerned to agree to a reasonable delay in the talks on a nuclear test ban — and it is our intention to resume negotiations prepared to reach a final agreement with any nation that is equally willing to agree to an effective and enforceable treaty.

(*b*) We must increase our support of the United Nations as an instrument to end the cold war instead of an arena in which to fight it. In recognition of its increasing importance and the doubling of its membership —

we are enlarging and strengthening our own mission to the UN.

we shall help insure that it is properly financed.

we shall work to see that the integrity of the office of the Secretary-General is maintained.

And I would address a special plea to the smaller nations of the world — to join with us in strengthening this organization which is far more essential to their security than it is to ours — the only body in the world where no nation need be powerful to be secure, where every nation has an equal voice, and where any nation can exert influence not according to the strength of its armies but according to the strength of its ideas. It deserves the support of all.

(c) Finally, this administration intends to explore promptly all possible areas of co-operation with the Soviet Union and other nations "to invoke the wonders of science instead of its terrors." Specifically, I now invite all nations — including the Soviet Union — to join with us in developing a weather prediction program, in a new communications satellite program, and in preparation for probing the distant planets of Mars and Venus, probes which may someday unlock the deepest secrets of the universe.

Today this country is ahead in the science and technology of space, while the Soviet Union is ahead in the capacity to lift large vehicles into orbit. Both nations would help themselves as well as other nations by removing these endeavors from the bitter and wasteful competition of the cold war. The United States would be willing to join with the Soviet Union and the scientists of all nations in a greater effort to make the fruits of this new knowledge available to all — and, beyond that, in an effort to extend farm technology to hungry nations — to wipe out disease — to increase exchanges of scientists and their knowledge — and to make our own laboratories available to technicians of other lands who lack the facilities to pursue their own work. Where nature makes natural allies of us all, we can demonstrate that beneficial relations are possible even with those with whom we most deeply disagree — and this must someday be the basis of world peace and world law.

## The Views of Business, Industry, and Labor

### Frank Pace, Jr., Chairman, General Dynamics Corporation

Frank Pace, Jr., Chairman, General Dynamics Corporation. During the Truman administration he was Director of the Bureau of the Budget and Secretary of the Army. The quoted material is from a speech, "What Price Security. How's My Country Doing?."[6]

[6] *Vital Speeches of the Day,* Vol. XXVI, No. 23 (September 15, 1960), p. 713.

delivered at the Annual Alumni Federation Luncheon, Columbia University, New York City, June 1, 1960.

How do we organize ourselves affirmatively to combat the evil of Communism?

When as a nation of a little over 3 million people we threw off the yoke of a dominating Britain, we were the bright hope of mankind.

In the 180 years since, we have carved an empire for ourselves out of an undeveloped continent, on principles set forth by farsighted forefathers who planted the seed of nation in our rebellion of birth; on the principles of liberty, justice, and dignity of the individual. Even our wars, we have felt, have been on the side of the angels.

Is this sufficient to cope with the menace of the known evil of the Soviet Union, the emerging evil of Communist China?

We know it is.

A free society benefits from the best thoughts, the best work, the best efforts of all its people. Democracy is a remorseless sifting process that inevitably makes the correct decisions, given enough time.

Pitted against a controlled society in peacetime, the democratic process appears hopelessly outdated, old-fashioned, inaccurate, and inefficient. The dictator speaks and a hundred thousand peasants become steel workers. To the lay observer, this appears to be a miracle of organization and administrative efficiency.

What we don't know is — is the steel any good; is the right kind of steel being produced; is the economy ready to absorb the steel that results; who is doing the work formerly performed by the hundred thousand peasants? The orders of the dictator may result in waste, ineptitude, and chaos, but in the closed society, it is possible to bury even mistakes of this magnitude.

We are more familiar with successes in the Communist dictatorships . . . such as the Russian performance with the Sputnik. These are exploited by a propaganda apparatus so large that it surpasses in size the organizations that in a free society perform the undistorted dissemination of the news. But the cold hard facts still are that Communist states are making giant strides, not only militarily but in the economic and psychological fields as well.

We have no time to lose.

Sometimes we tend to forget that we are operating on a more or less relaxed peacetime footing while the Communist societies are operating under continuing forced draft. Consider, if you will, World War II. During that time this nation constructed more than 30,000 four-engine bomber aircraft. This means that well over 120,000 aircraft engines for bombers alone were built in that four-year period. Steel, guns, tanks, uniforms, food, and bullets for ourselves and our allies, including Russia, were built in the greatest production effort the world has ever seen.

That war showed the world what an aroused democracy can do. Our problem now is that we can't seem to waken the sleeping democracy again. We can't seem to digest the idea that we are again fighting for our lives. We can't believe that something so wrong can prevail over something so right as the free way of life. Because freedom fits us loosely and comfortably, we forget that it was purchased dearly, that we must work to preserve it.

Because there are no missiles flying yet, we hope that perhaps it will all go away. Maybe Russia will dissolve in civil war as her populace gains in education and sophistication. Or Russia and China will have a falling out that will solve the problems of the West.

While possible, each of these eventualities is unlikely; and we cannot afford to rely on them in establishing our national strategy.

Likewise we should not look for a great leader to spring from the people at the last minute to rescue us. Great men are products of their people and of their times and can do little, indeed are not great, out of context.

We must waken again within ourselves that hot war urgency that has been our salvation in the past. The threat is subtle and difficult to counter. We must attack it with the weapons of understanding and hard work.

These are difficult concepts to sell in a democracy. They can't be encapsulated in a slogan; they can't be depicted in a poster. But they are our hope for survival.

We must make the effort to understand the issues in the United Nations; the issues in forming the national budget; the issues of defense, foreign affairs and the great problems of our time.

When I was in Australia recently, people I met would say, "Mr. Pace, how do you like our country? How is our country doing? Are we growing as we should?" And I thought to myself, "How long is it since I said, 'How's my country doing?'" Too long.

I think there is a tendency on the part of the citizenry to lose its sense of personal identity with and responsibility to our nation. We must get people to take a feeling of personal self-interest in the way that the country is being run; to probe; to question; to contribute.

I heard a marvelous phrase the other day. Thomas Jefferson, that great embodiment of the spirit of our young country, was being discussed and the phrase was used that Jefferson "plagiarized the atmosphere," drawing from all of the people and the spirit of the times a sense of greatness.

It is essential for us to recreate that atmosphere of greatness, that sense of destiny, so that a latter-day Thomas Jefferson can plagiarize the atmosphere of greatness in America and revivify the spirit that 180 years ago made us the bright hope of freedom-hungry people everywhere.

## George Meany, President, AFL-CIO

George Meany, President of the American Federation of Labor and Congress of Industrial Organizations since its founding in 1955. The quoted material is from *American Labor and World Affairs*, No. 84, August, 1960. (Washington, D.C.: AFL-CIO)

We of the united American labor movement — the American Federation of Labor and Congress of Industrial Organizations — have three main areas of activity in our efforts to aid our country in the fulfillment of its new historic role. These are: (1) Through our trade union strength and political actions, help build an ever better and stronger America, a prosperous and progressive land free from economic and social inequity and all racial and every other form of discrimination. (2) Through democratic processes, help our nation evolve and execute an effective democratic foreign policy. (3) Through co-operation with and assistance to the International Confederation of Free Trade Unions, to aid free labor everywhere in becoming a most powerful force for furthering social justice, national and human freedom, economic well-being, and world peace. . . .

Unlike preceding international crises, the present struggle

between the Communist dictatorships and the Free World is not a collision between two power blocs, in the old nineteenth-century sense, but between two conflicting ways of life — democracy (despite all its imperfections), and Communist totalitarianism with its all-embracing program of world conquest and transformation. Soviet imperialism seeks to subvert and conquer the free world and remold all society in line with its Communist preconceptions of a new social order. This vital difference between the old imperialisms and the new Soviet imperialism accounts for the continuous character of the present crisis as distinct from preceding ones. . . .

To preserve world peace, extend freedom, and defeat the Communist challenge, the democratic world must do more than build adequate military strength. The democratic nations should also seek closer political ties and scientific co-operation; improved economic conditions and expanded economic relations; improvement of the democratic way of life so as to make it more attractive to the peoples of the so-called un-committed countries; expanded and coordinated economic and technical assistance to the industrially underdeveloped countries in their efforts to raise their productive capacities and living standards and to strengthen their democratic institutions; elimination of colonialism; and promotion of friendship with the Soviet peoples as distinct from their oppressive Communist rulers.

## As the Church and Synagogue See the Issue

### "On Fighting Communism" — A Roman Catholic Editorial

*America* is a Jesuit-edited Roman Catholic magazine, published weekly in New York City. The quoted material is from an editorial in the issue for May 2, 1959 (Vol. Cl, No. 5), pp. 268–269.

. . . We should like to sketch in broad strokes the only kind of anti-Communism which seems to us to be at the same time informed and Catholic.

At the risk of offending sophisticated readers, we begin by

making the fundamental point that Communism is both a movement of social protest and a conspiracy aimed at world conquest. As a form of social protest, it appeals to the victims of capitalist oppression and colonial exploitation, promising them a better and happier life in a society devoted to equality and justice. As a conspiracy, Communism poses a double threat to the non-Communist world — the threat of direct, or military, aggression, and the threat of subversion, or indirect aggression.

It is scarcely necessary to argue that an intelligent and effective anti-Communist program must be well-rounded and all-embracing. It must be directed not only at blunting the appeal of Communism as a social protest, but also at exposing and checking its conspiratorial drive for power. Such was the program sketched in 1937 by Pope Pius XI in *Divini Redemptoris*. Referring to the anti-Communist role of the Catholic press, the Pope wrote that "its foremost duty is to foster in various attractive ways an ever better understanding of social doctrine." In addition to this "foremost duty," the press should also, he explained, "supply accurate and complete information on the activity of the enemy and the means of resistance. . . ."

On the anti-Communist program thus outlined, there ought to be general agreement among Catholics. Some of our coreligionists, however, seem surprised — when it is called to their attention — at the priority the Pope gives to propagating the Church's social teaching. Clearly such Catholics are not well acquainted either with the social implications of their faith or with the state of affairs in the world today. They don't understand that even should Khrushchev call for baptism tomorrow, Catholics would still be obliged to strive zealously for social justice. They don't appreciate, either, the appeal of Communism in underdeveloped countries, whose leaders are impressed both by the industrial progress of the Soviet Union and its official policy of racial equality. Such Catholics seem blind to the pressing necessity of demonstrating to the world, by our solicitude for justice here at home, the superiority of our way of life to the Communist way. . . .

[Waging] an anti-Communist war on the social front, though indispensable, is not enough. To the subversive activities of the Communist Fifth Column, it is only a partial answer; and to the Red Army, with its missiles and bombs, it is no answer at all.

In dealing with Communism as a conspiracy, two questions are of capital importance. One has to do with methods; the other with emphasis.

With regard to methods, anti-Communists differ on the importance to be attached to democratic procedures in combating the Communist plot. Some would cut constitutional corners to wage a more effective fight. Others insist on giving Communists the full benefit of all the rights and immunities they are sworn to destroy. Unless Communism is fought with clean democratic hands, say the constitutionalists, we risk being infected by the totalitarian poison we abhor. That this danger is not negligible appears today from the persistent effort in some quarters to turn "liberal" into a smear word and to stigmatize as "socialistic" all proposals for social reform. The blurring of ideological lines is not the least of the temptations which the earnest anti-Communists must stoutly resist.

There remains the question of emphasis. In some areas of the world the great threat of indirect Communist aggression is obviously greater than the danger of direct aggression. This is true of a country like Indonesia, as it is true of the Middle East and Africa generally. The opposite, however, is true of the United States, since over the past decade it has become agonizingly clear that far and away the bigger threat to our security is Soviet power as symbolized in the Red Army. That does not mean that our domestic Communists, no matter how discredited they are right now, can be safely ignored. On the contrary, they must be watched and exposed and checked at every point (and of course, our security agencies must be ever alert to Soviet espionage). But it would be a fatal error, we believe, to concentrate on the Soviet Fifth Column in our midst and to miss the greater threat from abroad.

That is the reason this Review has consistently supported big appropriations for defense and mutual security. That is why we have frowned on proposals for tax relief. That is why we have approved all sorts of foreign commitments — from the Truman Doctrine on Greece and Turkey, through Marshall Plan, to NATO and SEATO. We have thought — and still think — that the only hope of stopping further Communist expansion by force — is to maintain a clear margin of military superiority over the Soviet Union.

We have been disturbed, consequently, by the preoccupation

of some Catholics with our domestic Communists. Too often, we note, this preoccupation is accompanied by coolness toward NATO, by hostility toward foreign aid, by complaints about taxes, by opposition to desegregation, even by defeatist fears of Communist infiltration of Catholic schools and other Catholic organizations. In short, we are led sadly to suspect that some of the anti-Communism in Catholic circles is no more than a form of escapism from the anxieties and frustrations of a harsh and turbulent world.

We are fighting for our lives against a shrewd and implacable foe. We cannot afford to make mistakes. If with our knowledge of Communism we combine a realistic appraisal of existing situations; if, in addition, we never lose sight of the lessons of justice and charity read to us by all the recent Popes, we should be able, with God's help, to fight successfully, and with much greater unity, for values we hold dearer than life itself.

## "The Communist Conspiracy and American Freedom" — A Protestant View

The General Assembly of the United Presbyterian Church in the United States of America held its One Hundred and Seventy-third General Assembly in Buffalo, New York, May 17–24, 1961. The quoted material is from the *Minutes*[7] of this meeting.

The task of devising effective and appropriate means by which our nation can fulfill its destiny as a free society in the face of the threat of international Communism is real and urgent. Recent and sometimes vitriolic public controversy about persons and programs attempting to face this task suggests that it is time for thoughtful Americans of all faiths to consider seriously the responsibilities in this situation that confronts us.

The international Communist conspiracy is objectively real and vitally dangerous to the Christian Church, the United States, and the values of human dignity we accept.

Outside of the United States the evidence of Communist imperialism is abundantly clear — in China, in North Korea, in

[7] (Philadelphia 7: Office of the General Assembly, Witherspoon Building, August, 1961), pp. 432–434.

Viet Nam, in Tibet, in Czechoslovakia, in Poland, in Hungary, in Cuba, to cite only a few nations that have come under the tyranny. In some countries the Communist take-over has been accomplished by indirect military coup, in others by direct military intervention, in still others by the gaining of control of the centers of power by Communist agents.

Within the United States the Communist threat is very real, as manifest in the conviction, by the due process of law, of Communist agents for espionage — the conveying of military secrets to the Soviet Union. We also have reason to believe that sabotage — the destruction of military and communication installations by Communist agents — is a potential threat.

These real dangers of espionage and sabotage in our country can best be dealt with by specialized agents trained in the methods of prevention, direction, and apprehension. A thorough public awareness and support of such defenses of our internal security is necessary. However, an obsessive public preoccupation with these dangers diverts our energies from other important tasks.

The very real external danger of political, economic, and military machinations of international Communism — to us, to our allies, and to the uncommitted nations of the world — can best be confronted by a conscious Christian witness and by creative, coordinated programs of political action and economic co-operation from a position of strength.

The fear of subversion has led to much distrust. Public officials, clergymen, school teachers, and others whose loyalty to the United States is beyond question to those who know them, have been irresponsibly accused of being "card-carrying Communists" or "dupes." Reputations have been damaged and, in some instances, careers ruined, by undocumented charges and intentional innuendoes implying disloyalty to our country. Organizations engaged in controversial but legitimate efforts in the fields of civil rights and civil liberties have been labeled as "subversive" or worse by some of those who oppose their goals and their methods. Public policies in the areas of education, welfare and economics have been opposed as "Communist-influenced" without intelligent consideration of their objective value in meeting concrete problems in those areas.

Fear continues to work as the enemy of intelligence, responsibility, and decision. There are some indications that an unreasoning fear of Communism has vitiated and paralyzed the ability of some Americans to think intelligently and responsibly about either the objective reality of the Communist threat to freedom or the unfinished business of a free society. Certainly the debate of Americans with Americans about the alternative policies and programs has been unduly complicated and confused by the sowing of suspicion and distrust of the motives and loyalties of those supporting opposing positions.

Any distortion of truth in an effort to arouse the American public to any threat to American freedom is not an effective or a justifiable method in a free society. Loyal and responsible Americans should use honest criticism of such distortion whenever it occurs. It is imperative that Americans make the fine distinction between honest blunders of policy in the past, innocent associations with what turned out to be questionable organizations, and honest proposals for the future, on the one hand — and on the other hand, revealed or concealed loyalty to an alien nation or a hostile ideology. The former is part and parcel of an open society and ought to be accepted. The latter demands detection and ought to be rejected. Public suspicions, fear, and hysteria do not contribute to such a distinction.

The danger to the non-Communist world, including our own nation, is too great and real for us to waste our energies and dissipate our intelligence in costly wrangling born of mutual suspicion and distrust within our body politic. And the need to strengthen and enlarge the cause of freedom, justice, and order within our own borders and around the world is too urgent to vitiate the necessary debate over real alternative programs by undocumented charges and ideological slogans.

## "Judaism Versus Communism" by Rabbi Edgar F. Magnin, D.D.

Rabbi Edgar F. Magnin is a past President of the Los Angeles Rabbinical Association. He has been a lecturer at the University of

Southern California. A noted author and lecturer, Rabbi Magnin prepared the quoted statement especially for this book.

Whatever differences may exist among Orthodox, Conservative, and Reform Judaism, they all agree on one subject, namely, that Communism is a menace to society and that every effort should be made to challenge its contentions.

The report of the Commission on Justice and Peace of the Central Conference of American Rabbis in 1960, includes the following statement:

"Our aim must be a social order which will provide the maximum of security, education, and well-being consistent with the liberty and dignity of the individual and his right of free choice. We are unalterably opposed to Communism and other totalitarian ideologies which seek to propagate their views by aggression and subversion; which operate upon the unethical assumption that the end justifies the means; and which impose upon their own or subject peoples the tyranny of one man or one party rule."

There are five good reasons why a religious Jew should be opposed to Communism.

1. It is anti-religious, in fact, atheistic. Actually, it is a secular religion in and by itself that ridicules God and the sacred principles of Judaism and Christianity. It attempts to make religion appear as something passé and obsolete. It regards faith as an opiate of the people. Communism, as Abraham Kaplan points out in *The New World of Philosophy*, is the old myth in which the fall and redemption is replaced by the fall of capitalism and salvation by the Communist doctrine. Its leaders are a "priesthood" in and by themselves and they demand unalloyed and absolute faith in the cause they are supposed to represent.

2. The methods of Communism are amoral and in some cases immoral. They hold that the end justifies the means even if the means be violence, slavery, and cruelty. They indulge in lies and deceit. They mouth words like democracy while their government displays the very opposite attitude. They attack colonialism yet hold Hungary and other nations in suppression. They violate agreements on nuclear tests and are not ashamed of it.

3. Communism is a monster that wants to conquer the whole world in the name of materialism. As such it is ruthless and

inflexible. It will crush any and all opposition within or without to attain its end.

4. It is a form of despotism. The leaders are not elected. They are the "elect" as Kaplan put it. A few individuals control millions of people. They think nothing of speedy imprisonments, exile, and executions. The individual is just a cog in a wheel. He is a servant of the state.

5. Judaism is a religion of peace. Isaiah revealed the vision of the day when the lion shall lie down with the lamb . . . when nation shall not lift up sword against nation, neither shall they learn war any more. Every man would sit under his own vine and fig tree and none would be afraid.

In addition to the foregoing, Communism is hostile to the Jewish people everywhere. This policy was carried out by Stalin and has not been ameliorated by Khrushchev. Captain Joshua Goldberg, in his article on anti-Semitism in Russia, which appeared in Look Magazine, expresses the thought that the tsars killed Jewish bodies, the Soviets the Jewish soul. They have stifled all publication of Jewish books both in Hebrew and Yiddish. While some synagogues exist, they are few in number and are mostly attended by old people. The young are afraid to go lest they be discriminated against economically and in other ways. Jewish culture is at a standstill.

The present government of Russia is definitely against the nation of Israel and will not allow any of the Jewish people to emigrate to that land.

The synagogue and the church also should work out definite techniques in order to carry out a program of education and inspiration that will open the eyes of their followers to the evils of Communism. What is more important perhaps is to find a substitute for the vacuum that exists in the minds of people who have lost their faith and are seeking some other source of salvation.

It is not enough to attack Communism. We must have a positive point of view to present. This can be done through the pulpit, the religious school, and by the auxiliary organizations like the sisterhoods and brotherhoods.

The pulpit can not only challenge the false assertions and promises of Communism but should point out the virtues of democracy and the necessity for living it twenty-four hours a day every day of the year.

The religious school children should have definite courses of study on the place of religion in the life of America and other free countries.

The sisterhoods and brotherhoods can develop study circles and hold panel discussions and special programs on all phases of the subject.

If such a program, well arranged and properly worked out, can be pursued, great changes are bound to take place in the next few years in the thinking of many Americans.

## J. Edgar Hoover's Recommendations on "How to Stay Free"

J. Edgar Hoover, Director of the Federal Bureau of Investigation (FBI) since 1924. The quoted material is from one of Mr. Hoover's books.[8]

In our reawakening, we Americans can learn a great deal from the fight against Communism. Here are five special areas:

1. The Communists emphasize *ideological study,* meaning, of course, Marxism-Leninism. Such study has been the very foundation of their "monolithic unity": their power to keep people in line no matter how the "line" changes. Their study allows no deviation for free thought and independent action. Also, it provides them with a "common language," since all Communists give the same meaning to words and acts. This emphasis upon study has been the means whereby they have captured the minds of some of our young people who read and think and who are lacking in proper companionship.

It is sad but true that many young people have been drawn into Communist clubs or study groups. Often they are highly intellectual but lonely students and fall under a sinister influence. We know this from the experiences of hundreds of former Com-

---

[8] From *Masters of Deceit* by J. Edgar Hoover (pp. 333–337). Copyright © 1958 by J. Edgar Hoover. Reprinted by permission of Holt, Rinehart and Winston, Inc.

munists and from acts of near-treason we have been called upon to investigate.

American education, of course, does not make Communists; Communist education does. Communism, to survive, must depend upon a constant program of education, because Communism needs educated people, even though it distorts the use to which their education is put. Thus, we need to show our young people, particularly those endowed with high intellects, that we in our democracy need what they have to offer.

We, as a people, have not been sufficiently articulate and forceful in expressing pride in our traditions and ideals. In our homes and schools we need to learn how to "let freedom ring." In all the civilized world there is no story which compares with America's effort to become free and to incorporate freedom in our institutions. This story, told factually and dramatically, needs to become the basis for our American unity and for our unity with all free peoples. I am sure most Americans believe that our light of freedom is a shining light. As Americans we should stand up, speak of it, and let the world see this light, rather than conceal it. For too long we have had a tendency to keep silent while the Communists, their sympathizers, and their fellow travelers have been telling the world what is wrong with democracy. Suppose every American spent a little time each day, less than the time demanded by the Communists, in studying the Bible and the basic documents of American history, government, and culture? The result would be a new America, vigilant, strong, but ever humble in the service of God.

2. Then there is the training of *youth*, on whom the Communists place so much emphasis. To the Party, youth is not something auxiliary but an important training ground. We must meet this challenge. America must devote the best of her efforts to make youth responsible, conscious of its obligations, and eager to be good citizens. Experience and observation point to certain facts which we need to consider in providing for youth.

First, youth gravitates toward youth. The young person who feels left out may remain a "solitary." Or he may, according to his background and make-up, join a delinquent gang. He may join a Party front or club. Or he may find some other short cut to a sense of belonging. But every American youth has a right to find some place within a group that expresses rather than contradicts the real values of society.

Second, given half a chance, youth gravitates toward companionship with competent, generous, and experienced adults. Practically all my life I have been face to face with young people becoming involved in difficulties or coming under the Communist spell. Invariably I have discovered that they all had one thing in common. In their early years and in the periods of their lives when their transgressions began to take form, they could not talk things over with their parents. Their parents were either too busy, or not interested, or resented any difference of opinion. Or parents simply doled out "final" answers when the young people wanted to try to think things through.

Our youth want not only to talk to adults, they want to work with adults. It is a fine thing for them to have their own groups, but it is better if, in addition, they can participate in shared projects with adults. If the adults can show, in action, that it is possible to combine high idealism with solid practicality and patience, the results will enhance character and citizenship development manyfold.

3. The Communists stress *action*. This means carrying out our responsibilities now — not tomorrow, the next day, or never. To Communists the Party means continual action, not just talk, waiting for annual elections, meetings, or affairs. With us action must supplement good intentions in building the America of the future. We need to provide our youth with activity groups. To give them only a high standard of material advantages or a constant diet of recreation is not enough. Recreation must be made part of a life of responsibility, otherwise it becomes merely a preface to boredom. Our young people, as well as adults, need to be working members of our republic and citizens on duty at all times.

4. Communists accent the *positive*. In their deceptive and perverted way they are always purporting to stand for something positive. "Better," "higher," etc., are trade-marks in their language. We, too, in the true sense of the word, should strive for goals that are genuinely better, higher, and more noble, trying to improve

self, community, and nation. A strictly negative attitude or the philosophy of just staying afloat — all too common today — will never meet the impact of the Communist challenge.

5. Most important of all is *faith*. Let us not blind ourselves to the fact that Communists do have a "faith." True, it is falsely placed, but still it inspires them to sacrifice, devotion, and a perverted idealism.

The late Mother Bloor, the Party's woman "hero," often praised Walt Whitman's "The Mystic Trumpeter" as the poem she loved best. It seemed, she said, to prophesy the coming of a "new world":

> War, sorrow, suffering gone — the rank
> earth purged — nothing but joy left!
> The ocean fill'd with joy — the atmosphere
> all joy!
> Joy! joy! in freedom, worship, love! joy in
> the ecstasy of life!
> Enough to merely be! enough to breathe!
> Joy! joy! all over joy!

She is trying to identify Communism with the dream of a world of joy. She is exploiting Walt Whitman. Yet her feeling shows the lure of Communist "faith." If Communists can be so inspired from error, falsehood, and hate, just think what we could do with truth, justice, and love! I thrill to think of the even greater wonders America could fashion from its rich, glorious, and deep tradition. All we need is faith, *real faith*.

The Communist prides himself on being a revolutionary — and revolutionary he is in the sense of destruction, terror, and violence. Free men can learn here too: the truly revolutionary force of history is not material power but the spirit of religion. The world today needs a true revolution of the fruitful spirit, not the futile sword. Hypocrisy, dishonesty, hatred, all these must be destroyed and man must rule by love, charity, and mercy.

The Party's effort to create "Communist man," to mold a revolutionary fighter completely subservient to the Party's desires, is destined to fall. The power of bullets, tanks and repression will bulwark tyranny just so long. Then, as the Hungarian Freedom Fighters proved, man's innate desire for freedom will flare up stronger than ever. In Communism we see what happens when freedom is extinguished. This must give us renewed zeal to work untiringly to uphold the ideals of justice and liberty which have made this nation great.

With God's help, America will remain a land where people still know how to be free and brave.

## A Word of Advice from the Author

We have shared the advice of four Presidents, the thoughts of business and labor leaders, the convictions of great spokesmen for the Catholic, Protestant, and Jewish faiths, and of a man whose job it has been to combat subversion. The issue is before us. The danger is clear and present. We see that the problem is international, national, and local. The solution, likewise, must be projected at all levels. The question remains: What can we do individually — right now?

Here is a positive program for high school students — six suggested steps toward combating Communism while improving America:

**1. Take your studies and work more seriously.** Whatever you do, do it the very best you know how. Don't be satisfied with less than the best from yourself. A lazy, what-does-it-matter attitude is the sure path to defeat. A dedicated Communist can always whip a lazy or careless American. A Communist, however dedicated, is no match for an American ready and willing to do his best for his school, his family, and his community — which is to say for himself.

**2. Re-dedicate your life to positive values.** The world is divided into those who build and those who destroy. If you attend a church or a synagogue, try to do more than make a rare appearance on holidays. If you don't attend church, then live by the values in which you really believe, by what you know is right. These are the things that have made America strong, and they are what will keep us free.

**3. Learn all you can about Communism.** Know your enemy. Learn to recognize Communist lies for what they are. Be able to defend your own country and the Free World against the false charges made by the Right or Left extremists. Don't let yourself become a victim of either clever Communists or misinformed ultra-patriots. Become, rather, an informed, dedicated, alert citizen. Know more about the world outside the United States. Read more! Think more! Act more — intelligently!

**4. Take a new look at your own country.** Stop taking freedom and plenty for granted. Count your many blessings. Remember, literally millions of people throughout the world are suffering starvation or slavery — or both. We are the lucky ones. But our freedom and plenty are no accident. They have been forged out of faith, wisdom, vision, and hard work. Our fortunate present is the product of the blood, sweat, and tears of the millions of Americans of the recent past. Our parents, grandparents, and those who preceded them have bequeathed us all these wonderful things. Who are we to treat their gifts so carelessly?

**5. Work for a better America.** Don't let prejudice, cheating, graft, waste, and petty crime grow up around you while you stand silent. It *is* your business! It's every American's business. Take a critical attitude toward the evils in our own society and culture. This is desirable in itself and is a positive aid in our struggle with Communism. Stand up for what you believe. Speak up for our American way of life. Stand up for what our Constitution guarantees. Above all, be sure your own hands are clean, that your own actions square with democratic values.

**6. Organize for America.** When you graduate from high school and go to college or to work, don't permit Communists, pro-Communists, or other undemocratic elements of the Left or Right to take over the groups to which you belong. Be an active member and citizen. Organize for America. Vote. Make your voice heard.

# Appendix

# A

## GLOSSARY OF COMMUNIST JARGON AND DOUBLE TALK

One of the difficulties in understanding the Communists is that they give familiar words new meanings — often, as it turns out, meanings that are quite the opposite of the ideas these words normally convey. Unless we understand precisely what the Communist means — or does not mean — when he uses such terms as "peace," "democracy," and "imperialism," we are bound to be at best confused, at worst dangerously misled.

As we know, the Communists have adopted as their own many of our cherished concepts and our standard terms. The word "democracy" is a perfect example. Such terms the Communists empty of their original meaning. Then they fill these words with a new meaning of their own making and use them — without notice of the change — in an effort to convince the world that they stand for what we stand for.

But words and phrases are only useful as a reliable means of communication when we agree as to precisely what they mean. A whole field of scholarship called semantics has grown up concerned with just this problem. For our purposes, however, the question is relatively simple. Most of the specialists in Soviet and Communist affairs have over the years become experts in converting Communist jargon and double talk into basic English.

How major the conversion, how essential the process, may be judged from the fact that when the Communists use the term "democracy" they actually mean Communism! This "different" meaning is not likely to occur to the uninformed. So we would do well to brief ourselves on the essentials of Communist jargon and double talk. To this end the following terms, selected as representative key terms which the Communist constantly employs, have been examined carefully to determine the way in which they have been and are being used by the Communists.

The results of this effort are startling. Obviously, Communists and Americans attach different meanings to many terms.

| Term or jargon employed by the Communists | Actual meaning of Communist double talk |
| --- | --- |
| Aggression | Any military activity or defensive plans of the Free World. |
| Agitation | Communist activity designed to cause unrest, confusion, and Communist sympathy in the Free World. |
| Capitalist encirclement | The NON-Communist nations' defensive arrangements. |
| Coexistence | The absence of nuclear war. (Not: Co-operation, conciliation, or implied compromise). |
| Collective leadership | The Kremlin inner cabinet run by Khrushchev. |
| Democratic centralism | Preliminary "democratic" discussion, followed by absolute compliance with the decision of the Party. |
| Democracy | Communism |
| Deviationism | Any independent thought; the slightest departure from the Communist line of the moment. |
| Dialectic | The Communist manner of reasoning — a convenient substitute for standard logic. |
| Dictatorship of the proletariat | Absolute Communist Party control. |
| Imperialism | The foreign relations of the "capitalist" nations, especially actions which check Soviet ag gression. |

| | |
|---|---|
| Neutralism | Anti-Americanism |
| New democracy | A stage of Communism in China |
| Opportunism | Anti-Communism |
| Party line | Latest Communist strategy and tactics. |
| Peace | A Communist-dominated world where no one challenges Marxist-Leninist theory or Moscow-Peking practice. |
| People's democracy | Communism in Eastern Europe. |
| Proletariat | The working people of the world — so long as they are not anti-Communist. |
| Proletarian internationalism | "Communists of the world unite!" |
| Propaganda | Information put out by the nations of the Free World. |
| Purges | Arbitrary removal from the Communist Party because of disagreement with the views of the existing Party leadership. |
| Socialism | Communist state practice in the nations behind the Iron Curtain. |

# B

## A COMPACT BOOKSHELF ON COMMUNISM

Is it possible to suggest six or seven books that will provide the average high school teacher or student with reliable basic information about the complex field of Communism?

The following books together provide a wealth of information. They do more than that: they provide an important guide to understanding; they cut through much of the myth, nonsense, and propaganda which surround this subject. They will *not* answer all questions nor solve many of our complex problems. They do provide perspective on the challenge and greater understanding of the fundamental issues which divide the Communist world from the free, open societies.

\* \* \*

Adams, Arthur E. (Editor), *Readings in Soviet Foreign Policy: Theory and Practice*. Boston: D. C. Heath and Company, 1961.

An excellent, authoritative treatment of the Soviets in world affairs, 1918 to date. Forty reports, articles, and short documents by a host of authors ranging from American and European specialists to such prominent figures as Stalin and Churchill.

Arranged chronologically and topically. Includes treatment of "The Sino-Soviet Alliance," "Strategy and Tactics," "Post-Stalin Policy in Western Europe," and other topics.

Important in understanding the motivation, objectives, policies, and trends of the Soviets in world affairs. Particularly significant in suggesting the nature of the enemy we face.

Barnett, A. Doak, *Communist China and Asia: Challenge to American policy*. New York: Published for the Council on Foreign Relations by Harper & Brothers, 1960.

Adds the essential Peking perspective to the Communist challenge. An objective view of this critical area and its complex problems by a specialist on the Far East, presently Professor at Columbia University.

Includes, among others, the following chapters: "The Challenge of Communist China," "Communist China, a Totalitarian Political Power," "Economic Development," "The Roots of Mao's Strategy," "Evolving Tactics in Foreign Policy," "Military Strength and the Balance of Power," "Communist Subversion and the Political Struggle."

Brings the Moscow-Peking axis and the many-sided threat to the United States and the free nations into clearer view.

Carew-Hunt, R. N., *The Theory and Practice of Communism.* New York: The Macmillan Company, 1957.

A concise, clearly written, critical evaluation of Marxism-Leninism-Stalinism by the late British authority. Examines the philosophy, assumptions, and postulates on which the Soviet system and the Communist view of the world rest.

Points out the areas of confusion, unreality, absurdity, and untruth in the theories of Communism. At the same time stresses the strengths and significance of ideology as an operational factor in Soviet and Chinese Communist behavior.

An essential point of departure for a basic understanding of the world of Communism.

Hoover, J. Edgar, *Masters of Deceit.* New York: Holt, Rinehart, and Winston, 1958

A very important book on Communism in the United States by a man who ought to know. Covers background, nature, and scope of the Communist conspiracy in this country; the way the Party works; what it means to be a Communist; the appeals of Communism; and what we can do about it.

The most authoritative, non-partisan, non-political treatment available in any language.

Inkeles, Alex, and Kent Geiger, *Soviet Society: A Book of Readings.* Boston: Houghton Mifflin Company, 1961.

A thorough-going, critical look at the Soviet system and life in the Soviet Union. Comprised of authoritative reports and articles by more than fifty of the top government and academic specialists on the Soviet Union in this country and in Europe; augmented by a few revealing Soviet documents.

The topics, each by a specialist in his field, include: "Recent Trends in Soviet Education," "The Durability of Soviet Totalitarianism," "The Economic Challenge to the American Way of Life," "Leisure-Time Activities," "Soviet Living Standards," "A Survey of Russian Science," and "The Peasant and Soviet Agricultural Policy."

Seventy-three such topics are organized systematically into six major chapters or divisions — (1) Background: Resources and Development; (2) Ideology and Power; (3) Economic

Life; (4) The Mind and Spirit; (5) Everyday Living; and (6) A Forward Look.

Here are the facts plus some expert interpretation and conclusions valuable in countering Soviet propaganda and correcting uninformed opinion. Informative and absorbing reading.

*Oxford Regional Economic Atlas: The USSR and Eastern Europe.* Oxford University Press, 1956 (reprinted 1960).

An indispensable reference guide to the physical, cultural, and economic geography of the Soviet Union. Some 50 maps and charts in color with explanatory text. Arranged in three parts: (1) general reference maps, (2) topical maps (agriculture, minerals, industry, transportation, population), and (3) gazetteer (gives references in terms of longitude and latitude for some 5,500 place names).

Swearingen, Rodger, *What's So Funny, Comrade?* New York: Frederick A. Praeger, 1961.

A critical footnote on life in the Soviet Union today and on the way the Kremlin wants the Russian people to view the United States and the world. Some 150 cartoons from the official Soviet humor magazine *Krokodil,* 1958–1961.

A devastating self-criticism on the problems of Soviet society with a satirical, running commentary pointing up the distinction between Soviet propaganda and the facts. An inside look at life behind the Iron Curtain.

# C

## KEY SOURCES OF CURRENT, UP-TO-DATE INFORMATION

*The Bulletin* (Published monthly in English by the Institute for the study of the USSR in Munich, Germany).

Political, economic and cultural analysis of Soviet affairs. Contributors include former Soviet scholars (now residing in the West) as well as outstanding European and American specialists on World Communism.

*The Current Digest of the Soviet Press* (Published weekly by the Joint Committee on Slavic Studies Appointed by the American Council of Learned Societies and the Social Science Research Council, Columbia University, New York.)

A selection from the contents of the Soviet press, carefully translated in full into English or objectively condensed by competent editors. Essential resource material, invaluable information on official Soviet documents and speeches as well as on the Communist treatment of events at home and abroad. Useful in following the changing Soviet propaganda line.

*Problems of Communism* (Published every two months by the United States Information Agency, Washington, D.C.)

United States Government and academic specialists on the Soviet Union, Communist China, and Eastern Europe analyze the challenge and prospects of the world of Communism. Authoritative and well written in a semi-popular style.

*Survey: A Journal of Soviet and East European Studies* (Published quarterly in London — Summit House, 1–2 Langham Place, London W.1)

An excellent scholary treatment emphasizing the important ideological and cultural side of Soviet affairs and Communism. Contributors include most of the recognized authorities in the field. Effectively refutes Communist cultural and peace propaganda with facts and expert analysis. Representative topics: "Friendship University," "Islam in the Soviet Union," "The Origins of Literary Control," and "Two Roads to Communism." Not easy reading, but well worth the effort.

*The China Quarterly* (Published in London — Illford House, 133 Oxford Street, London W.1)

This publication does for Communist China what *Survey* does for the Soviet Union. Some examples of topics covered: "Communist China's Agricultural Calamities," "The Situation in Tibet," "Sino Soviet Competition in North Korea," and "Buddhism under the Communists." Again, not easy reading, but well worth the effort.

Among the journals, magazines, and newspapers useful in keeping up to date on the rapidly changing strategy and fortunes of the World of Communism, the following may be noted: (1) *Foreign Affairs* (a quarterly journal of international affairs which often includes significant articles on the Soviet Union and World Communism); (2) *Newsweek, Time,* and *U.S. News and World Report* (weekly news magazines containing much useful information as well as authoritative reports on critical topics; (3) *Life* and *Look* (useful for weekly pictorial coverage and for occasional substantial articles on Russia, China, and Communism); (4) *The New York Times, The London Times, The Manchester Guardian,* and *The Christian Science Monitor. The New York Times'* "News of the Week in Review" is especially recommended.

# Selected Readings

## CHAPTER 2

### Books

Milovan Djilas, *The New Class: An Analysis of the Communist System.* New York: Praeger, 1957.

R. N. Carew Hunt, *The Theory and Practice of Communism.* New York: The Macmillan Company, Revised edition, 1957.

Joseph A. Shumpeter, *Capitalism, Socialism and Democracy.* New York: Harper, 1950.

### Periodicals

John K. Jessup, "The Story of Marxism: its Men, its March," *Life,* October 20, 1961.

Alvin S. Rubenstein, "Tito's Homemade Communism," *The Reporter,* January, 1961.

Harry Schwartz, "Stalin and Stalinism Five Years After," *The New York Times Magazine,* March 2, 1958.

## CHAPTER 3

### Books

Robert Daniels (Editor), *A Documentary History of Communism — from Lenin to Mao.* New York: Random House, 1960.

R. N. Carew Hunt, "The World Communist Movement" in Grove C. Haines (Editor), *The Threat of Soviet Imperialism.* Baltimore: The Johns Hopkins Press, 1954.

Stefan Thomas Possony (Editor), *A Century of Conflict: Communist Techniques of World Revolution.* Chicago: Regnery, 1953.

Hugh Seton-Watson, *From Lenin to Khrushchev: A History of World Communism.* New York: Praeger, 1960.

### Periodicals

Max Eastman, "The Communists' Master Plan for Conquest," and Eugene Lyons, "The 'Shock Troops' and How They Fight"; in "World War III Has Already Started," *Reader's Digest,* January, 1961.

## CHAPTER 4

### Books

Raymond H. Bauer and others, *How the Soviet System Works: Cultural, Psychological and Social Themes.* Cambridge: Harvard University Press, 1957.

Merle Fainsod, *How Russia is Ruled.* Cambridge: Harvard University Press, 1953.

Vladimir Katkoff, *Soviet Economy 1940–1965.* Baltimore: Dangery Publishing Company, 1961.

John S. Reshetar, *A Concise History of the Communist Party of the Soviet Union.* New York: Praeger, 1960.

### Periodicals

"Party Congress: How Russia is Ruled," *Newsweek,* October, 1961.

W. W. Rostow, "Where Russia Goes From Here," *U.S. News and World Report,* November 2, 1959.

Nate White, "Two Kinds of Growth — The USSR: Economic Giant?" *The Christian Science Monitor,* January 18, 1961.

## CHAPTER 5

### Books

John Gunther, *Inside Russia Today.* New York: Harper, 1958.

Alex Inkeles and Kent Geiger (Editors), *Soviet Society: A Book of Readings.* Boston: Houghton Mifflin, 1961.

Rodger Swearingen, *What's So Funny, Comrade?* New York: Praeger, 1961.

### Periodicals

Stewart Alsop, "What I Saw in Khrushchev's Uneasy Empire," *Reader's Digest,* May, 1960.

"Another Look at Today's Russia (Two staff reporters accompanied Secretary of Agriculture Benson)," *U.S. News and World Report,* Vol. 47, (October 26, 1959), pp. 96–103.

Donald Connery and John Launois (photographer), "The Warm Hearts in a Bleak Land," *Life,* July 21, 1961.

"Khrushchev's Man-In-the-Street — What He's Like; How He Lives" (Interview with Hans Adler, American economist), *U.S. News and World Report,* Vol. 49, (October 10, 1960), pp. 88–90.

Philip E. Mosely, "How the Kremlin Keeps Ivan in Line," *The New York Times Magazine,* February 19, 1961, p. 16+.

W. L. White, "How Russia Treats the Jews," *Reader's Digest,* June 1961.

## CHAPTER 6

### Books

Robert C. North, *Moscow and the Chinese Communists.* Stanford: Stanford University Press, 1953.

Peter S. H. Tang, *Communist China Today: Domestic and Foreign Policies.* New York: Praeger, 1957.

Richard L. Walker, *China Under Communism: The First Five Years.* New Haven: Yale University Press, 1955.

### Periodicals

Theodore H. E. Chen, "Education and Indoctrination in Red China," *Current History,* September, 1961.

Chao Kuo Chun, "Progress in Chinese Agriculture," *Current History,* December, 1960.

Dai Shen-Yu, "Government and Law in Communist China," *Current History,* September, 1961.

Peggy Durdin, "The Happy Life in Red China," *New York Times Magazine,* September, 1960.

"Eyewitness Story of Red China Today," (A Swiss authority just out of Communist China reports on conditions), *U.S. News and World Report,* November 20, 1961.

Wu Yuan-Li, "Chinese Industrialization at the Crossroads," *Current History,* September, 1961.

## CHAPTER 7

### Books

Arthur E. Adams, *Readings in Soviet Foreign Policy: Theory and Practice.* Boston: D. C. Heath and Company, 1961.

Doak Barnett, *Communist China and Asia: A Challenge to American Policy.* New York: Vintage Books, 1960.

George Kennan, *Soviet Foreign Policy, 1917–1941.* New York: D. Van Nostrand Company, 1960.

Philip E. Mosely, *The Kremlin and World Politics: Studies in Soviet Policy and Action.* New York: Vintage Books, 1960.

## Periodicals

Max Eastman, "The Communists' Master Plan for Conquest," and Eugene Lyons, "The 'Shock Troops' and How They Fight" in "World War III Has Already Started," *Reader's Digest,* January, 1961.

Philip E. Mosely, "Is it 'Peaceful' or 'Coexistence?' " *The New York Times Magazine,* May 7, 1961.

Marshall D. Shulman, "The Real Nature of the Soviet Challenge," *The New York Times Magazine,* July 16, 1961.

Colonel Truman Smith, "The Infamous Record of Soviet Espionage," *Reader's Digest,* August, 1960.

Charles Stevenson, "How the Soviets Stole the March on Us in Africa," *Reader's Digest,* November, 1960.

Lester Velic, "Chinese Red Star Over Latin America," *Reader's Digest,* March, 1961.

Don Wharton, "Poison from Red Printing Presses," *Reader's Digest,* November, 1961.

"Will Russia and China Break?" A Panel of Experts, *U.S. News and World Report,* October 24, 1960.


# CHAPTER 8

## Books

J. Edgar Hoover, *Masters of Deceit:* The Story of Communism in America and How to Fight It. New York: Holt, 1958. (Also available in paperback edition published by Pocket Books, Inc.)

Benjamin Gitlow, *The Whole of Their Lives:* Communism in America, a personal history and intimate portrayal of its leaders. New York: Scribner, 1948.

Herbert A. Philbrick, *I Led Three Lives:* Citizen — "Communist" — Counterspy. New York: McGraw-Hill, 1952.

Don Whitehead, *The FBI Story:* A report to the people. New York: Random House, 1956.

# Suggestions for Review
# and Further Study

## CHAPTER 1

*Terms to Understand*

1. Communist theory 2. Soviet defector 3. collective farm 4. White Paper 5. military attaché 6. Moscow-Peking policies 7. intelligence reports 8. recognize government 9. burning issue 10. Marxist-Leninist theory 11. competitive coexistence 12. Bolsheviks 13. ideology 14. strategy 15. tactics 16. Communism

*Persons and Things to Identify*

1. Iron Curtain 2. Bamboo Curtain 3. Communist China 4. J. Edgar Hoover 5. World Communist movement 6. Five Year Plan 7. Khrushchev 8. FBI 9. Soviet Union

*Questions for Discussion*

1. (*a*) What is the world of Communism? (*b*) Explain what is included in this term.

2. (*a*) What reasons does Peggy give for not studying Communism (See Introduction)? (*b*) What reasons for studying Communism are given by Frances? (*c*) by the author? (*d*) Which reason (for or against) do you think most important? (*e*) Why?

3. From what sources can information about Communists be obtained: (*a*) what they think, (*b*) their plans, (*c*) their system, (*d*) life in Communist-ruled lands?

## CHAPTER 2

*Terms to Understand*

1. class struggle 2. middle class 3. revolutionmakers 4. surplus value 5. fellow traveler 6. synthesis 7. opportunist 8. sympathizer 9. imperialism 10. feudalism 11. collective ownership 12. historical materialism 13. economic penetration 14. guilt by association 15. New Democracy 16. nationalization 17. limited war 18. peasant base 19. colonialism 20. deviationism 21. socialism 22. atheism 23. dupe 24. capitalists 25. subversion 26. commune 27. Marxism 28. dialectic 29. thesis 30. antithesis 31. fascist 32. dictatorship of the proletariat 33. totalitarian machine 34. collectivization of

agriculture 35. regimentation of workers 36. labor theory of value 37. supply and demand 38. parliamentary means 39. free enterprise system 40. proletarian revolution

## Persons and Things to Identify

1. Brook Farm 2. Free World 3. Cominform 4. Yugoslavia 5. Communist Party 6. People's Democracies 7. Trotsky 8. Stalin 9. Lenin 10. Marx 11. Tito 12. Engels 13. National Communism 14. Communist Party Congress 15. Mao Tse-tung

## Questions for Discussion

1. (*a*) What did Marx consider the central theme of human history? Explain. (*b*) Why have things not turned out as Marx expected? (*c*) How did Lenin establish Communism in Russia? (*d*) Has the Communist state "withered away"? Explain. (*e*) What are the chief characteristics of the Communist economic system? (*f*) Why is Communism called a world-wide conspiracy? (*g*) Using the items listed on pp. 14–15, explain in each case the difference between ideal and practice.

2. (*a*) What is dialectical materialism? (*b*) the labor theory of value? (*c*) Point out things wrong with this theory.

3. Explain Lenin's theory of imperialism.

4. How does socialism differ from Communism?

5. (*a*) Explain differences in the views of Trotsky and Stalin on the Communist world revolution. (*b*) Why did they differ?

6. Why has Khrushchev taken the view that another World War is not inevitable?

7. (*a*) Why did Tito break with Stalin? (*b*) How is Tito's National Communism similar to (different from) the Moscow brand? (*c*) Why has this country given Tito economic and military aid?

8. (*a*) What are the unique characteristics of Maoism? (*b*) Explain why Chinese Communism has these characteristics.

9. Discuss the ten beliefs a Communist must accept. Evaluate each in terms of American ideals.

10. To what different kinds of people does Communism appeal? Explain why in each case.

11. Why is the Free World combating Communism more effectively today than fifteen years ago?

12. (*a*) Why is it difficult to identify a Communist? (*b*) How can one identify Communist sympathizers? (*c*) Why should one not brand as a Communist a person whose views differ from one's own?

13. Explain what is meant in each case: (*a*) a fellow traveler, (*b*) a sympathizer, and (*c*) a dupe.

## CHAPTER 3

*Terms to Understand*

1. fascism  2. coexistence  3. cell  4. warmongers  5. power center
6. defector  7. fifth column  8. secret police  9. "inner cabinet"  10.
Moscow orbit  11. Stalinist clique  12. democratic centralism

*Persons and Things to Identify*

1. Comintern  2. United Nations  3. Korean War  4. Southeast Asia
5. Malenkov  6. Mikoyan  7. Malinovsky  8. Kuomintang  9. Politburo  10. Third International  11. U.S. Lend-Lease  12. Stalin-Hitler
Pact  13. Party Committee  14. *Communist Manifesto*  15. *Das
Kapital*  16. Chou En-Lai  17. Lin Piao  18. Kremlin  19. Nazis  20.
Peking  21. Djilas  22. Poland  23. Hungary  24. Albania  25. Beria
26. Suslov  27. Koslov  28. Leninist Zig-Zag line  29. World Communist line  30. Japanese Non-Aggression Pact  31. Spirit of Geneva
32. World Federation of Trade Unions  33. Twenty-one Conditions
34. National People's Congress  35. Central People's Government

*Questions for Discussion*

1. (*a*) What was the Comintern?  (*b*) What were its goals?  (*c*)
How were these to be achieved?

2. (*a*) Point out major zigs and zags in Soviet foreign policy since
1917.  (*b*) How do you account for these?

3. What are the long-range goals of World Communism?

4. (*a*) How did the Comintern further Communist goals?  (*b*) Why
was it abolished?

5. (*a*) How is the Communist Party different from a regular
political party in this country?  (*b*) How does Moscow control Communist Parties in other lands?

6. What evidence can be cited to support the statement that the
World Communist movement has become less powerful since World
War II?

7. What did each of these men contribute to the World Communist
movement: (*a*) Marx, (*b*) Lenin, (*c*) Trotsky, (*d*) Stalin, (*e*) Khrushchev?

8. Why is it difficult to know "who runs the Kremlin"?

9. (*a*) What two major positions are held by Khrushchev?  (*b*)
Why is each important?  (*c*) Why has he downgraded Stalin?  (*d*)
What is the rôle of each of Khrushchev's chief advisors?

10. (*a*) Who are the leaders of the Chinese Communist Party?
(*b*) What is the rôle of each?

## CHAPTER 4

### Terms to Understand

1. scorched earth policy 2. preventive terror 3. punitive unemployment 4. thought control 5. sovnarkhoz 6. heavy industry 7. consumer goods 8. kolkhoz 9. sovkhoz 10. satellite 11. troika 12. rayon 13. oblast 14. rural soviet 15. labor camp 16. secret police 17. purge 18. bureaucracy 19. regionalism 20. automation 21. astronaut 22. socially dangerous elements 23. collective farm 24. progressive pay rates 25. fire power 26. space race 27. heatsensing satellite 28. missile thrust 29. delivery systems 30. nuclear capability 31. anti-missile missile

### Persons and Things to Identify

1. Kerensky 2. Mensheviks 3. Presidium 4. Secretariat 5. Ukraine 6. Sputnik 7. Duma 8. Kulaks 9. NEP 10. KGB 11. AUCCTU 12. Provisional Government 13. League of Nations 14. Council of Ministers 15. Gross National Product 16. Gagarin 17. United Front 18. Supreme Soviet 19. Central Committee 20. The Plan 21. Gosplan

### Questions for Discussion

1. (a) Why was the tsar's government overthrown in March 1917? (b) What groups took part in this revolution? (c) Why were the Bolsheviks able to seize power in November 1917? (d) Why did the Allies intervene?

2. (a) Why did the USSR join the League? (b) reach agreements with Nazi Germany and Japan? (c) How did the Western Allies come to be allied with the Soviet Union?

3. (a) What gains were made by the Soviet Union after World War II? (b) How did Khrushchev come to power?

4. (a) Describe the administrative organization of the USSR: (1) republics, (2) oblasts, (3) rayons, (4) rural soviets. (b) How does the Party control the government at each level?

5. (a) What is the purpose of the Iron Curtain? (b) How is it viewed outside the Soviet Union and satellites?

6. (a) Why do nearly all eligible voters vote in a Soviet election? (b) Why is this large vote meaningless?

7. (a) What evidence is there that people in Communist-controlled lands are opposed to the system? (b) How did Stalin suppress opposition? (c) Khrushchev? (d) Why have the Soviets maintained labor camps?

8. (a) Why was Soviet economic planning at first centralized? (b) later decentralized? (c) What are advantages and limitations of the latter?

9. (a) What considerations must be taken into account in comparing the economies of the Soviet Union and this country? (b) What are the chief goals of Soviet economic planning? (c) How has Khrushchev sought to increase agricultural production? (d) Compare the status of the Soviet farmer on a state farm and on a collective farm.

10. (a) What three men jointly manage a Soviet factory? (b) What are the functions of the local labor union? (c) Describe the organizational structure of labor unions in the Soviet Union. (d) Why are there no strikes?

11. Compare the military strength of the USSR and the United States.

12. (a) On what types of projects have Soviet scientists focused their attention? (b) How does over-all progress in science in the Soviet Union compare with that in the West?

13. (a) What are the major Soviet achievements in the space race? (b) the major achievements of this country? (c) What are the differences in emphasis?

14. Evaluate the nuclear capabilities of the Soviet Union and this country.

## CHAPTER 5

### Terms to Understand

1. steppe  2. dacha  3. stilyagi  4. hooliganism  5. nibo nicho  6. closed cities  7. turnover tax  8. philistine outlook  9. people's court  10. "humor underground"  11. standard of living  12. freedom of the press  13. opiate of the people  14. sobering-up station  15. nihilistic attitudes

### Persons and Things to Identify

1. Komsomal  2. *Krokodil*  3. Russification  4. Russian Orthodox Church  5. Park of Culture and Rest  6. American Relief Administration  7. Metropolitan Gregory  8. House of Culture

### Questions for Discussion

1. (a) What impressions of the Soviet Union were reported by Stevenson and Nixon after their visits? (b) Compare typical cities of the same size in this country and in the USSR.

2. (*a*) In terms of living standards, what three major groups are found in the Soviet Union? (*b*) What types of people are in each group? (*c*) Compare living standards for a lower middle class family in the two countries. (*d*) Point out differences in salaries and prices in the two countries.

3. (*a*) What is the turnover tax? (*b*) Why are income tax rates low in the Soviet Union? (*c*) Why do Russian women fill a variety of jobs?

4. (*a*) Describe the Soviet school system. (*b*) Contrast educational goals in this country and in the Soviet Union. (*c*) Contrast the purposes served by the press in this country and in USSR.

5. (*a*) Describe recreational opportunities in the USSR (*b*) Contrast these with opportunities in this country.

6. (*a*) What do Russians read? (*b*) Why do they read so much? (*c*) What types of material are not available?

7. (*a*) What steps have been taken to stifle religion and worship? (*b*) Why has the Government not abolished religion?

8. (*a*) What evidence is there of discrimination against colored peoples in the Soviet Union? (*b*) against Jews? (*c*) other minorities?

9. (*a*) Is juvenile delinquency a problem? (*b*) How does the Soviet government seek to discourage divorce?

10. (*a*) What crimes are punishable by death? (*b*) What is meant by "anti-social, parasitic behavior"? (*c*) How is it punished? (*d*) Is alcoholism a problem in the Soviet Union? (*e*) What is being done about it?

11. (*a*) What is the attitude toward this country and its people of the Soviet government? (*b*) of the Russian people? (*c*) How is the attitude of the people conditioned by Soviet propaganda?

12. Have Russians a sense of humor? Explain.

## CHAPTER 6

### Terms to Understand

1. Middle Kingdom 2. agrarian reformers 3. arable land 4. jet fighters 5. border incursions 6. "shock" campaign 7. Autonomous Regions 8. "great leap forward" 9. protracted war 10. guilt by association 11. germ warfare 12. nuclear reactor 13. cooperatives 14. village elders 15. technology 16. cadres 17. proletarian internationalism

### Persons and Things to Identify

1. Sun Yat-sen 2. Chiang Kai-shek 3. Yalta Agreement 4. Sinkiang

5. Yenan   6. Borodin   7. Taiwan   8. Formosa   9. Manchuria   10. Tibet   11. Hong Kong   12. Lao Tzu   13. Confucius   14. People's Liberation Army   15. "Hundred Flowers" season   16. Joint Institute of Nuclear Research

## Questions for Discussion

1. (a) Why did the Russian Revolution of 1917 have a great impact on China? (b) How did Communists take advantage of the on-going Chinese Revolution? (c) What steps were taken by Chiang Kai-shek to combat Communism? (d) Where did Chinese Communists establish themselves? Why?

2. (a) Describe relations between the Nationalists and Chinese Communists during World War II. (b) Why were the latter able to take over China following the war? (c) How has this take-over turned out for China?

3. (a) Compare the political organization of Communist China and the Soviet Union. (b) Compare the economic development of the two countries. (c) What difficult economic problems confront the Chinese? (d) How effectively are they coping with them?

4. (a) Compare life in Chinese cities and rural areas today and twenty-five years ago. (b) Why do the Chinese put up with the Communist regime? (c) Why were the People's Communes established? (d) How well have they worked?

5. (a) Why have the Communists tried to up-root family loyalty? (b) attacked Confucianism?

6. (a) What is meant by "protracted war"? (b) With what weapons is the Chinese army equipped? (c) How does this force compare to that of the Soviet Union or the United States?

7. (a) What are the science goals sought by Communist China? (b) How are scientists responding to pressure from the Party? (c) Is the emphasis on applied science in the best interest of over-all scientific progress?

8. (a) Why do educated Chinese have mixed feelings about the West? (b) Has the Party been able to make most Chinese anti-American?

9. (a) Why have tensions developed between Red China and the Soviet Union? (b) In what areas?

## CHAPTER 7

## Terms to Understand

1. foreign policy   2. self-determination   3. multilateral   4. super-state

5. naked force   6. the big lie   7. people's diplomacy   8. Summit meetings   9. "salami" techniques   10. embargo list   11. "middle kingdom"   12. "positive neutralism"   13. "non-alignment"   14. espionage   15. bilateral   16. renegade   17. "semi-colonial" country   18. neutralist bloc   19. Castro's kind of revolution   20. Fidelismo

## Persons and Things to Identify

1. Truman   2. Molotov   3. MacArthur   4. Beneš   5. Nasser   6. Rakosi   7. Ghana   8. Yemen   9. Nkrumah   10. Clausewitz   11. North Korea   12. South Korea   13. 38th parallel   14. Red Bloc   15. Laos   16. Cambodia   17. Thailand   18. Burma   19. Malaya   20. Indonesia   21. Philippines   22. Nehru   23. Congo   24. Sukarno   25. Cuba   26. Panama   27. Haiti   28. Security Council (UN)   29. Hungarian freedom fighters   30. Manhattan Project   31. Central Intelligence Agency   32. Aswan High Dam   33. "Panch Shila"   34. Federal Republic of Germany   35. German Democratic Republic   36. Dominican Republic   37. Nicaragua

## Questions for Discussion

1. (a) What are the goals of Communist foreign policy? (b) What methods are used to achieve these goals? (c) Contrast United States and Soviet foreign policy goals and methods used to achieve them. (d) What good are summit meetings? (e) Does the Soviet Union believe in the UN? (f) desire disarmament?

2. (a) What does the Soviet Union mean by coexistence? (b) Why do Soviet diplomats lack the power to make decisions and reach compromises? (c) What lessons can be learned from the Korean War? (d) Why did the Soviet Union intervene in Hungary in 1956?

3. (a) Why does the Soviet Union have a vast espionage program? (b) How successful has it been?

4. (a) How did the Communists take over Czechoslovakia? (b) Hungary? (c) Why has Soviet propaganda been effective in underdeveloped and uncommitted areas? (d) How can this country combat it?

5. (a) How do the Soviets use trade and aid as foreign policy weapons? (b) What goals do they have in mind? (c) Why do Soviet trade and aid sometimes have unforeseen consequences for the nation "helped"? (d) Contrast purpose, scope, and focus of United States and Soviet trade and aid.

6. (a) What tensions have developed between Red China and the Soviet Union? (b) Why? (c) Why are these tensions not likely to divide the two countries?

7. (a) Why is China anti-imperialist? (b) Why does Red China have imperialist aspirations of its own? (c) Compare Soviet and Chinese foreign policies.

8. (a) Why does the Soviet Union wish to oust the Western Allies from Berlin? (b) Why is it seeking to penetrate Africa? (c) How successful have the Communists been in Africa? (d) Why? (e) What is our policy in Africa?

9. Why is Southeast Asia vulnerable to Communist penetration?

10. (a) What is neutralism? (b) Why do some nations follow this policy? (c) Why does this country feel that a policy of neutralism is unrealistic? (d) Why are some of the neutrals beginning to question the wisdom of neutralism?

11. (a) Why are the Communists enthusiastically supporting Castro and his revolution? (b) How is Fidelismo being spread in other Latin American lands? (c) With what success?

## CHAPTER 8

### Terms to Understand

1. iron discipline   2. cryptographic machine   3. Browderism   4. Communist front

### Persons and Things to Identify

1. House Committee on Un-American Activities 2. Senate Internal Security Sub-Committee 3. Subversive Activities Control Board 4. Internal Security Act of 1950 5. Communist Control Act of 1954 6. Senate Investigating Committee 7. Worker's Party of America 8. Lenin School 9. William Z. Foster 10. Earl Browder 11. CPUSA 12. *Daily Worker* 13. Communist Political Associations 14. Smith Act of 1940

### Questions for Discussion

1. (a) When were Communist Parties first established in this country? (b) How were the two Parties unified? (c) How did the united Party come under the domination of Moscow?

2. (a) How successful was the Worker's Party of America in the 1920's? (b) What was its relation to the Communist Party? (c) What evidence is there that CPUSA in the 1930's followed the Moscow line? (d) Why was CPUSA dissolved when the Soviet Union and this country became allies in World War II? (e) Why was CPUSA reconstituted after the war?

3. Compare CPUSA with a traditional political party in terms of (a) ideology, (b) organization, (c) responsibility of members, (d) goals and methods, (e) where final authority is located.

4. Can a person be both a loyal United States citizen and a Communist? Explain.

5. (a) What is a Communist front organization? (b) How can such an organization be detected?

6. (a) What groups in this country are Communists seeking to influence? (b) How?

7. In what three respects are Communist activities within the United States a threat to this country? Explain.

8. What four approaches are being used by the United States Government in its efforts to check Communist influence within the country? Explain.

## CHAPTER 9

### President Hoover

1. What does this President regard as the real sources of our country's strength? Do you agree?

2. What is his evaluation of the status of science and technology in the Free World and in the Soviet Union?

3. What are his views about the ability of the United States to meet the threats posed by possible aggressor nations?

### President Truman

1. According to the President, what is the basic goal of the Kremlin's foreign policy?

2. How does he feel that the free nations can best keep the Communists from achieving this goal?

3. What conditions must be met if a real peace in Korea is to be achieved?

### President Eisenhower

1. What does this President regard as the chief appeal of Communism to uncommitted peoples?

2. What does he place first in our scale of values?

3. In what ways has this country held Communist imperialism in check?

4. What has the United States done to help strengthen the economies of Free World nations?

5. What are the fundamental principles on which our foreign policy rests?

### President Kennedy

1. What does this President say about our foreign policy goals in Asia, Africa, and Latin America?

2. What other methods than aggression and subversion might be used by Soviet Russia and Communist China to achieve greater status?

3. What suggestions are made by the President for increasing this country's ability to carry out its rôle in world affairs through (a) strengthened military tools, (b) improved economic tools, (c) sharpened political and diplomatic tools?

### Mr. Pace

1. What does this author regard as the inherent advantages of a free society?

2. Does he believe that dictatorships are as efficient as described in their own propaganda?

3. Does Mr. Pace feel that Americans are doing well enough in terms of production, concern for understanding issues of the day, accepting responsibility? Explain.

### Mr. Meany

1. In what three ways, according to this author, can American labor help the United States become a stronger and better land?

2. How does he feel that Communist imperialism is different from 19th century imperialism?

3. What must the democratic nations do to meet this challenge?

### A Roman Catholic View

1. What are the two "faces" of the Communist movement?

2. In the opinion of the author, is the greater threat of the Communist conspiracy from within or without?

3. If one accepts his conclusion, what types of measures should be supported?

### A Protestant View

1. What evidence is cited to show the menace of the Communist conspiracy abroad? at home?

2. How has fear of Communism worked "as the enemy of intelligence, responsibility, and decision" in combating the Communist conspiracy in this country?

### Judaism Versus Communism

1. List and explain five reasons why Judaism is opposed to Communism.

2. What evidence is cited to show that Communism is hostile to the Jewish people everywhere?

3. What can be done to combat Communism?

## J. Edgar Hoover

1. The Communists stress ideological study. How can Americans become more articulate about our traditions and ideals?

2. How can we make American youth "responsible, conscious of its obligations, and eager to be good citizens"?

3. Why should youth be made "working members of our republic"?

4. Why is it important to strive for goals "to improve self, community, and nation"?

5. Why is faith important in combating Communism?

# Maps, Charts, and Pictures

A. Communist World West (*map*)

B. Red Square

C. (top to bottom) Karl Marx, Leon Trotsky, Stalin-Lenin statue

D. Political System of the Soviet Union (*chart*)

E. World Youth Forum

F. (top) USSR Output as a percentage of U.S. Output (*chart*)
   (bottom) Growth of New Capital Investment in U.S. and USSR (*chart*)

G. (top) Outdoor display, Red Square
   (bottom) Men and women working, Leningrad

H. (top) Agricultural cartoon
   (bottom) Collective farm

I. Communist World East (*map*)

J. (top) Mao Tse-Tung
   (bottom) Meeting in Tibet called by Military Control Committee

K. (top) Chinese boy working on commune farmland
   (bottom) Chinese women factory workers

L. (top) Commune workers discuss Communist theory
   (bottom) Mechanized harvesting of wheat on commune

M. East Berlin guard leaping over the barricade

N. (top) Russian troops parading in Red Square
   (bottom) The Nuclear Arms Race (*chart*)

O. (top) Neutralist leaders
   (bottom) Soviet-built model of Aswan Dam used in hydraulic research

P. (top to bottom) Khrushchev and Castro; Demonstrations in support of Cuba: in Moscow; in Peking

# Permissions and Picture Credits

Grateful acknowledgment is made to the following publishers, authors, and other copyright holders, for permission to reprint copyrighted material: *America*, for selections from the editorial "On Fighting Communism"; American Association for the Advancement of Science, for a selection from Sydney H. Gould, ed., *Sciences in Communist China;* E. P. Dutton and Company, for a selection from *The Russians as People* by Wright Miller; Harper & Brothers, for selections from *Inside Russia Today,* by John Gunher; Harvard University Press, for a selection from *Red Flag in Japan* by Rodger Swearingen and Paul Langer; Holt, Rinehart, and Winston, for selections from *Masters of Deceit* by J. Edgar Hoover; *Life,* for selections from "Misery, Oppression, Fear Inside China's Communes" by James Bell; Los Angeles *Examiner,* for "student opinion poll" and essays on the study of Communism in high school; *National Geographic,* for selections from "Russia as I Saw It," by Richard M. Nixon; Frederick A. Praeger, Inc., for selections from *The New Class* by Milovan Djilas; The *Saturday Evening Post,* for a selection from "Will Africa Go Communist" by Stewart Alsop; *Vital Speeches of the Day,* for selections from speeches by Herbert Hoover and Frank Pace, Jr.; World Peace Foundation, for a selection from *Negotiating with the Russians;* Yale University Press, for a selection from *The Changing World of Soviet Russia* by David J. Dallin.

    ✿    ✿    ✿

Grateful acknowledgment is made to the following for permission to reproduce the pictures indicated:
Front cover, Eastfoto; back cover, H. Armstrong Roberts; Insert A, Lilli Mautner; B, Sovfoto; C, Sovfoto, Wide World; E, Sovfoto; F, Redrawn from *Fortune,* October, 1961, courtesy of *Fortune* Magazine; G, H. Armstrong Roberts, Wide World; I, Lilli Mautner; J, Wide World, Eastfoto; K, Wide World; L, Sovfoto, Wide World; M, Wide World; N, Sovfoto; O, Wide World, Sovfoto; P, Wide World, Sovfoto, Eastfoto.